A Bibliography of the
Socioeconomic Aspects of Medicine

A Bibliography of the Socioeconomic Aspects of Medicine

Theodora Andrews

Libraries Unlimited, Inc.
Littleton, Colo.

1975

LIBRARIES UNLIMITED, INC.
P.O. Box 263
Littleton, Colorado 80120

Library of Congress Cataloging in Publication Data

Andrews, Theodora.
    A bibliography of the socioeconomic aspects of
medicine.

    Includes index.
    1. Medical care--Bibliography. 2. Social medicine
--Bibliography. 3. Medical economics--Bibliography.
4. Hygiene, Public--Bibliography. I. Title.
[DNLM: 1. Delivery of health care--Bibliography.
2. Public health--Bibliography. 3. Socioeconomic
factors--Bibliography. ZWA100 A571b]
Z6675.E2A53   016.3621   74-34054
ISBN 0-87287-104-5

TABLE OF CONTENTS

PART I
GENERAL REFERENCE SOURCES

PART II
SOURCE MATERIAL BY SUBJECT AREA

INTRODUCTION

A great deal of attention has been paid lately to the socioeconomic aspects of health care. Many diverse groups feel that these are trying times and that something should be done about the problems of health care delivery and public health in general. The rapid growth of the literature of the field reflects such attitudes. It is frequently said that we are experiencing a "health care crisis." Whether or not the problems that confront us have actually reached a crisis stage, most individuals agree that there is much room for improvement and that awareness of the various facets of the subject may help bring about needed results.

The materials selected for this bibliography include those that have social, political, and economic implications. It may occur to some that the title of this publication is similar to that of the American Medical Association's *Medical Socioeconomic Research Sources* (described in entry No. 53). The two works are not particularly similar except insofar as they cover the same subject areas. The AMA's publication is a monthly indexing tool covering periodical literature, whereas this bibliography presents reviews of reference materials and monographs. The subjects treated are outlined in the table of contents. Some scientific materials have been included, but for the most part the titles listed are suitable for use by those without special scientific or medical training.

The bibliography is limited to English-language materials, primarily American. Most of the works listed here have been published since 1969, although a few older titles have also been included.

I have attempted to make a rather complete listing of useful materials that librarians consider "reference books," such as dictionaries, manuals, guides, handbooks, bibliographies, etc. In addition, a great many of the monographic titles included have reference value and cover the problem areas in a representative way. Many of the books present controversial solutions to problems; an attempt has been made to include titles that reflect various points of view and that cover several facets of the problems in question.

In addition to reference books and monographs, a few pamphlets, periodical articles, and annuals are listed. There are special sections on statistical publications, periodicals, and indexes and abstracts. The annotations for yearbooks, annuals, and frequently revised titles are based on the latest issue available at the time of writing.

Many materials on drug abuse have been listed, primarily because this important problem area has received a great deal of attention in the last few years. The number of books available in the field is very large; for this bibliography I have attempted to select titles that represent current thinking and diverse points of view.

It is hoped that librarians who wish to build collections in the fields of health care and related areas will find this bibliography valuable. The titles selected are suitable for university, college, public, and many special libraries. In addition, faculty members who teach or who are preparing to teach courses in this field may find the material presented here to be helpful. Such courses are on the increase in schools of health science and also in the social science departments of universities. Finally, hospital administrators and other members of the health care industry may find the book useful.

During the past year or so, the author has had occasion to help Purdue University faculty members involved with courses on health care and related areas; they have in turn provided valuable assistance in the preparation of this publication.

Theodora Andrews

PART I

GENERAL REFERENCE SOURCES

1. MEDICAL TERMINOLOGY

1. Blessum, William T., and Charles J. Sippl. **Computer Glossary for Medical and Health Sciences.** New York, Funk and Wagnalls, 1972. 262p. illus. $6.95. LC 79-188734.

This valuable book is a basic tool for beginners in the field. It will serve as a refresher source for those who are more familiar with the terminology. The bulk of the book is definitions; in addition there is an appendix on "The Impact of Computers on Medicine and the Health Sciences" and a glossary of acronyms.

2. Byers, Edward E., comp. **10,000 Medical Words: For Secretaries, Stenographers, Typists, Medical Librarians, Technicians, and Students.** New York, Gregg Division, McGraw-Hill Book Co., 1972. 122p. $3.15. LC 72-2487. ISBN 0-07-009503-5.

The objective of this pocket-sized book is to provide the user with a convenient source for spelling and dividing medical terms. The words are listed alphabetically showing the division into syllables. No definitions are included. Easy words have been omitted. In addition to the main list there is a section of medical abbreviations with the meanings indicated. The book is particularly useful because of the convenient compact size.

3. Carlin, Harriette L. **Medical Secretary Medi-Speller.** Springfield, Ill., Charles C. Thomas, 1973. 244p. bibliog. $4.95pa. LC 72-81689. ISBN 0-398-02579-7.

There are other reference books, dictionaries, and handbooks available for medical secretaries. This one is a bit different, however, in that it is more of a spelling book. There are few definitions, although the words are categorized into the main fields of transcription. Occasionally a definition is given, in cases when word pronunciation is very similar but the meaning is different. The sections are arranged as follows: (1) General terminology, (2) Anatomy, (3) Surgical pathology, (4) Radiology, (5) Diseases/Syndromes, (6) Surgical procedures, (7) Instruments, (8) Clinical pathology, and (9) Commonly misspelled English words. The book should assist the secretary in turning out a greater volume of accurate work.

4. Chatton, Milton J., ed. **Handbook of Medical Treatment.** 13th ed. Los Altos, Calif., Lange Medical Publications; Oxford, Blackwell Scientific Publications, 1972. 648p. index. $6.50. LC 62-13251.

This concise publication has been kept to pocket size by omitting some of the less common disorders and most of the limited diagnostic information included in previous editions. However, new innovations in therapy have been incorporated and new drugs have been included and evaluated. Each of the 23 chapters takes up a different type of disorder such as "Diseases of the Heart," "Diseases of the Nervous System," etc., and each was written by a well-known expert. In addition the appendix includes some useful materials such as "Desirable Weight Tables" and Heart-Lung Resuscitation."

5. Frenay, Sister Agnes Clare. **Understanding Medical Terminology.** 5th ed. St. Louis, Catholic Hospital Association, 1973. 361p. illus. bibliog. index. $6.50. LC 72-97662. ISBN 0-87125-006-3.

Although there are several publications on medical terminology available, this one seems as useful as any, particularly for the students in one of the health related fields such as pharmacy, nursing, medical technology, physical therapy, or hospital administration. This title is also of use to the general public as it is written on a basic understandable level. The book has been quite useful as a text for courses in medical terminology and is quite relevant to professional practice in the health science fields.

The work is arranged with a beginning chapter which is an orientation to the terminology; then there follows 15 chapters, each covering terms related to various biological disorders such as cardiovascular disorders, digestive disorders, etc. There is a second part of four chapters which treats terms applying to various fields of medicine such as physical medicine, nuclear medicine, etc. The text is illustrated and contains a number of useful tables. Many new medical terms are included relating to orthopedics, cardiovascular and blood disorders, immunology, laboratory, radiologic, and nuclear procedures.

6. Herbert, W. J., and P. C. Wilkinson, eds. **A Dictionary of Immunology.** Oxford and Edinburgh, Blackwell Scientific Publications, 1971. 195p. SBN 0-632-07750-6.

This small dictionary lists over 1500 words which are briefly defined to serve the needs of the undergraduate student, the biologist, clinician, and biochemist. The definitions are simple enough to be understood by one with a minimum background of biological knowledge. An attempt has been made to give current usage in the field. Included are short descriptions of diseases with immunological features, human and animal vaccines, abbreviations in current use, and some obsolete terms which will help in the interpretation of older literature. The book should prove useful in college, university, and medical libraries.

7. Koch, Michael S. **Biomedical Thesaurus and Guide to Classification.** New York, CCM Information Corporation, 1972. 181p. bibliog. LC 72-91852. SBN 8409-0333-2.

This thesaurus was developed by the author, who is a medical librarian, over a period of many years. It will be of value to both practitioners and researchers in information handling. The terms listed were drawn from three major sources of medical subject headings: the National Library of Medicine printed catalogs of 1950-1959, the Library of Congress list of subject headings, and the National Library of Medicine Medical Subject Heading List (MeSH). In addition, appropriate classification numbers from both the NLM and LC classification schedules are given. The thesaurus consists of about 5,000 headings.

The basic aim of the compilation is to provide a guide to the subject analysis of biomedical book collections. It also provides a correlation between subject headings and pertinent classification numbers. A secondary purpose is to present a list that will furnish an overview of the terminology for users, particularly for those who are unfamiliar with the subject field. Thirdly, the thesaurus provides terms employed by NLM and LC back to 1950 and before, which is of importance in research of a historical nature.

There are several potential users of the list: medical and health-related libraries, medical faculties, colleges and university libraries where pre-clinical and biological science courses are offered, public libraries (particularly those that have public health collections), and special libraries with a secondary interest in health problems.

8. Larson, Leonard A., Executive Editor, and Donald E. Herrmann, Assistant Executive Editor. **Encyclopedia of Sport Sciences and Medicine.** Under the sponsorship of the American College of Sports Medicine, the University of Wisconsin, and in cooperation with [other organizations]. New York, Macmillan, 1971. 1707p. index. bibliog. $39.95. LC 70-87898.

This publication, which is international in scope, summarizes the scientific literature of this interdisciplinary field and serves as a definition of the sports medicine field which is somewhat in the development stage at the present time.

The encyclopedia contains over 1,000 articles which present data on all the influences that affect the human organism before, during, and after participation in sports. Since the editors feel that any force, stress, or environmental factor that influences the human being in such instances is within the scope of sport sciences and medicine, the context of physical activity has been enlarged to include the social, emotional, physical, and intellectual characteristics, abilities, and capabilities of the individual independently, the individual within the group, and the group as a whole. Consequently, the coverage of the encyclopedia is quite broad. Such areas as environment, emotions and the intellect, drugs, prevention of disease, safety rehabilitation, and physical activity and the handicapped individual are included along with the more obvious areas. Also some detailed information is included regarding individual sports, the basic skills required, evaluation and skill measurement.

Over 500 writers, authorities in science and medicine, contributed to the encyclopedia. An effort was made to include authors from many countries. A variety of approaches have been used in the writing, depending on the available sources. These include experimental, clinical, and theoretical or experimental approaches. For instance, certain articles have been written theoretically because of a lack of research data.

The publication is impressive and well written. It should prove useful to a large number of groups which include physicians, physical education teachers, coaches, trainers, health educators, physical therapists, recreation leaders, and many others. Also it will provide useful resources information for college and university courses dealing with human development through physical activity. The book is written at a rather high level, but it has considerable value as a general reference book.

The encyclopedia is organized into 10 general areas, and under each the signed articles appear. References are included in most cases. Articles vary in length from about ¼ page to 2 or 3 pages. There is a detailed subject index which makes material on specific topics easy to locate. Also an author index has been furnished which includes the names of authors of the articles and also the names of the authors in the citations. The publication is unique in that no other work of this kind and scope is available.

9. McConnico, Charles T. **The Medical Transcriptionist Handbook.** With fore-
    words by Margaret C. Cevely and R. LeRoy Carpenter. Springfield, Ill.,
    Charles C. Thomas, 1972. 238p. index. $8.75. LC 73-165891.
    ISBN 0-398-02367-C.

Because of the increasing demand for competent medical transcriptionists, this handbook was produced to assist with their training. The text is presented in a simple style, and is suitable for self-teaching. Study of the material is presumed to provide the transcriptionist with an understanding of medical terms, the content of medical reports, unfamiliar medical words by analysis of their elements, medical synonyms, various surgical instruments and procedures, laboratory procedures, suture materials, anesthetics, bandages and dressings, etc. Providing this understanding is a rather ambitious task, and the material in the book is presented in a somewhat oversimplified fashion. However, there is a need for this kind of reference work, and the handbook may prove useful to other individuals in the paramedical field also. Libraries serving the medical and paramedical fields will probably want to own the book.

10. Osol, Arthur, ed. **Blakiston's Pocket Medical Dictionary.** 3d ed. New York,
    Blakiston Division, McGraw-Hill Book Co., 1973. 964p. $6.95. LC 72-10063.

This publication is a shortened version of the third edition of *Blakiston's Gould Medical Dictionary.* Terms were chosen for inclusion that were deemed to be most important to nurses, medical assistants and secretaries, dental assistants, pharmacists, medical laboratory technicians, and students. The arrangement is a bit different from that of earlier editions where phrase entries were grouped into general categories. In this edition each phrase is entered and defined in its own alphabetic location; that is, there are no subentries. Pronunciation is included. Special effort was put forth to include information on and to identify drugs. There are a number of tables appended. These include tables of arteries, bones, muscles, nerves, synovial joint and ligaments, and veins. Services of specialists in diverse fields of the health professions were sought in compiling this work. It should prove well worth the small price.

11. Schmidt, J. E. **Paramedical Dictionary: A Practical Dictionary for the Semi-
    Medical and Ancillary Medical Professions.** Springfield, Ill., Charles C.
    Thomas, 1969, 423p. $8.75. LC 69-19180.

The dictionary is designed for such paramedical workers as physical therapists, public health officers, laboratory technicians, medical secretaries, social workers, dieticians, dental assistants, and others who are not medically trained and cannot use a comprehensive physician's medical dictionary. Pronunciation is indicated, and there is an appendix of useful information including weights and measures and a short list of medical abbreviations. The compilation is adequate and useful for the groups named and laymen, although advanced professionals will want a more scholarly compendium.

12. Schmidt, J. E. **Visual Aids for Paramedical Vocabulary.** Springfield, Ill., Charles C. Thomas, 1973. 182p. $6.95. illus. LC 72-84149. ISBN 0-398-02609-2.

The purpose of this book is to provide a painless way of learning medical terminology. The format of the text is basically a simplified discussion of medical subjects through which the reader can gain knowledge of the vocabulary. Also included at the end of each chapter is a list of words for review and a commentary on derivation and allied matters. Also exercises and questions are provided to assist with the learning process. Visual aids in the form of drawings have been included to make word meanings more clear. Most of these are anatomical drawings. There are chapters on the sources of medical words, the anatomy of medical vocabulary, the human body as a whole, and illustrations of common fractures. The bulk of the book, however, is devoted to a discussion of the following systems: skeletal system, circulatory system, digestive system, urinary system, sensory system, muscular system, nervous system, respiratory system, reproductive system, and endocrine system. The presentation is effective and does seem to offer a less trying method of vocabulary building. The book is particularly valuable for paramedical personnel and laymen.

13. Smith, Genevieve Love, and Phyllis E. Davis. **Medical Terminology: A Programed Text.** 2d ed. New York, John Wiley and Sons, Inc., 1967. 289p. $6.25pa. LC 66-30383. ISBN 0-471-80196-8.

This publication is useful for anyone who desires a background in medical terminology. It is particularly intended for self study for those in medical and paramedical fields such as nurses, medical secretaries, medical technologists, medical librarians, etc. Upon completion of the test, used in the intended programed manner, the student should be able to build medical words from Greek and Latin prefixes, suffixes, and word roots; also be able to recognize medical words from the Greek and Latin parts; and use a medical dictionary intelligently.

14. Smith, Genevieve Love, and Phyllis E. Davis. **Quick Medical Terminology.** In consultation with Shirley E. Soltesz. New York, John Wiley and Sons, Inc., 1972. 248p. $3.95pa. ISBN 0-371-80198-4.

This programmed text has been designed for the self-teaching of medical terms. No special background is required for users, other than a high school education. Review sheets for each chapter are provided. Also, there is a glossary of word parts and an additional list of word parts if the student wishes to further expand his medical vocabulary. It is claimed that when the user finishes the book he will have formed over 500 medical terms using the word building system of combining Greek and Latin prefixes, suffixes, word-roots, and combining forms. In addition, new words can be understood following this system.

15. Steen, Edwin G. **Dictionary of Abbreviations in Medicine and the Related Sciences.** 3d ed. Philadelphia, F. A. Davis, 1971. 102p. bibliog. $1.90.

The scope of this edition of the dictionary has been widened, and more definitions included than in the earlier ones. There is a real need for this kind of publication as the use of abbreviations needs to be standardized since some chaos exists. There has been no attempt, however, to say which of several abbreviations in common use is preferred or correct. All are given. Some useful appendices are

included. There is a list of symbols, a list of abbreviations of titles of the principal medical journals (probably not complete enough for librarians to make much
use of), and a bibliography of source books.

16. Thomas, Clayton L., ed. **Taber's Cyclopedic Medical Dictionary**. 12th ed.
    Philadelphia, F. A. Davis, 1973; London, Blackwell Scientific Pubs., Ltd.;
    Canada, McGraw-Hill Ryerson Ltd.; India, Burma, and Ceylon, The
    Kothari Book Depot. 1v. (various paging). illus. $9.50. LC 62-8364.

The high quality of earlier editions of this work is still evident. The type for this
edition was set by computer which allowed for last-minute additions, making the
material unusually up-to-date. New tables and illustrations have been included,
and obsolete terms have been dropped. For these definitions older editions must
be consulted. The dictionary is intended for all persons concerned with the promotion of health, care of the sick, and prevention of disease. Areas covered are
medicine in general, nursing, diagnosis and treatment, drugs, foods, chemistry,
and many allied sciences. Most definitions are concise, but a few take up a
column or more. An extensive appendix section is included which presents such
material as a list of poison control centers in the U.S. and Canada, a table for
radiological emergencies, dietary information, a five language outline for basic
medical diagnosis and treatment, physiological standards for blood, and many
other useful lists and tables. Dorland's and Stedman's dictionaries are more complete and scholarly, but this work contains much useful information presented in
somewhat simpler fashion.

2. LAWS, LEGISLATION, AND REGULATIONS

17. Anderson, Oscar E., Jr. **The Health of a Nation: Harvey W. Wiley and the Fight for Pure Food.** Chicago, University of Chicago Press, 1958. 333p. illus. bibliog. index. $6.00 LC 58-11945.

This book is a biography of Dr. Harvey W. Wiley, a chief chemist of the U.S. Department of Agriculture and the central figure in the fight for the Federal Pure Food and Drug Act of 1906. The book tells of Wiley's early life in Indiana and his work which began in the 1870s and ended in 1930 with his death. Wiley was a scientist who saw the need for controlling fraudulent and harmful practices such as the indiscriminate use of chemical preservatives, the sale of worthless or dangerous patent medicines, and the adulteration of food and drugs. There was a great deal of opposition to Wiley's views from special interest groups, but public indignation was aroused by his reports, and the reform legislation was passed. The author, who is a historian, has presented a well-documented and reasonable account of the crusade.

18. Bander, Edward J., and Jeffrey J. Wallach. **Medical Legal Dictionary.** Dobbs Ferry, N.Y., Oceana Publications, 1970. 114p. bibliog. $5.00. LC 73-83743.

A selected list of medical legal terms are defined in simple fashion. The emphasis is on practicality. Along with the definitions a great many references are given to other more extensive texts and/or cases. Several appendices are included which contain miscellaneous useful material. A bibliography is furnished and also lists of annotations on medical legal matters from three leading general legal sets, *Proof of Facts, American Law Reports,* and *Negligence and Compensation Cases Annotated.* There is also a section affecting the relationship of doctors and lawyers in medical legal matters.

Since the dictionary is so brief it may be necessary to consult some of the suggested sources rather frequently. However, the book should prove a good finding tool.

19. Blake, John B., ed. **Safeguarding the Public: Historical Aspects of Medicinal Drug Control.** Papers from a Conference sponsored by the National Library of Medicine and the Josiah Macy, Jr., Foundation. Baltimore, Johns Hopkins Press, 1970. 200p. bibliog. index. $7.50. LC 76-84651. SBN 8018-1054-X.

This book provides historical perspective on one of the important scientific and social problems of medicine today, protecting and promoting the quality and efficacy of medicinal drugs. The papers, comments, and discussion presented provide points of view from medical and social historians, pharmacologists, legal experts, and representatives of the drug industry and government. The speakers were asked to consider especially problems relating to controls of the purity, quality, safety, and efficacy of prescription drugs rather than problems relating to out-and-out quackery, narcotic control, or price control. There are four sections presented as follows, each with several papers: (1) European backgrounds, (2) Scientific backgrounds, (3) Private professional controls, and (4) Federal regulations.

20. Curran, William J. **National Survey and Analysis of Certification-of-Need Laws: Health Planning and Regulation in State Legislatures, 1972.** Special legislative report. Chicago, American Hospital Association, 1973. 38p. bibliog. $1.50. LC 73-75138. ISBN 0-87258-118-7.

This survey was presented at the Conference on Health Planning, Certificates of Need, and Market Entry, sponsored by the American Enterprise Institute for Public Policy Research, June 15, 1972. The debate about whether the health care industry should be regulated by law in a manner similar to that of the so-called public utilities industries has been carried on for some time. Public regulation now seems to be acceptable if not desirable. This publication presents material on the status of this matter in the various states. The following topics are covered: the legislative initiative; the enacted laws; other legislative activity; legislative history and political trends; constitutional foundation for regulation; coverage of the laws; construction and services necessitating certification; administration, relationship to health planning; the review process; and health planning and standards of review. The following tables are included: (1) Legislative and regulatory action, (2) Coverage of certification program, and (3) Quality of review process.

21. Hassan, William E., Jr. **Law for the Pharmacy Student.** Philadelphia, Lea and Febiger, 1971. 285p. bibliog. index. $6.50. LC 78-135682. ISBN 0-8121-0320-3.

This book is intended primarily as a text for pharmacy students, but will be of interest to others who have a need to know about the laws governing the sale and use of drugs, business and administrative law, and related matters. These laws have undergone considerable change the past decade or so. There is a revised Federal Food, Drug, and Cosmetic Law, and also new regulations governing drug labeling, drug experimentation, and drug control. In addition the Medicare Law, the Public Information Act, and the Truth in Lending Act have been passed as well as some new state laws.

22. Inquiry. **The Role and Responsibility of a State in Promoting Good Health for Its People.** Proceedings of the Illinois Governor's Invitational Conference, Center for Continuing Education, Chicago, February 18-19, 1972. Chicago, Blue Cross Association, 1973. 90p. (Inquiry, vol. 10, no. 1, Supplement, March, 1973).

This publication presents the papers of the Conference which were published as a supplement to the periodical *Inquiry.* The material will be of most value to those in state administrations who are currently reviewing their responsibilities for health affairs. Five papers are included with comments and discussions on the following topics: Financing of health care, health facilities and health service, planning a more effective health care system, health manpower and the education of health personnel, and organization and administration for health affairs.

23. Moritz, Alan R., and R. Crawford Morris. **Handbook of Legal Medicine.** 3d ed. St. Louis, C. V. Mosby Co. 1970. 238p. illus. bibliog. index. $8.75. LC 73-126807. SBN 8016-3507-1.

This handbook has played a part in creating an atmosphere of harmony between the legal and medical professions which has been to the ultimate benefit of society. It is a sensible, brief, and understandable book. Information on newer developments are included such as: (1) medical, professional, civil, and criminal liability, (2) the physician, coroner, and violent death, (3) unusual features of suicides, (4) injuries attributable to ionizing radiation, (5) alcohol determination tests, (6) psychiatric analysis of criminal intent, (7) narcotics, and (8) organ transplants and human experimentation. A glossary is included.

24. U.S. Food and Drug Administration. Office of Administration. Division of Management Systems. **Food and Drug Administration Committees.** Washington, G.P.O., 1970. 113p.

This booklet was designed to provide information on the major committees within the Food and Drug Administration and on outside committees with which FDA personnel are associated. The publication states, however, that changes within the organization have been frequent. In spite of this, the lists should be of considerable assistance. There are several sections as follows: public advisory committees, interdepartmental committees, departmental committees, interbureau committees, international committees, non-governmental committees, and NIH study sections.

25. Willig, Sidney H. **The Nurse's Guide to the Law.** New York, McGraw-Hill Book Co., 1970. 264p. bibliog. index. $6.95. LC 79-76826.

The objective of this book is to aid in the development of personal and general guidelines that will assist the practicing nurse when she senses some irregularity in prospective action. Also educators in both collegiate and hospital nursing programs find it necessary to advise the nursing student concerning the elementary principles of pertinent law, and this book can be used to good advantage. Some of the matters taken up are legal requirements attached to specific practical activities, such as buying or caring for medical supplies, equipment, drugs (including narcotics), and the significance of civil rights, and public care legislation. Also of concern are matters that arise from contractual difficulties or tortious conduct, such as negligence, invasion of privacy, and the like. The treatment is brief, and the book will not serve as a do-it-yourself legal guide. However, it will be of value in alerting nurses to their rights and duties. The contents of the book are as follows: (1) Evolution of law and existing legal systems, (2) Legal, professional, and public status of the nurse, (3) The nurse as an agent, an independent contractor, and an employee, (4) Delegation, (5) Tort law: Unintentional torts, (6) Tort law: Intentional torts, (7) The defamatory torts: Libel and slander, (8) Contracts, (9) Agreements of guaranty, warranty, and special performance, (10) The nurse and criminal law, (11) Drugs and narcotics violations, (12) Statutes of limitations, (13) Fiduciary responsibility of the nurse, and (14) The trial. Also included is a glossary of legal terms and some other appended material such as a code of ethics.

3. RESEARCH AND GRANT INFORMATION

26. **Annual Register of Grant Support, 1973/74.** Deanna Sclar, ed., and the staff of Academic Media. Orange, New Jersey, Academic Media, 1973. 828p. index. LC 69-18307. ISBN 0-87876-037-7.

This annual publication is a comprehensive guide to fellowships, grant support programs of government agencies (including some foreign), foundations, and business and professional organizations. This year's edition has been considerably expanded to include grant programs from such new sources as labor unions, major industrial firms, and educational associations. The aim of the publication is to provide the academic and professional community with comprehensive, up-to-date information on all existing forms of financial aid. A great many types of grant support programs are covered, including advanced study, clinical research, in-service training, and also additional programs were added this year for those involved in fields of health and medicine, civic improvement, social welfare, and environmental action.

There are several sections: (1) General, (2) Humanities, (3) Social sciences, (4) Sciences, (5) Health and medical sciences, (6) Area studies, and (7) Environmental studies. Each entry under these sections contains such information as organization name, type of grant support, purpose, eligibility, financial data, duration, application information, deadline, address, and any existing special stipulations. Indexes are by subject, organization, geographic location, and personnel.

27. Flook, E. Evelyn, and Paul J. Sanazaro, eds. **Health Services Research and R & D in Perspective.** Ann Arbor, Michigan, Health Administration Press, 1973. 311p. bibliog. index. $7.50. LC 73-86625.

This volume summarizes the research that has been done in the field of health services. The findings of the most important individual studies and conclusions of the investigators are discussed. The aim of the publication is to place in perspective the evolution of health service research and R & D as we now know them by looking at their historical development and to attempt to see the way of future development. About one-third of the book is a bibliography. References are made to the citations in the text material. The citations are limited to publications in the 20th century through early 1973.

Chapter headings are as follows: (1) Health services research: origins and milestones, (2) Influence of philanthropic foundations and professional organizations, the federal government, and various commission reports, (3) Politics and health services research: a cameo study of policy in the health services in the 1930s, (4) Health services research in academia: a personal view, (5) Academic disciplines and health services research, (6) Federal health services R & D under the auspices of the National Center for Health Services Research and Development, (7) International health services research. The research publications cited in Chapter 1 have been classified as follows: health manpower; health facilities, organization and administration of health services; evaluation and quality of health services, utilization of health services; economics, costs, and financing of health care; social-behavioral aspects of health care; nursing health services research; dental health services research; pharmacy-related health services research; health care technology; research methods; and the emerging concept of health services research.

28. The Foundation Center. **The Foundation Directory.** 4th ed. Marianna O. Lewis, ed. New York, Columbia University Press, 1971. 642p. index. LC 60-13807. ISBN 0-87954-000-1.

The directory lists 5,454 nonprofit non-governmental agencies that make grants of $25,000 or more in the year of record or possessed assets of $500,000 or more. The listing is by state and presents so far as available: the legal name of the foundation, address, data on establishment, names of the donor, officers, trustees, an outline of general purposes, fields of interest, specific limitations, and for the most recent year the assets, amount of new gifts to the foundation, total expenditures, and grants. Also included in this edition for the first time is the person to whom communications should be addressed and the number of grants and their total value. There are three indexes: (1) Fields of interest, (2) Donors, trustees, and administrators, and (3) Foundations. The directory has been used by many persons and agencies, particularly those seeking funds, but also foundation trustees and executives have found it valuable.

The Foundation Center has since 1972 published a periodical, *Information Quarterly,* which offers updating of the listings in the directory.

29. **Grants Register, 1973-1975.** Edited by Ronald Turner. London, St. James Press; New York, St. Martin's Press, 1973. 685p. index. $17.50. LC 77-12055. ISBN 0-900997-13-3.

This reference work is published every two years to provide information on award opportunities primarily for students at or above the graduate level, academic staff, and those requiring further professional or advanced vocational or occupational training. Sources for assistance from government agencies and international, national, or private organizations are included. The following kinds of assistance are given by the organizations included: (1) Scholarships, fellowships, and research grants, (2) Exchange opportunities, vacation study awards and travel grants, (3) Grants-in-aid—including equipment, publication, and translation grants, and grants and funds for attending seminars, courses, conferences, etc. (4) Grants for all kinds of artistic or scientific projects, (5) Competitions, prizes, and honoraria, (6) Professional and vocational awards, and (7) Special awards. The work covers awards for nationals of the United States, Canada, United Kingdom, Ireland, Australia, New Zealand, South Africa, and the developing countries. However, more than one third of the awards listed are international in scope. A subject index for each country is furnished.

30. Katz, Jay. **Experimentation with Human Beings: The Authority of the Investigator, Subject, Professions, and State in the Human Experimentation Process.** With the assistance of Alexander Morgan Capron and Eleanor Swift Glass. New York, Russell Sage Foundation, 1972. 1159p. bibliog. index. $20.00. LC 70-188394. SBN 87154-438-5.

This large volume is organized rather like a law school casebook, but it is not intended for law students exclusively. It is addressed to both graduate and undergraduate students in many disciplines. The case studies are from medicine, psychology, sociology, biology, and law. The problems raised by human research are explored along with the attempts that have been made to resolve them. The authority which should be vested in the chief participants of the human experimentation process are explored, chiefly the investigator, the subject, the professions, and the state. The treatment is very comprehensive as a large number of problems and questions are presented and discussed. The aim of the book is to encourage the reader to sort out the conflicts and begin to formulate rules and procedures which will minimize the possibility of harm to the human being without impeding the acqusition of scientific knowledge. The author is a psychiatrist and Professor of Law and Psychiatry at Yale Law School.

31. Smithsonian Institution, Science Information Exchange. **Catalog of Health Services Research: Abstracts of Public and Private Projects, 1969-70.** Springfield, Va., National Technical Information Service, U.S. Department of Commerce, 1971. 1v. (various paging). index. DHEW Publication No. 72-3009. PB-207-129.

This catalog is a successor to *Health Economics Studies Information Exchange* published in 1968 by the Health Economics Branch, Division of Medical Care Administration, U.S. Public Health Service. The catalog presents resumes of current health services research and development projects. The resumes are arranged under six topics: (1) Policy, planning, and research methodology, (2) General health care administration, (3) Manpower: Planning and management, (4) Hospital management and planning, (5) Health services, and (6) Specific problem areas. Several indexes are included: subject, contractor, investigator, and supporting agency.

32. U.S. National Institutes of Health. **Public Health Service Grants and Awards.** Fiscal year 1973 funds. Pt.I, National Institutes of Health Research Grants. Washington, G.P.O., 1973. 257p. DHEW Publication No. (NIH) 74-197. $1.95. Stock No. 1740-00367.

This publication is prepared annually. It identifies and presents key items of information on research grants made by the National Institutes of Health. There are six other parts as follows: Part II, NIH research training grants, and medical library grants; Part III, NIH research contracts; Part IV, NIH health manpower education programs; Part V, Programs of the Food and Drug Administration; Part VI, Summaries of NIH programs by state and organization; Part VII, Programs of the Health Services and Mental Health Administration.

The data is presented in tables, most of which present tabulation of each program by principal investigator or director of the project, as well as by the state or city of the organization having responsibility for the work. In addition, each part contains summary material to indicate the extent of the financial support given by the agency administering the program.

4. INDEXES, ABSTRACTS, AND BIBLIOGRAPHIES

33. **Abstracts for Social Workers.** National Association of Social Workers. Quarterly. 1965– .

This publication covers nearly 200 journals in the field of social work and related areas. It includes sections on the aged, alcoholism and drug abuse, economic security, family and child welfare, health and medical care, mental health, and mental retardation in addition to other topics.

34. **Abstracts of Hospital Management Studies.** Cooperative Information Center for Hospital Management Studies, the School of Public Health, University of Michigan. Quarterly. 1964– .

The object of this publication is to acquaint the reader with studies and research in the field of hospital management and help him obtain copies of the reports he wants. A great many of the entries are for academic theses, although there are also many for periodical articles and research reports. The last issue each year is a cumulated one. The publication is of particular value to health professionals, researchers, educators, students, and administrators.

35. **Abstracts on Health Effects of Environmental Pollutants.** BioSciences Information Service of Biological Abstracts. Monthly. 1972– .

This abstract publication furnishes current information on environmental pollution primarily for scientists. It is supported by two machine-readable data bases and is comprised of selected material from BIOSIS and MEDLARS. Each issue contains bibliographic information and abstracts of about 1,000 research articles. There are author, subject, and CROSS indexes similar to those used in *Biological Abstracts.* In addition, there are annual cumulative author, subject and CROSS indexes. Material included is limited to these areas: (1) Occupational health and industrial medicine, (2) Chemicals or substances in the environment with emphasis on their effects on human health, (3) General reviews and original papers reporting potentially harmful effects of pollutants on humans, (4) Studies of lower vertebrates used as indicators of the substances toxic to man; and vertebrates and invertebrates as vectors in the food chain, (5) Reports of analytical methods for examining biological tissues or fluids.

36. **Air Pollution Abstracts.** U.S. Environmental Protection Agency, Office of Air Quality Planning and Standards. Monthly. 1970– .

The primary purpose of this publication is to inform personnel of the E.P.A. and others who are professionally interested in air pollution, of selected technical literature. However, in addition to the technical material there is also coverage of economic, legislative, administrative, and social aspects of the problem.

37. American Medical Association. **Medical and Surgical Motion Pictures: A Catalog of Selected Films.** 2d rev. ed. Chicago, American Medical Association, 1969. 572p. index.

This catalog contains information on 4,800 films which will be of particular value for the education of medical students, interns, residents, physicians, and individuals in fields allied to medicine. The catalog is divided into three sections: (1) Films for the basic sciences, (2) Clinical medicine and surgery, and (3) Paramedical sciences. The film descriptions include: title; statistics as to size, running time, black and white or color, silent, optical or magnetic sound, year of release, and language versions other than English; author, sponsor; producer; distributor; and an abstract of content with a statement as to approval by other organizations or evaluation from the *Journal of the American Medical Association* reviews. There is an index by title and distributor.

38. Ash, Joan. "Current Reference Works in Public Health." **American Journal of Public Health.** vol. 62, no. 7 (July 1972) pp. 1014-1017. ,
This annotated bibliography will help those who are attempting to make a literature search in the field of public health. It brings together tools from peripheral and related disciplines. Those titles most likely to be needed by public health workers are marked with an asterisk. Special topics included are: statistics, environmental health, medical care and health administration, occupational health, epidemiology and infectious and communicable diseases, maternal and child health, school health, and public health nursing.

39. Blake, John B., and Charles Roos, eds. **Medical Reference Works, 1679-1966: A Selected Bibliography.** Chicago, Medical Library Association, 1967. 343p. index. Medical Library Association Publication No. 3. $10.00. LC 67-30664.
This annotated bibliography is a revision of "A Bibliography of the Reference Works and Histories in Medicine and the Allied Sciences," published in the Medical Library Association's *Handbook of Medical Library Practice,* 2d ed., 1956. It is a fine comprehensive compilation, useful for all bio-science libraries. Some references considered to be of special usefulness to smaller medical libraries have been marked with an asterisk. The work is in three parts: the first, general medicine; the second, history of medicine; and the third (and longest), special subjects. The listing is being kept up-to-date with supplements. The section on public health is of particular interest.

40. **Business Periodicals Index.** H. W. Wilson Co. Monthly except August with cumulations. 1958– .
This index covers about 125 periodicals. It is a subject index to English language periodicals in the fields of accounting, advertising and public relations, automation, banking, communications, economics, finance and investments, insurance, labor, management, marketing, taxation, and specific businesses, industries, and trades. A good deal on medical subjects is included.

41. **Child Development Abstracts and Bibliography.** Published by the University of Chicago Press for the Society for Research in Child Development. 3 times per year. 1927– .
Each issue of this periodical contains a subject and author index, an abstract section, and a section of book reviews. All aspects of the subject are covered, including clinical medicine and public health, and sociology and social psychology.

42. **Current Bibliography of Epidemiology: A Guide to the Literature of Epidemiology, Preventive Medicine, and Public Health.** National Library of Medicine (co-sponsored by the American Public Health Association). Monthly. 1969– .

This publication provides a comprehensive and continuing index to the current medical periodical literature for physicians and investigators in community medicine and others concerned with the causes, prevention, and control of disease. There are two parts in each issue: Section 1, Selective Subject Headings, which includes the current references related to some 200 topics of interest to administrators, investigators, and teachers; and Section 2, Diseases, Organisms, Vaccines, which includes references related to causes, prevention, and control of specific diseases. The publication is prepared from the MEDLARS tapes for *Index Medicus.* Annual cumulations are planned.

43. **Dissertation Abstracts International.** Section A, Humanities; Section B, Sciences. Xerox University Microfilms. Monthly. 1938– .

This publication is a compilation of abstracts of doctoral dissertations submitted to the publisher by more than 300 cooperating institutions in the U.S. and Canada. A list of the institutions is given in each issue. However, not all institutions send all their doctoral dissertations, and they began submitting them at different times. Copies of the dissertations listed are available for purchase from the publisher as microfilm or Xerox prints. There is a keyword title and author index in each issue and there are some cumulated indexes. Section B contains the health sciences dissertations and includes such subject areas as hospital management and public health as well as the strictly scientific materials.

44. **Excerpta Medica Section 17. Public Health, Social Medicine, and Hygiene.** Excerpta Medica Foundation. 10 times per year. 1955– .

This abstracting journal which is part of the Excerpta Medica International Medical Abstracting Service, covers material in the general areas indicated and also includes material in the following subjects: statistics, communicable diseases, social hygiene, industrial medicine, dental hygiene, sanitation, military medicine, atomic warfare, nutrition, veterinary hygiene, and medical zoology.

45. **Excerpta Medica Section 35. Occupational Health and Industrial Medicine.** Excerpta Medica Foundation. 10 times per year. 1970– .

This publication is part of the Excerpta Medica International Abstracting Service. It indexes and abstracts materials in the following areas of the subjects indicated: legislation, social security, medical examination, work and leisure activities, labor, ergonomics, micro, physical, and chemical environment, sanitation, skin, respiratory tract, infections and toxins, cancerogenesis, mutagenesis, teratogenesis, mental health, accidents, disablement, rehabilitation, and medical treatment.

46. **Excerpta Medica Section 36. Health Economics and Hospital Management.** Excerpta Medical Foundation. 10 times per year. 1970– .

This journal, which is part of the comprehensive Excerpta Medica set of international medical abstracting services, indexes and abstracts material in such areas as general aspects of health care, health care organization, macroeconomics, health care systems and costs, insurance, hospital management and organization, and the like.

47. **Excerpta Medica Section 40. Drug Dependence.** Excerpta Medica Foundation. Monthly. 1973– .

This publication indexes and abstracts international literature pertaining to the non-medical use of drugs and related subjects. More than 5,000 journals are covered. The following subject areas are included: general materials, drugs with material arranged by type of drug, individual response, diagnosis, medical treatment, rehabilitation, epidemiology, social aspects, and prevention.

48. **Excerpta Medica Section 46. Environmental Health and Pollution Control.** Excerpta Medica Foundation. Monthly. 1971– .

This publication indexes and abstracts literature pertaining to environmental health, pollution control, and related subjects. More than 15,000 scientific journals and periodicals are screened for articles. These journals are in the fields of engineering, chemistry, the biomedical sciences, economics, physics, meteorology, and agriculture. Each issue includes an author and subject index which are cumulated annually at the end of each volume. The publication is of interest to engineers, managers, documentalists, and scientists working in the field of pollution control or environmental hygiene.

49. **Hospital Abstracts.** Great Britain. Her Majesty's Stationery Office, Department of Health and Social Security. Monthly. 1961– .

This publication surveys the world literature in the hospital field. The arrangement is by subject. There is an annual author and detailed subject index.

50. **Hospital Literature Index.** American Hospital Association. Quarterly. 1945– . (title varies).

This is an author and subject index to hospital literature covering such areas as administration, planning, and financing of hospitals and related health care institutions, and the administrative aspects of the medical, paramedical, and prepayment fields. There are annual and five-year cumulations. The cumulative issues list the periodicals indexed, an impressive number. They are all English language publications. This work is a very good, complete index of all aspects of hospital literature.

51. **Index Medicus.** U.S. National Library of Medicine. Monthly. 1960– .

This is a comprehensive bibliographic listing of articles appearing in current biomedical journals. All medical subjects are covered. Approximately 2,200 periodicals from all over the world are indexed. There is a subject and author section and a separate *Bibliography of Medical Reviews* in each issue. Also a complete key to title abbreviations and a list of subject headings used are issued annually in January each year.

A cumulated edition is published annually.

52. **International Pharmaceutical Abstracts.** American Society of Hospital Pharmacists. Semimonthly. 1964– .

This publication is devoted to all phases of the development and use of drugs and to the professional practice of pharmacy. It presents abstracts of articles from a large number of periodicals which are of interest to practitioners, research scientists, industrial pharmacists, professors, students, and those interested in public health. Each issue contains a subject index. In addition, there is a semi-annual cumulated subject index and an annual author index. The abstracts are arranged by subject and each issue has a section on sociology, economics, and ethics which is of special note.

53. **Medical Socioeconomic Research Sources.** American Medical Association, Archive-Library Department. Monthly. 1971— .

A forerunner of this index began in 1962 and was called *Index to the Literature of Medical Socioeconomics.* From the beginning the publication was valuable as it filled a gap in indexing. Many of the journals included are not indexed in *Index Medicus.* Each monthly issue lists under subject headings references to articles from a wide variety of sources covering the economics and sociology of health care. Each issue has an author index. There is an annual cumulation which contains a list of journals and serials indexed during the year, subject heading used, and a subject section and author index with the format of the monthly issues. It is easy to scan the subject section for articles of interest.

54. **Mental Retardation Abstracts.** U.S. Department of Health, Education and Welfare, Rehabilitation Services Administration, Division of Mental Retardation. Quarterly. 1964— .

Most of the abstracts included abstract research studies, although there are sections on treatment and training aspects and programmatic aspects. The latter includes planning and legislative facets, and community and recreational facets.

55. **Monthly Catalog of United States Government Publications.** U.S. Superintendent of Documents. Monthly. 1895— .

This is a current bibliography of publications issued by all branches of the government, including both the congressional and the department and bureau publications. The arrangement is by issuing agency. Each issue contains general instructions for ordering documents, and other general information. For each publication listed is given its full title, date, paging, price, Library of Congress card number, etc. There is an annual index by subject and agency, and since 1945 there has been a monthly index in each issue.

56. **Personnel Literature.** U.S. Civil Service Commission Library. Monthly. 1942— .

This publication abstracts material received in the Library of the Civil Service Commission. It includes books, pamphlets, periodical articles, dissertations, microforms, and other materials. The entries are arranged alphabetically by subject. There are several sections of interest such as health manpower; insurance, health; medical care; and public administration.

57. **Population Index.** Office of Population Research, Princeton University and Population Association of America, Inc. Quarterly. 1935— .

This publication is an annotated bibliography of books and periodical articles on all phases of population problems. It covers the literature of the world. Selection is on the basis of intrinsic merit, current interest, and the paucity or richness of the literature for the various areas and problems. Coverage is less complete in peripheral fields, and selection is less rigid in underdeveloped areas. The arrangement is by class, with annual cumulated indexes by author and country. Each issue contains a few articles of current interest.

58. **Population Sciences: Index of Biomedical Research.** U.S. National Institute of Child Health and Human Development, Center for Population Research. Monthly. 1973– .

This index is based on citations selected for the corresponding monthly issue of *Index Medicus.* It should provide a useful resource for those concerned with keeping abreast of the biomedical research literature in the population sciences. There is a subject section and an author index. The subject section is divided into a number of sections including, for example, anatomy and physiology, drug and radiation effects, contraceptive drugs and devices, reproductive behavior, and many others.

59. **Poverty and Human Resources Abstracts.** Sage Publications. Quarterly. 1966– .

This periodical contains abstracts of the most important current literature. It is used by businessmen, federal agencies and grantees, social service organizations, research groups, students, and faculty. It covers human, social, and manpower problems and solutions; minority group problems; slum rehabilitation; and rural poverty.

60. **Psychological Abstracts.** Nonevaluative Summaries of the World's Literature in Psychology and Related Disciplines. American Psychological Association. Monthly. 1927– .

The comprehensive publication covers over 8,000 journals, technical reports, and monographs in the field of psychology, with abstracts listed under 17 major classification categories. The section on "Treatment and Prevention" includes material on counseling, community mental health, crisis intervention, social casework, rehabilitation, hospital progress, and institutionalism.

61. **Public Affairs Information Service: Bulletin.** Public Affairs Information Service. Weekly with cumulations. 1915– .

This publication indexes books, pamphlets, government publications, reports of public and private agencies, and periodical articles. English language publications only are included. The fields covered are economic and social conditions, public administration, and international relations. There are quarterly and annual cumulations published.

62. **Readers' Guide to Periodical Literature.** H. W. Wilson Co. Semi-monthly Sept.-June; monthly in July and August; with cumulations. 1900– .

This index is a cumulated author and subject listing of periodical articles of general interest from American periodicals of broad, general, and popular character. Also included are some nontechnical magazines representing the important scientific subject fields. A good deal of material on public health is included. Entries are under author, subject, and occasionally title.

63. **Social Sciences Index.** H. W. Wilson Co. 4 times per year with cumulations. June 1974— .

This publication is an author and subject index to some 260 periodicals in the fields of psychology, physical anthropology, area studies, classical studies, economics, geography, history, nursing, political science, environmental sciences, sociology and related subjects. The coverage is international with the emphasis on American periodicals. It should be noted that this new index is based on a well-known *Social Sciences and Humanities Index* (1916—) and beginning with June 1974, H. W. Wilson is publishing also *Humanities Index* . The coverage in both new indexes is considerably expanded in comparison with the old *Social Sciences and Humanities Index.*

64. **Sociological Abstracts.** Sociological Abstracts, Inc. 7 times per year. 1952— .

This publication is co-sponsored by the American Sociological Association, Eastern Sociological Society, the International Sociological Association and the Midwest Sociological Society. Over 400 serials are covered. A section on the sociology of health and medicine is included. This ia a major index publication in the field of sociology.

65. **Speed: The Current Index to the Drug Abuse Literature.** Madison, Wisconsin, Student Association for the Study of Hallucinogens, Inc. (STASH) and the National Coordinating Council on Drug Education. Semi-monthly. 1973— .

This publication comes as part of the *Grassroots* subscription (see review #439) but may be subscribed to separately also. Bibliographic data on drug abuse articles from about 4,000 professional journals, books, and monographs are supplied rather promptly. The arrangement is by subject and/or form. No indexes have been supplied to date. The publication is most useful as a selection aid for monographs or as a current awareness tool for periodical articles.

66. U.S. National Library of Medicine. **Current Catalog.** U.S. Public Health Service. Monthly with quarterly and annual cumulations. 1966— .

This publication is a bibliographic listing of citations to publications cataloged by the National Library of Medicine. The monthly issues are arranged in six sections: (1) Name section, (2) Technical report name section, (3) Serials section, (4) Audiovisual section, (5) Added volumes, and (6) Directory of express cataloging service publishers sections. About 15,000 monographs, periodicals, technical reports, and audiovisual materials are listed each year.

The December 1973 issue will be the last monthly issue published. The quarterly and annual issues are to be continued. The "Added volumes" section will be continued in the quarterly issues.

67. U.S. National Library of Medicine. **Selected References on Environmental Quality as It Relates to Health.** GPO . Monthly. 1970— .

The publication cites articles selected from 2,200 biomedical journals. Many scientific articles are cited, but some are on social aspects of the subject. There is an author and a subject section. The monthly issues cumulate annually.

5. STATISTICS

68. American Hospital Association. **Hospital Statistics, 1972.** Chicago, American Hospital Association, 1973. 224p. index. $3.50.
The statistics presented in this publication are based on questionnaires sent to all hospitals registered in the United States. The material is presented in tables, and the data is very detailed.

69. American Medical Association. Center for Health Services Research and Development. **Reference Data on Socioeconomic Issues of Health.** Compiled by Robert J. Walsh. 1972 ed. Chicago, American Medical Association, 1972. 148p. bibliog. $1.00pa.
This small booklet presents a wide range of statistical data and analyses of problems of the health care community. Most of the data is in chart, graph, or tabular form; however, the analyses are in textual format. The bibliography is a list of the sources used, and itself should prove useful as a guide to more information.

70. **American Statistics Index.** Congressional Information Service. Annual with monthly supplements. 1973– .
This reference source provides access to the statistical publications of the U.S. government pertaining to the American people. Coverage of data on economic activity and natural resources is to begin with the 1974 volume. This publication serves a great need. It makes location of statistical information much easier than it was formerly.

71. **Book of the States, 1972-1973.** Volume 19. Lexington, Ky., Council of State Governments, 1972. 629p. index. $13.50; with two supplements, $19.50. LC 35-11433.
This book provides a source of information on the structures, working methods, financial and functional activities of the state governments. It also deals with the public service performed by them. The supplementary volumes list elected officials and legislators and administrative officials classified by functions. There is a health and welfare section. Many statistical tables are included, but the book is mainly text material.

72. Bourke, Geoffrey J., and James McGilvray. **Interpretation and Uses of Medical Statistics.** Oxford and Edinburgh, Blackwell Scientific Publications, 1969. 162p. illus. index. $4.75. SBN632-05370-4.
This book is intended to assist those who have little knowledge of statistics but who have need to keep abreast of advances in medicine and allied subjects and interpret basic notions of statistical inference presented therein. It will help the reader to become acquainted with terms and methods commonly employed in analysis and presentation of data.

73. Health Insurance Institute. **Source Book of Health Insurance Data, 1973-74.** 15th ed. New York, Health Insurance Institute, 1974. 76p. index. LC 60-187.

This pamphlet publication is a statistical report of the private health insurance business in the United States. Six major forms of health insurance are covered: hospital, surgical, regular medical, major medical, disability (loss of income) insurance, and dental insurance. The statistical data presented (mostly in tabular and graphic form) has been compiled from the reports of insurance companies and other health insuring plans, government agencies, and hospital and medical associations. Chapter headings are as follows: key health insurance statistics, the development of health insurance, extent of coverage under health insurance, trends in health insurance benefits, trends in health insurance premiums, medical care costs in the United States, and trends in morbidity. There is also a glossary.

74. Institute of Life Insurance. **Life Insurance Fact Book 1972.** New York, Institute of Life Insurance, 1972. 126p. charts. index. Free. LC 47-27134.

This useful compilation has been published annually for 27 years. It presents, mostly in charts, graphs, and tables, a record of the life insurance business. There is also interpretive text material. Generally speaking, only U.S. life insurance data is included, although some information is given on the foreign business of U.S. companies. This is a very good source of much statistical information. Original primary source references are indicated so that these publications may be consulted for additional data.

75. Jensen, Marilyn Anne. "Selected Sources of Current Population, Vital, and Health Statistics." **Bulletin of the Medical Library Association.** Vol. 60, No. 1 (January 1972) p.14-21.

This annotated bibliography includes government and non-government sources of statistics in the subject areas indicated. Publications giving local, regional, state, national, and international statistics are included. The arrangement is geographical and secondly by issuing body. Below the national level sources are given for California only, but similar publications are available for other states. Most of the sources given are for current statistics although some historical ones are included. The list is not comprehensive but is well-selected.

76. Kilpatrick, S. James, Jr. **Statistical Principles in Health Care Information.** Baltimore, University Park Press, 1973. 228p. bibliog. index. $12.50. LC 72-5213. ISBN 0-8391-0632-7.

This book was written for those who need a grasp of statistical principles in the health care professions such as physicians, nurses, hospital administrators, allied health workers, and behavioral scientists. No mathematical background is necessary; essential theory and methodology are presented and practical applications in hospital and laboratory management and health care included. Chapter titles are as follows: (1) Nature, use, and analysis of hospital and health care data, (2) Collection, presentation, and interpretation of health care information, (3) Rates, ratios, and indices, (4) Epidemiology and the design of surveys, (5) Distributions; location and dispersion, normal variation, (6) Elementary probability, (7) Estimates and confidence limits; use of tables, (8) The underlying distribution of statistics from repeated samples, (9) Significance tests,

(10) Decisions in health care, (11) Role of the computer in health care administration and research, and (12) Design of investigation.

77. Lilienfeld, Abraham M., Morton L. Levin, and Irving I. Kessler. **Cancer in the United States.** Cambridge, Mass., Harvard University Press, 1972. 546p. bibliog. index. (American Public Health Association Vital and Health Statistics Monographs). $12.00. LC 72-80658. SBN 674-09425-5.

The data in this volume came from the 1960 Census figures. It is concerned with the mortality from 86 different cancer sites, and morbidity data has been examined in depth and analyzed. A great amount of statistical data, particularly in tabular form, has been presented as well as text material. The contents is as follows: (1) Introduction, (2) Mortality trends, 1930 to 1959-61, (3) Mortality by age, sex, and color, (4) Mortality and marital status, (5) Mortality by geographic region, (6) Mortality, urbanization, and socioeconomic status, (7) Mortality among the foreign born and in their countries of origin, (8) Summary of mortality data for selected sites, (9) Suggested research and future prospects.

The authors feel that there is a continuing need for "national bookkeeping" in terms of monitoring the trends of mortality in various population groups, and perhaps also some continuing analysis of the geographic distribution of the various types of cancer.

78. **Monthly Labor Review.** U.S. Bureau of Labor Statistics. Monthly. 1915— .

This periodical includes articles on labor and related subjects, including employment, labor force, wages, prices, productivity, unit labor costs, collective bargaining, workers' satisfaction, social indicators, and labor developments abroad. There are regular features such as a review of developments in industrial relations, significant court decisions in labor cases, book reviews, and current labor statistics. The latter is given in tabular form. The material published is indicative of trends in the labor field. Information on medical care spending is included occasionally.

79. **Municipal Year Book, 1973.** Volume 40. Washington, International City Management Association, 1973. 366p. index. LC 34-27121.

This publication is called an "authoritiative resume of urban data and developments." The purpose of the book is to provide local officials with relevant information on questions and issues of urban management. It contains both primary and secondary data. The material is divided into sections as follows: trends, urban management: issues and activities, intergovernmental relations, municipal finance, public manpower, public safety, and directories. Many tables of statistical information are included. The directories section includes listings of officials and organizations.

80. U.S. Bureau of the Census. **County and City Data Book, 1972.** A Statistical Abstract Supplement. Washington, GPO, 1973. 1020p. $12.50 LC 72-4576. Stock No. 0324-00121.

This volume contains data on counties, cities, metropolitan areas, urbanized areas, unincorporated places, regions, divisions, and states. There are many tables of data, maps and charts, and statistical appendices. The sources of the data are given.

81. U.S. Bureau of the Census. **Statistical Abstract of the United States.** Washington, GPO. Annual. 1879– .

This well-known publication is the standard summary of statistics on the social, political, and economic organization of the United States. It contains much material, usually in tabular form, for reference and also serves as a guide to other sources. Much of the data is from government sources, but some is from private agencies.

82. U.S. Center for Disease Control. **Morbidity and Mortality.** Weekly Report. U.S. Center for Disease Control. Weekly. 1952– .

The data presented in this publication is based on material furnished by state health departments. Most of the data is presented in tabular form, but in addition, accounts of case investigations and outbreaks of epidemics are reported. Current trends are indicated and international notes included.

83. U.S. Health Services and Mental Health Administration. National Center for Health Services Research and Development. **Health Service Use: National Trends and Variations, 1953-1971.** By Ronald Andersen and others. Washington, GPO, 1972. 57p. DHEW Publication No. (HSM) 73-3004. HE 20.2102.

This report has two purposes. The first is to document the public's use of health services in the U.S.; the second is to consider major policy issues regarding the distribution of medical care according to such factors as age, income, race, and residence. The data is based on random samples of families. In addition, data was provided also by physicians, clinics, hospitals, insuring organizations, and employers regarding the families' medical care and health insurance in order to verify and add additional details. The report is divided into sections dealing with various aspects of medical care such as: regular source of care, physician care, hospital care, surgical procedures, obstetrical care, dental care, Medicaid benefits, disability days, and physical contacts. Also included are appended materials outlining the methods used in the study.

84. U.S. Health Services and Mental Health Administration. National Center for Health Statistics. **Health Resources Statistics: Health Manpower and Health Facilities, 1972-73.** Washington, GPO, 1973. 569p. index. DHEW Publication No. (HSM) 73-1509. LC 66-62580.

This report is published annually to provide current and comprehensive statistics on a wide range of health topics. It is hoped that this data will be of value for planning, administrating, and evaluating health programs. Part 1 of the publication gives statistics on health occupations of various types such as physicians, dentists, and nurses and those known as "allied health" occupations. Part 2 gives statistics on inpatient health facilities such as hospitals, nursing care, and related homes. Part 3 presents data on outpatient and nonpatient health services such as clinical laboratories, family planning services, etc. Sources of the statistics are indicated.

85. U.S. Health Services and Mental Health Administration. National Center
for Health Statistics. **Hospitals: A County and Metropolitan Area Data
Book.** Data compiled from the 1969 master facility inventory. Washington,
GPO, 1973. 245p. DHEW Publication No. (HSM) 73-1215-1. $3.10.
LC 78-609001.

This publication is made up almost entirely of tables which present information
on hospitals. Such data as number of beds, occupancy rate, admissions, and type
of ownership for various kinds of hospitals is presented. The tables are presented
by state, standard metropolitan area, and county.

86. U.S. Health Services and Mental Health Administration. National Center
for Health Statistics. **Nursing Homes: A County and Metropolitan Area
Data Book.** Data compiled from the 1969 master facility inventory.
Washington, GPO, 1973. 135p. DHEW Publication No. (HSM) 73-1215-2.
$2.10. LC 78-609001. Stock No. 1722-00280.

This publication is made up almost entirely of a number of tables which present
information on nursing and personal care homes. It provides such information as
number of homes, number of beds, number of personnel, personnel-to-resident
ratio per 100 residents, beds-to-population ratio per 1,000 population aged 65
and over, and ratio of beds to full-time equivalent personnel per 100 beds. The
tables are by state, standard metropolitan statistical area, county, and geographic
region.

87. U.S. Social Security Administration. Office of Research and Statistics.
Medical Care Expenditures, Prices, and Costs: Background Book.
Washington, GPO, 1974. 90p. DHEW Publication No. (SSA) 74-11909.
$1.20. LC 73-600318. Stock No. 1770-00232.

Much concern has been shown because medical care costs have risen so much
faster in recent years than most other costs in the economy. As a result, the
health industry became a primary target of the Economic Stabilization Program.
The first edition of this publication (January 1972) presented summary data on
medical care costs and prices. The focus of this revised edition is on the effect of
the Economic Stabilization Program on health care spending. It summarizes the
available data on how medical care costs have responded to a period of economic
controls. Chapter headings are as follows: (1) Medical care expenditures,
(2) Medical care price trends, (3) Hospital prices and costs, (4) Physicians' fees
and income, (5) Dentists' fees and income, (6) Skilled nursing facilities and
charges, (7) Private health insurance. The material is presented in text and tabular form. The sources of the data are included. General trends are pointed out
and analyzed.

88. Wasserman, Paul, Eleanor Allen, Charlotte Georgi, and Janice McLean, eds.
**Statistical Sources: A Subject Guide to Data on Industrial, Business,
Social, Educational, Financial, and Other Topics for the United States and
Selected Foreign Countries.** Rev. 3d ed. Detroit, Gale Research Co., 1971.
647p. $27.50. LC 72-127923.

This guide may be used to aid in locating current statistical data. The sources are
arranged alphabetically by subject. Librarians, business executives, government

officials, executives of associations and professional societies, research workers, and students will find the work of value.

89. **World Almanac and Book of Facts.** Newspaper Enterprise Association, Inc. Annual. 1868– .
This familiar publication contains a great deal of factual and statistical information of interest in the health care field. New developments and research in medicine, birth and death rates, information and statistics about diseases, hospital statistics, medical education, insurance, drug store sales, drug discoveries, and drug abuse information are among the subjects covered.

6. PERIODICALS

90. **Addiction and Drug Abuse Report.** A Confidential Newsletter Covering All Aspects of Drug Abuse, Its Prevention, and Treatment of Its Victims. In two parts. Grafton Publications, Inc. Monthly. 1970— .

The aim of this newsletter is to keep readers up-to-date on the constantly changing addiction scene, the progress of treatment methods, and community action in the field. A good deal of attention is given to alcoholism as well as to other drug abuse. The publication is particularly useful for those working closely with addicts.

91. **American College of Surgeons. Bulletin.** American College of Surgeons. Monthly. 1916— .

This bulletin contains mostly news and official announcements and statements of the organization. In addition, there are frequently articles of socioeconomic interest.

92. **American Dental Association. Journal.** American Dental Association. 13 times per year. 1913— .

This official journal includes original articles, news, editorials, announcements, letters, book reviews, death notices, advertising, material on laws and proposed legislation, and matters of professional interest as well as association affairs.

93. **American Journal of Hospital Pharmacy.** American Society of Hospital Pharmacists. Monthly. 1943— .

This journal is the official publication of the American Society of Hospital Pharmacists and combines with it the American Journal of Clinical Pharmacy. The main object of the publication is to assist pharmacists practicing in hospitals and related institutions in the improvement of institutional pharmaceutical services in the interest of better patient care. Articles are on a rather wide range of topics. These include management, administration, systems, planning, professional practice and problems, and clinical articles. There are special features in each issue such as law notes, news, and drug information.

94. **American Journal of Nursing.** American Journal of Nursing Company. Monthly. 1901— .

Each issue of this periodical has a number of articles on a wide range of topics. In addition, there are special features, news, and editorials. Special features include drug data, equipment, book reviews, and the like. This is the leading periodical for nurses, but there is much in it of interest to those in the public health field.

95. **American Journal of Public Health.** American Public Health Association. Monthly. 1911— .

This periodical is the official publication of the American Public Health Association. It contains organizational news and announcements. In addition, it publishes high quality articles on public health, editorials, letters to the editor, book reviews, death notices, employment opportunities, and contains advertising. Of recent years, a good deal of material on the environment has appeared.

96. **American Medical Association. Journal.** American Medical Association. Weekly. 1883— .
This publication is the official journal of the American Medical Association. It contains organizational news and announcements as well as clinical and professional articles, letters from readers, editorials, book reviews, questions and answers, selected abstracts of articles from other journals, death notices, and a good deal of advertising.

97. **American Pharmaceutical Association. Journal.** American Pharmaceutical Association. Monthly. New Series. 1961— .
This periodical is one of the journals published by the American Pharmaceutical Association. It contains organization news and announcements, professional (rather than scientific) articles, letters from readers, book reviews, personal news, and advertising. Also included is a page for the Student A. Ph.A. Group.

98. **Archives of Environmental Health.** American Medical Association. Monthly. 1960— .
This journal is the official publication of the American Academy of Occupational Medicine and the American College of Preventive Medicine. Each issue contains a number of articles on such subjects as pollution, respiratory disease, carcinogens, effects of toxic materials, and industrial health and hygiene. In addition, there are letters to the editor, news items, book reviews, editorials, and brief notes on articles currently appearing in other periodicals.

99. **Association of Food and Drug Officials of the United States. Quarterly Bulletin.** Editorial Committee of the Association of Food and Drug Officials of the United States. Quarterly. 1937— .
This bulletin publishes papers presented at meetings of the Association, such as the Annual Conference, and sectional and local conferences of Food and Drug Officials. Complete proceedings of the meetings of the National Association, abstracts of meetings of sectional and local organizations, and news items relative to food and drug control appear from time to time.

100. **Attack on Narcotic Addiction and Drug Abuse.** New York State Narcotic Addiction Control Commission. Quarterly. 1967— .
This tabloid-sized news publication contains information on developments in drug related problems in New York State. There are articles about legal matters, treatment of addicts, education, rehabilitation, and like matters. Also directories of agencies that provide help to the drug user are included from time to time.

101. **Bulletin on Narcotics.** United Nations, Division of Narcotic Drugs. Quarterly. 1949— .
This international journal is published in English and French. Selected articles are subsequently published in Spanish and Russian, and a summary of each volume is issued in Chinese every year. The publication covers all aspects of drug control,

the work of international groups responsible in this field, developments in treatment, rehabilitation and social reintegration of addicts. Some scientific articles are published, and when included, they describe original research.

102. **Canadian Journal of Public Health: Revue Canadienne de Santé Publique.** Canadian Public Health Association. Bimonthly. 1910— .
This journal has a balance of articles of both technical and scientific content and the philosophical or general type. Occasionally there are issues on special topics. The periodical is a medium for communication among members of the Association as well as a journal that presents formal articles.

103. **Community Mental Health Journal.** Behavioral Publication, Inc. Quarterly. 1965— .
This journal is devoted to new approaches in mental health research, theory, and practice as they relate to the community, broadly defined. The articles are scholarly, and some knowledge of social science terminology may be necessary for complete understanding of what is presented.

104. **Contemporary Drug Problems: A Law Quarterly.** Federal Legal Publications, Inc. Quarterly. 1971— .
While most of the articles in this periodical are concerned with the legal aspects of drug abuse, some material is included on education, policy, social problems, treatment, employment, and other aspects of the drug problem. Book reviews are included.

105. **Drug Enforcement.** Drug Enforcement Administration, U.S. Department of Justice. Quarterly. 1973— .
This publication continues the *BNDD Bulletin.* Articles on miscellaneous matters of drug enforcement are presented with many photographs. There is a section on notable cases and also photographs and descriptions of persons wanted by the Drug Enforcement Administration.

106. **Emergency Health Services Digest.** U.S. Public Health Service, Health Services and Mental Health Administration, Division of Emergency Health Services. Approximately annual. 1969— .
This digest is published to help those engaged in the planning, programming, and delivery of emergency health services keep abreast of useful literature. It contains summaries of current articles which have appeared in professional journals and other periodicals. The digests are arranged by subject.

107. **Environment.** Scientists' Institute for Public Information. 10 times per year. 1958— .
This periodical contains articles for the layman on all matters relating to environmental problems. Also included are letters, book reviews, and news of current events.

108. **Environmental Science and Technology.** American Chemical Society. Monthly. 1967— .

This publication contains research articles, features, news, trends, notes on new products and manufacturers' literature, book reviews, editorials, letters, meeting notices, and the like.

109. **FDA Consumer.** U.S. Food and Drug Administration. 10 times per year. 1967– .
This official magazine of the Food and Drug Administration was previously known as the *FDA Papers.* It publishes reports that summarize actions under the Food, Drug and Cosmetic Act, also regional reports, and explains the stand FDA takes on many issues. There are articles on such subjects as treatment for drug abuse, nutrition, vitamins, and drug development.

110. **FDA Drug Bulletin.** U.S. Food and Drug Administration. Monthly. 1971– .
This newsletter presents news and reports of clinical interest especially for practicing physicians and other health professionals. Information about new drugs is presented, often prior to their marketing. Also new information about older drugs is reported.

111. **FDC Reports—The Pink Sheet: Drugs and Cosmetics.** FDC Reports, Inc. Weekly. 1939– .
This publication is a specialized newsletter for executives in the drug, cosmetic, and related industries. There are trade and government memos, stock reports, reports on sales and earnings of companies, reports of conferences and meetings, legislation, and information about people and companies. Much news is reported that is not readily found elsewhere; it is a "scandal sheet" of sorts.

112. **Family Health.** Family Health Magazine, Inc. Monthly. 1969– .
This interesting, rather new publication specializes in family health matters and is written in popular style for the general public. Several widely known physicians are on the editorial board, including Christian Barnard and Morris Fishbein. There are articles and special sections on general health problems, mental health, child care, nutrition, veterinary medicine, and many other topics.

113. **Federal Register.** U.S. Office of Federal Register, National Archives and Records Service, General Services Administration. Distributed by GPO. Daily, Monday through Friday (no publication on Saturdays, Sundays, and official holidays). 1936– .
This publication makes available to the public regulations and legal notices issued by the Executive Branch of the Federal Government. These include presidential proclamations and executive orders and federal agency documents of public interest. Monthly, quarterly, and annual indexes are published. The material in the *Federal Register* is codified and later published in the *Code of Federal Regulations.*

114. **Food, Drug, Cosmetic Law Journal.** Commerce Clearing House. Monthly. 1946– .
This journal records the progress of the law in the field of food, drugs, and cosmetics, and provides a discussion of it as a service to the public. Each issue contains five or six articles on various aspects of the law with the intent of creating

a better knowledge and understanding of it, promoting due operation and development of it, and bringing about remedial action.

115. **Geriatrics.** Lancet Publications, a division of the New York Times Media Co. Monthly. 1946– .
This journal publishes clinical articles on diseases and conditions that most commonly affect older individuals. Also, each issue contains information on such things as government programs for the elderly, current developments in medicine and allied fields, and new government regulations. In addition, there is an editorial section, book reviews, and a section of abstracts of geriatric articles from other current journals.

116. **Health Resources News.** Health Resources Administration, U.S. Public Health Service. Monthly. 1973– .
This newsletter presents information about the education of health professionals, the development of health resources, research, health statistics, official news about the issuing agency, and related material.

117. **Health Services Reports.** U.S. Health Services Administration. Bimonthly. 1878– .
This periodical was formerly called *Public Health Reports.* It contains scientific papers concerned with the delivery of health care services and other facets of health care, and technical reports on research studies. Also, papers on new programs, projects, ideas, and news of the health field are included.

118. **Hospital Progress.** Catholic Hospital Association. Monthly. 1920– .
This publication is the official journal of the Catholic Hospital Assocation. It contains articles of an administrative and managerial nature as well as papers which express official positions of the association. In addition, there are a number of recurring features such as letters to the editor, book reviews, a calendar of events, a law forum, news and reports, and news about people and places.

119. **Hospital Topics.** Hospital Topics, Inc. Monthly. 1923– .
Each issue of this periodical has two or three featured articles on subjects such as hospital practice, management, financing, planning, organization, and the like. There are, in addition, a great many special departments which present columns on the operating room, financial problems, the pharmacy, hospital law, housekeeping, new products, new literature, films, and related topics.

120. **Hospital Week.** American Hospital Association. Weekly. 1965– .
This newsletter gives up-to-date information on such matters as legislation and trends that affect health care, particularly of interest to hospitals.

121. **Hospitals.** American Hospital Association. Semimonthly. 1936– .
This periodical is an official publication of the American Hospital Association. Each issue contains a number of articles, many of them on administration, management, and personnel. Also included are sections on food service, education and training, nursing, and the pharmacy. In addition, there are regular features such as a calendar of meetings, questions and answers, a discussion of

accreditation problems, federal news, books reviews, personnel changes and deaths, and general news.

122. **Inquiry: A Journal of Medical Care Organization, Provision, and Financing.** Blue Cross Association. Quarterly. 1964— .
Each issue contains several articles on the economics of health care, the emphasis being on health insurance. The articles are particularly concerned with original research, demonstrations, or the concepts and philosophy surrounding the organization, provision, and financing of medical care. Articles discussing innovative programs or policies are particularly sought. There is a good section of book reviews included.

123. **International Journal of the Addictions.** Marcel Dekker. Six times per year. 1966— .
This journal is sponsored by the Institute for the Study of Drug Abuse. It publishes scholarly articles on all aspects of addiction, including narcotics, alcohol, and tobacco. Each issue also contains a section of research notes which presents brief sketches that describe research being carried out.

124. **The Journal.** Alcoholism and Addiction Research Foundation, Toronto. Monthly. 1972— .
This tabloid sized publication is designed to familiarize professionals and other interested persons with recent developments in the alcohol and drug dependence field. It reports and interprets news in the areas of research, treatment, education, enforcement, and social policy.

125. **Journal of Environmental Education.** Dembar Educational Research Services. Four times per year. 1969— .
This journal is "devoted to research and development in ecological communications." Each issue presents a number of articles, most dealing with some aspect of education. In addition, there is a book review section, field news, and an editorial section.

126. **Journal of Health and Social Behavior.** American Sociological Association. Quarterly. 1960— .
This journal publishes scholarly articles in the fields of health, sociology, psychology, and related areas. Also, book reviews and letters to the editor are included.

127. **Journal of Psychedelic Drugs.** STASH Press. Semiannual. 1968— .
This journal is a cooperative venture between the Haight-Ashbury Free Medical Clinic and the Student Association for the Study of Hallucinogens (STASH). The goal of the journal when established was to provide a method for dissemination of honest, objective drug information and to alert workers in the field to the rapidly changing drug abuse pattern which developed in the Haight-Ashbury district of San Francisco and spread to other parts of the country. In more recent issues, emphasis has been on special themes and the "politics of drug abuse." Film reviews and bibliographies are included from time to time.

128. **Medical Care.** Official Journal of the Medical Care Section, American Public Health Association. J. B. Lippincott. Six times per year. 1963– .
This official publication serves as an international medium for publication of articles in the broad field of medical care and attempts to encourage progress in the research, planning, organization, financing, provision, and evaluation of health services. Original papers and brief communications are published.

129. **Medical Care Review.** Bureau of Public Health Economics, School of Public Health, University of Michigan. Monthly, except September. 1944– .
This publication was formerly called "Public Health Economics and Medical Care Abstracts." It contains brief reviews or abstracts of articles that appear originally in other periodicals. There are three main sections: news, abstracts, and recent publications. The news section is broken down as follows: legislation, government programs, insurance, personnel, illness, drugs and appliances, reports and comments, and other countries. The abstract section is broken down into such subsections as: general materials, basic data, personnel, facilities, organization of payment, and organization of services. The "Recent Publications" section is a bibliography with no annotations.

130. **Medical Economics.** Medical Economics Co. Fortnightly. 1923– .
This journal publishes articles on economic problems from the physician's point of view. Such subjects as fees, malpractice, investments, retirement funds, office personnel, peer-review plans, insurance, etc., are discussed in the articles. There are also special sections of memos from the editor, letters to the editor, money management, and other similar features.

131. **Medical Marketing and Media: The Monthly Intercom of the Medical Marketplace.** Navillus Publishing Co. Monthly. 1966– .
This journal, formerly called *Pharmaceutical Marketing and Media,* contains articles of professional interest, material on laws and proposed laws and regulations, news and opinions, and information of particular interest to drug manufacturers and marketers.

132. **Medical Times.** Romaine Pierson Publishers, Inc. Monthly. 1872– .
This publication for physicians publishes several featured articles each month that alert practitioners to problems, new treatments, and the like. There are also a number of special sections on such matters as investing, travel, meetings, malpractice, new products, education, letters to the editor, and diagnosis.

133. **Medical World News.** McGraw-Hill, Inc. Weekly, except for June 29, July 27, August 17 and 31 issues. 1968– .
This periodical, which is primarily for physicians, contains articles to inform about recent developments in treatment and practice. Included are articles on laws and regulations, business, liability, and the like as well as those on scientific developments. There are letters to the editor, editorials, and a names in the news section.

134. **Mental Health Digest.** U.S. National Institute of Mental Health. Distributed by GPO. Monthly. 1969– .

This publication prints condensed versions of articles appearing in the current mental health literature. It reflects the whole spectrum of mental health liter-ature. It reflects the whole spectrum of mental health and presents a broad sam-pling of scientific material and professional points of view. Also, news digests are sometimes included.

135. **Metropolitan Life Insurance Company. Statistical Bulletin.** Metropolitan Life Insurance Company. Monthly. 1920— .
This free publication contains a few articles on subjects such as mortality, longev-ity, diseases, and public health trends. Also, many statistical charts and graphs are included.

136. **Milbank Memorial Fund Quarterly: Health and Society.** Milbank Memorial Fund. Quarterly. 1923— .
This is a basic journal in the field of sociology and health. It contains scholarly papers and reports on the various projects supported by the fund which cover a wide range of research activities. Papers are included in the fields of public health, medicine, psychology, psychiatry, social psychology, sociology, education, demography, health education, fertility, and population control.

137. **Modern Hospital.** McGraw-Hill. Monthly. 1913— .
This periodical contains all kinds of information about hospitals. There are arti-cles and information on trends in hospital management, new laws and proposed legislation and regulations, association news, finances, business practice, labor-atory design, hospital equipment, the pharmacy, food service, new products, and news about people.

138. **Modern Medicine.** Modern Medicine Publications. Biweekly. 1933— .
Each issue contains a few articles on medical developments and matters of pro-fessional interest. In addition, there are letters to the editor, a report on matters in Washington, abstracts from other medical journals, a list of new books, new products, and a section on diagnostic assistance.

139. **NABP Newsletter.** National Association of Boards of Pharmacy. Monthly. 1963— .
This newsletter contains information of most interest to educators in the phar-maceutical field as it contains material on trends and financing of education, laws and regulations affecting training, licensing, and news of the various phar-maceutical associations. Some personal news is also included on appointments and the like.

140. **Narcotics and Drug Abuse—A to Z: A Monthly Newsletter.** Croner Publica-tions. Monthly.
Each issue of this newsletter usually contains the following sections: A feature article, press review, foreign news, legislative reports, last minute news, and book reviews.

141. **National Drug Reporter.** National Coordinating Council on Drug Educa-tion. Semimonthly. 1971— .

The publisher of this newsletter is the country's largest private nonprofit drug consortium of 130 national professional, law enforcement, government, youth and service organizations, and corporations. The aim of the Council is to make a coordinated effort to find workable approaches to drug abuse prevention. The newsletter contains information on pertinent national projects, laws and proposed legislation, meetings, publication, and other related matters.

142. **The Nation's Health.** American Public Health Association. Monthly. 1971– .
This publication is the official newspaper of the Association. It contains public health news, association news, editorials, policy statement, commentaries, occasional book reviews, and job openings.

143. **Notes and Tips.** Harper and Row, Publishers, Inc. Medical Department. Monthly. 1970– .
This publication, which is primarily for physicians, contains sections on drug notes, diagnostic aids, abstract-reviews, and money matters. Frequently there are brief sketches and cover photographs of medical schools and centers. The "Money Matters" section is of most interest to those concerned with health care economics.

144. **Nuclear Safety.** U.S. Atomic Energy Commission. Bimonthly. 1959– .
This journal covers significant developments in the field of nuclear safety. The scope is limited to topics concerned with the analysis and control of hazards associated with nuclear reactors, operations involving fissionable materials, and the environment. Primary emphasis is said to be on safety in reactor design, construction, and operation; however, safety considerations in reactor fuel fabrication, spent-fuel processing, nuclear waste disposal, handling of radioisotopes, and environmental effects of these operations are also included. The articles are interpretive in type. There is a section on current events.

145. **PMA Newsletter.** Pharmaceutical Manufacturers Association. Weekly. 1959– .
This newsletter publishes information, particularly on legislation and regulations, that affect the pharmaceutical industry. It contains a good deal of material of socioeconomic interest.

146. **Psychology Today.** Communications/Research/Machines, Inc. Monthly. 1967– .
This magazine, which is about psychology, society, and human behavior, publishes articles of somewhat popular appeal on a wide range of topics. Professional psychologists write the articles for the most part, but they are for the public. The publication helps bridge the gap between the professional and the general reader. Many articles deal with medical problems, physiology, and sociology, although psychology is the main emphasis.

147. **Public Welfare: Journal of the American Public Welfare Association.**
American Public Health Association. Quarterly. 1945– .

Each issue of this journal contains articles on various aspects of welfare services. These include such areas as philosophies, management, law, financing, career education, and community problems. Articles frequently deal with medical problems and public health. Book reviews are included.

148. **Quarterly Journal of Studies on Alcohol: Pt. A, Originals.** Journal of Studies on Alcohol, Inc., at Rutgers Center of Alcohol Studies. Quarterly. 1940— .
This journal publishes reports of research for all scientific fields which relate to alcohol. This includes medicine, pharmacology, sociology, psychology, criminology, mental health, and other fields. Besides the research papers, there is a section of notes and comments and current events. Since 1968 the journal has been issued in two parts. This one, which contains original articles, and Part B which includes abstracts of current literature and other documentation.

149. **Quarterly Journal of Studies on Alcohol: Pt. B, Documentation.** Journal of Studies on Alcohol, Inc., at Rutgers Center of Alcohol Studies. Quarterly. 1940— .
This section of the journal contains abstracts of current literature on the subject of alcohol, an index of subjects and authors (included in each issue), newly accepted articles to be published in Part A of the journal, new titles of periodical literature (from other journals), and new titles of books and other documents, and book reviews.

150. **Radiation Data and Reports.** U.S. Environmental Protection Agency, Office of Radiation Programs. Monthly. 1960— .
This publication presents data and reports provided by Federal, State, and foreign governmental agencies, and other cooperating organizations. Both interpretive manuscripts and those that present original data are published.

151. **Social Science and Medicine: An International Journal.** Pergamon Press. Monthly. 1967— .
This journal publishes scholarly articles to aid the dissemination of important research and theoretical work in all areas of common interest to the sociobehavioral sciences and medicine, including psychiatry and epidemiology. Interrelationships between the various branches of medicine and the social sciences are emphasized. Book reviews, proceedings of symposia, and details of research (planned and in progress) are additional features.

152. **Social Security Bulletin.** U.S. Social Security Administration. Monthly. 1938— .
This official publication of the Social Security Administration reports current information and statistics on the operation of the program and also reports on new pertinent research. News notes are included as are a list of recent publications of interest. Beginning in 1949, an annual statistical supplement has been published with the bulletin.

153. **Today's Health.** American Medical Association. Monthly. 1922– .
This popular publication contains articles for the public on matters of public
health, hygiene, and all matters of such concern. There is much on family health,
and also a good deal of interest to young people and children. There are many
special features such as columns on cosmetics, dental health, and general questions and answers. Also included is a good deal of health related news.

154. **Trustee: Journal for Hospital Governing Boards.** American Hospital Association. Monthly. 1948– .
This journal is for individuals who are serving on hospital governing boards and
who need to keep up-to-date on administrative questions. Concise articles
examine the problems of today's health care system.

155. **Voice of the Pharmacist.** American College of Apothecaries. Semimonthly.
1958– .
This newsletter presents professional news for the practicing pharmacist. Information on such matters as new laws and proposed legislation, continuing education,
economic affairs, and pharmaceutical organization news is included.

7. DIRECTORIES

156. American Medical Association. **Directory of National Voluntary Health Organizations.** 7th ed. Chicago, American Medical Association, 1971. 110p. index. $2.50.

A voluntary health agency is defined as "any nonprofit association organized on a national, state, or local level; composed of lay and professional persons; dedicated to the prevention, alleviation, and cure of a particular disease, disability, or group of diseases and disabilities. It is supported by voluntary contributions primarily from the general public and expends its resources for education, research, and service programs relevant to the disease and disabilities concerned."

The directory lists various agencies giving address, key personnel, major purpose, organizational structure, finance and fund raising information, and programs of each. The listings are arranged alphabetically by subject interest and include such topics as alcoholism, allergic diseases, birth defects, cancer, diabetes, drug abuse, sex education, and many others. A.M.A. policy statements and guidelines are included.

157. **American Medical Directory.** 25th ed. Chicago, American Medical Association, 1969. 3 vols. $90.00.

The first volume of this directory is an alphabetical index of physicians of the United States, its possessions, and U.S. physicians temporarily located in foreign countries. Volumes two and three are geographical registers of physicians arranged alphabetically within each state and city. In volume one, only the city of practice is given following the names. In volumes two and three, other brief information about each physician is given by code, such as whether or not he is a member of the American Medical Association, professional mailing address, year of birth, medical education obtained, year of license, etc.

158. **Directory of Medical Specialists Holding Certification by American Specialty Boards.** 15th ed. Chicago, Published for the American Board of Medical Specialties by Marquis Who's Who, 1972. 2 vols. index. $47.00. LC 40-9671. ISBN 0-8379-0515-X.

This directory lists the medical specialists of the United States who have been certified by American Specialty Boards. Details are given on the requirements for certification, and also included is other information on each of the Boards.

The bulk of the publication is the listing of the physicians arranged according to the Specialty Board in alphabetical sequence. Within each Board section, names are listed according to alphabetic arrangement of the states and localities, and finally alphabetically by the name of the biographee. Brief information is given in abbreviated form about each physician. There is also an index by name.

This is a very useful listing when one is seeking a specialist in a given geographic area.

159. Medical Library Association. **Directory.** Compiled to July 1, 1972. Chicago, Medical Library Association, 1972. 96p.

This directory, which is published every two years, contains lists of honorary, sustaining, associate, active, and institutional members with addresses. An asterisk has been placed beside names of members who are certified by the Association. The organization has a number of foreign members, both personal and institutional ones.

160. Moreland, Sara L., with the assistance of Ella B. Donaldson. **1971 Directory, Health and Allied Sciences Libraries and Information Sources.** Chicago, Midwest Regional Medical Library, The John Crerar Library, 1971. 217p. index.

The bulk of this directory is a listing of health science libraries in Illinois, Indiana, Iowa, Minnesota, North Dakota, and Wisconsin, arranged alphabetically by the name of the library. Brief information is given about each as follows: address, name of the librarian and assistant, subject fields, number of volumes held, services available, and publications. There are geographic and subject indexes, and information on interlibrary loan procedures is appended. The publication is particularly valuable for librarians who are seeking sources for interlibrary loans.

161. Schick, Frank L., and Susan Crawford, eds. **Directory of Health Science Libraries in the United States, 1969.** Chicago, American Medical Association and the Medical Library Association, 1970. 197p. index.

The libraries listed are arranged alphabetically by name under the names of the states. Very brief information is given about each institution, some of it by code, as follows: name of institution, address, name of librarian, telephone number, type of institution and administrative control, holdings, personnel, main users, and hours open. The index is by name of institution. The directory is the result of a survey. It is planned that other surveys and publications will follow. The present volume is a step in the direction of identifying the health science libraries that exist in the U.S.

162. U.S. Food and Drug Administration. Division of Hazardous Substances and Poison Control. **Directory, Poison Control Centers.** Washington, GPO, 1971. 50p. $.35. (FDA) 72-7001. 1712-0129.

This small directory is a listing, alphabetically by state, of facilities which provide for the medical profession, on a 24-hour basis, information concerning the treatment and prevention of accidents involving the ingestion of toxic substances. For each state, the state coordinator is indicated, which is usually the State Department of Public Health. Following, by city, is the name of the facility providing the service (usually a hospital), the address, phone number, and names of the directors in charge who are usually physicians, pharmacists, or nurses.

163. U.S. Library of Congress. National Referral Center. **A Directory of Infor-
mation Sources in the United States: Biological Sciences.** Washington,
GPO, 1972. 577p. index. $5.00. LC 72-2659. ISBN 0-8444-0023-8.
Stock No. 3000-000060.

This directory updates and extends the biological science coverage of a 1965 publication called *A Directory of Information Resources in the United States:
Physical Sciences, Biological Sciences, Engineering,* issued by the Center under
its earlier name: National Referral Center for Science and Technology. There is
approximately a fourfold increase in the coverage of the directory over the
earlier one. The directory lists a wide variety of agencies that may be considered
information centers. It includes societies, institutes, government agencies, libraries, hospitals, departments of universities, and industrial laboratories. The
arrangement is alphabetical by name of the agency. About each is given: address,
phone, areas of interest, holdings, publications, and information services.

PART II

SOURCE MATERIAL BY SUBJECT AREA

1. HEALTH CARE DELIVERY

164. Altman, Isidore, Alice J. Anderson, and Kathleen Barker. **Methodology In Evaluating the Quality of Medical Care. An Annotated Selected Bibliography, 1955-1968.** Rev. ed. Pittsburgh, University of Pittsburgh Press, 1969. 214p. index. (Contemporary Community Health Series.) $3.95. LC 62-22364.

This publication follows an earlier edition which covered the literature from 1955 to 1961. There are 397 references and abstracts which give a view of the activity in the field and are a guide to literature sources. Both book and periodical references are included. The citations are listed under four headings: (1) Standards and Recommendations (usually set by organized professional groups), (2) Elements of Performance, (3) Effects of Care (measurement of quality), and (4) General Approaches. The list seems to be rather complete for the period covered for English language papers.

165. American Hospital Association. **AHA Guide to the Health Care Field. 1973.** Chicago, American Hospital Association, 1973. 584p. index. $15.00.

This publication, which is revised annually, was formerly part 2 of the Annual Guide Issue of the journal, *Hospitals,* also published by the American Hospital Association. It is probably the most important reference source available for information on health care institutions; the American Hospital Association; organizations, agencies, and educational programs in the health care field; and sources of products and services used in hospitals. The largest section of the guide is a directory of the hospitals and a listing of long-term care facilities which are arranged by state and secondarily by city. A good deal of information about each hospital is given, making use of a code. An AHA membership list is included; also a list of health organizations, agencies, and educational programs; and a buyers' guide which lists alphabetically by subject category, products and services most commonly used in hospitals. The publication is very valuable and much used.

166. American Public Health Association. Program Area Committee on Medical Care Administration. **A Guide to Medical Care Administration.** Vol.1, **Concepts and Principles.** Prepared by Beverlee A. Myers. Rev. ed. New York, American Public Health Association, 1969. 114p. bibliog. $3.00. LC 72-82743.

This publication is the first volume in a projected series. The purpose of this one is to "provide a comprehensive view which will serve as a starting point for the discussion of the problems and issues in medical care today." A major objective of the work is to develop a unified framework which will integrate the differing viewpoints on medical care. In the first half of the book, the concept of medical care is discussed and the essential elements defined. In the second part, medical care programs are defined, and basic principles of administration are outlined. An interesting appendix is included which is a historical chronology of the evolution of medical care in the U.S. The book should be useful to health officers, community health planners, and legislators; administrators, directors and board members of health centers, prepayment plans, voluntary health agencies, and other medical care programs; and faculty and students of public health.

167. American Public Health Associatiation. Program Area Committee on Medical Care Administration in cooperation with the Division of Medical Care Administration of the U.S. Public Health Service. **A Guide to Medical Care Administration.** Vol.II, **Medical Care Appraisal—Quality and Utilization.** Prepared by Avedis Donabedian. New York, American Public Health Association, 1969. 221p. bibliog. $3.50. LC 65-26944. SBN 87553-012-5.

A large part of this volume is based on a workshop on the operational aspects of medical care appraisal which was held in 1966. The work is supplemented by an annotated bibliography on "Methodology in Evaluating the Quality of Medical Care" by Alice J. Anderson which covers 1962 to 1968. The text of the book is a very comprehensive discussion of the theoretical and operational aspects of medical care appraisal. Attention is given to the appraisal of the process of medical care and the assessment of outcomes. The guide is most useful to those who have administrative responsibility, responsibility for clinical performance, and to those who are interested in further research.

168. American Public Welfare Association. **Public Welfare Directory, 1972.** David Karraker, ed. Chicago, American Public Welfare Association, 1972. 246p. $15.00. LC 41-4981. SBN 910-106-03-7.

The directory, which is published annually, outlines the administrative structure of public welfare and related programs at federal, state, and local levels. It is a resource publication to assist public and voluntary agencies in serving more effectively. The first section is on federal agencies, the next on state, local, and territorial agencies, and the last on Canadian agencies. Under each entry, key personnel and other information is given about each.

169. Anderson, Odin W. **Health Care: Can There Be Equity? The United States, Sweden and England.** New York, Wiley-Interscience, 1972. 271p. bibliog. index. $11.95. LC 72-7449. ISBN 0-471-02760-X.

This timely book is a comparative study of the health service systems of the three countries named in the title. The comparison is interesting because the system in the United States is loose, that of Sweden semistructured, and that of England centrally controlled. The differences and the similarities are demonstrated. All three countries have had increased admissions to general and mental hospitals, increases in expenditures for services, increases in total costs of health care systems, and an increased percentage of national income devoted to health care costs. The book is divided into four parts as follows: (1) The framework, (2) Health services and the liberal-democratic context in three countries, (3) Organization and performance from 1950 to 1970, (4) The endless search for the dream. Also included is an appendix of comparative tables relating to health care in the three countries. The author, who is an outstanding authority in this field, points out that all three countries are striving toward increased coordination, integration, and planning. He does not advocate centralized federal funding. He believes that the U.S. will have a responsible health care system as long as the sources of funding are diffused. He also believes that a single source of funding may bring about equality, but that the price of doing so may be obsolete, worn-out facilities, inadequate numbers of trained personnel, and a medical profession frustrated by the financial constraints. Also, he observes that neither British nor American government is noted for generosity in financing health and welfare programs, and that increased costs are most likely.

This is a thoughtful book which should be of considerable interest to hospital administrators, trustees, medical staffs, legislators, newspaper publishers, sociologists, social workers, and many others concerned with health care delivery.

170. Annual Symposium on Hospital Affairs. 13th, held May 1971. Proceedings. **Health Maintenance Organizations: A Reconfiguration of the Health Services System.** Conducted by the Graduate Program in Hospital Administration and Center for Health Administration Studies, Graduate School of Business, University of Chicago, 1971. 90p. $5.50.

This publication, which presents the papers delivered at a Symposium meeting, brings together some thinking on the somewhat controversial topic, Health Maintenance Organizations. These organizations basically have four characteristics, an enrolled group of persons, an organized group of health professionals and facilities, a financial plan, and an organization which is supposed to manage the program. Titles of the papers are as follows: (1) Health maintenance organizations— the concept and structure—introduction, (2) Restructuring the health delivery system—will the health maintenance strategy work? (3) Analysis of the HMO proposal—its assumptions, implications, and prospects, (4) Start-up problems of health maintenance organizations, (5) Implications of the health maintenance organization concept. The questions and answers which arose from the discussion periods are also included in the publication.

171. Arnold, Mary F., L. Vaughn Blankenship, and John M. Hess, eds. **Administering Health Systems: Issues and Perspectives.** Chicago, Aldine-Atherton, 1971. 444p. bibliog. index. $9.50. LC 70-92060.

Because our society has entered a period of rapidly accelerating social change, this book was brought about. Although the editors feel that the scientific and technical capabilities in our society cannot find solutions to all problems, we are on the threshold of new scientific discoveries that will perhaps make it possible to control population, extend life, heal and prevent diseases, and to expand man's cognitive capabilities. They recognize that these new discoveries create new problems and that we must face the difficulties of keeping them within bounds.

The book presents interpretations of the forces and issues that are believed to be significant for the administrator of health organizations in the changing health system. A health systems approach to the problem is taken. The book is divided into four sections that focus on (1) the participants in the health system, (2) the political context of health administration, (3) planning as a means of rationalizing the system, and (4) a wide variety of organizational perspectives.

Very diverse aspects of the subject are dealt with by various experts in the field. There are papers on such topics as the professional association and collective bargaining, effects of professionalism on health systems, the hospital administrator's role, emerging patterns of federalism, the ecological perspective, and many others. Health administrators, students, and educated readers will find the book of interest.

172. Bauerschmidt, Alan D., and Richard W. Furst. **Forecasted Changes in the Health Care Industry.** Bureau of Business and Economic Research, College of Business Administration, University of South Carolina, 1973. 88p. (Occasional Studies No. 3). $2.50.

This report presents findings of a study that was made to forecast change in the health care industry in the next twenty years. It was discovered early in the research that no marked differences existed between the industry in South Carolina and that projected for the whole United States, so the results can be considered as applicable to them both. The noted Delphi methodology was used. For those who are unfamiliar with this technique, a chapter is included which explains it. The predictions for the future indicate that no great breakthroughs in medical knowledge will occur in the next decade or so. However, diagnosis, treatment and preventive methods will be improved. Also, no revolutionary changes in health care delivery are contemplated. Instead, a continuous evolutionary process of change is projected. However, the expectation is that at the end of the twenty-year period, the health care industry pattern will be quite different from the present. The turmoil over health care costs will peak in still greater governmental control.

173. Baumslag, Naomi, ed. **Family Care: A Guide.** Baltimore, Williams and Wilkins, 1973. 392p. bibliog. index. $7.95pa. LC 73-4556. SBN 683-00412-3.

This book was written primarily for medical students and faculty who are involved with courses on "family medicine," a course recently added in medical schools. The material presented is mainly concerned with how family care is practiced. The following subjects are discussed: (I) The family, (2) Home and the community, (3) Obstetrics, (4) Pediatrics, (5) Child abuse, (6) Prescribing, (7) Diet and the diabetic, (8) Testing and the laboratory, (9) Exfoliative cytolopathology, (10) Measuring, (11) Environmental pathology, (12) Family dentistry, (13) Family records, (14) The unwanted patient. The book will be of interest to public health officials and laymen as well as to professionals in the health field.

174. Bionetics Research Laboratories, Inc. **Marketing of Health Maintenance Organization Services.** Washington, GPO, 1973. 1v.(various paging). DHEW Publication No. (HSM) 73-13006. $4.00pa. 1721-00005.

Ordinarily a Health Maintenance Organization program must satisfy the following criteria: (1) It should provide a comprehensive range of services, (2) It should be prepaid and capitation based, and (3) There should be a voluntary, enrolled beneficiary population. This study was undertaken and supported by the Department of Health, Education and Welfare because of this last-mentioned criterion. The aim of it was to provide interested individuals with a better understanding of, and a methodological approach to, the marketing process. It is necessary for the succes of HMOs to achieve an enrollment base adequate to insure economic viability, so marketing is important.

The report is in six parts: (1) Guidelines for HMO marketing, (2) The beneficiary population, (3) Existing systems and services, (4) Market definition, (5) A marketing strategy and model is developed in terms of which judgments and decisions can be made on the marketing approach and from which information can be developed to monitor marketing progress, and (6) Appendices.

175. Blue Cross Association and the National Association of Blue Shield Plans. **Selected Studies in Medical Care and Medical Economics.** Chicago, Blue Cross Association, 1973. 205p. index. free. pa.

This publication is prepared annually at the request of the National Association of Insurance Commissioners. The data for the listing is obtained through a mail survey. This report contains over 400 abstracts of current research projects obtained from individuals and agencies who are doing work currently in fields of hospital and medical economics and health care organization and administration. The term "research" has been used loosely to include a variety of research, developmental, or demonstration projects.

The projects reported have been organized into eight broad major categories as follows: health planning, health economics, organization of the delivery system, service components, utilization, education, professional and population characteristics. An index of investigator's names is included.

176. Bryan, James E. **The Role of the Family Physician in America's Developing Medical Care Program: A Report and Commentary.** A publication of the Family Health Foundation of America. St. Louis, Warren H. Green, Inc., 1968. 57p. $2.00. LC 68-31185.

This report presents the trend of the discussions held at some Family Health Foundation of America's conferences which took place from 1965 to 1967. The conferences brought out that American medicine seems to have lost sight of its essential objective: to provide continuing comprehensive care to the whole man. The feeling was that a whole new breed of physician must be developed to do this. The report articulates what this physician will be expected to do, what education will be necessary, and attempts to establish his function and status in the medical complex.

177. Bullough, Bonnie, and Vern L. Bullough. **Poverty, Ethnic Identity, and Health Care.** New York, Appleton-Century-Crofts Educational Division, Meredith Corp., 1972. 226p. bibliog. index. $7.95. LC 73-175285.

The authors point out that while American health care delivery has long been in need of reform, and its deficiencies recently receiving public scrutiny, it is particularly hard on the poor and the members of minority groups. Data is presented to show this. It is important to point out, however, that many take the view that our system is almost equally bad for all socioeconomic groups. The following topics are covered: (1) The health care delivery problem, (2) Immigrant minority groups, (3) Black Americans, (4) The Spanish-speaking minority groups, (5) The native Americans, (6) Poverty and hunger transcend racial lines, (7) Mental health and mental illness, (8) Discrimination and segregation, (9) Improving health care delivery.

178. Cary, Ed. **In Failing Health: The Medical Crisis and the A.M.A.** Indianapolis and New York, Bobbs-Merrill, 1970. 257p. index. bibliog. $7.95. LC 79-98286.

The author points out that while many feel that American medical service is the finest in the world, statistics do not bear this out. He outlines the historical background of medical care in the U.S. and particularly the American Medical Association's part in it. The poor and their problems are dwelt upon. This book, like so many others, dwells heavily on the problems and the inequities, attempts to fix the blame (in this case the A.M.A. receives a large share), and offers little in the way of reform except to say that the money now spent on medical care (approximately $300 per year per person), while adequate, is not used wisely, and suggests that the federal government should resolve the problems with legislation.

179. Chacko, George K., ed. **Alternative Approaches to National Delivery of Health Care.** Proceedings of the Symposium on Health Care of the Operations Research Society of America at the 138th Annual Meeting of the American Association for the Advancement of Science, Dec. 28, 1971, Philadelphia, Pa. Arlington, Va., ORSA Health Application Section, 1972. 201p.

Four major alternatives for the national delivery of health care are offered. These are as follows: (1) The legislative viewpoint presented by a professional staff member of the U.S. Senate Health Subcommittee, (2) The executive viewpoint presented by the Deputy Assistant Secretary for Health Legislation, (3) The American Medical Association viewpoint presented by a member of the AMA Council of Legislation, and (4) The insurance viewpoint presented by the President of Equitable Assurance Society of America. Also presented are the views of discussants who were selected for their knowledgeability and representation of professional affiliations different from those of the speakers. Appropriate portions of the actual text of various legislative bills currently before Congress are on adjacent pages to the discussion. In addition, a presentation is included from a scientist from the USSR who spoke on medical care in that country. The publishers do not endorse any approach or concept, but merely present the views.

180. Ciba Foundation. **Medical Care of Prisoners and Detainees.** Amsterdam, London, New York; Elsevier, Excerpta Medica, North-Holland, 1973. 238p. index. (Ciba Foundation Symposium 16, New Series). LC 73-82148. ISBN, Excerpta Medica: 90-219-4017-5. ISBN, American Elsevier: 0-444-15013-7.

A group of well-known lawyers, psychiatrists, physicians, prison administrators, sociologists, and others took part in this symposium. They came from North America, Europe, and North Africa. The papers discuss how legislation affecting the physical and mental well being of prisoners might be implemented and improved. The management of disturbed and violent offenders, experiments on prisoners, tension in camps, and other problems are also taken up. The titles of the papers are as follows: (1) Ethics, the doctor, and the prisoner, (2) Medical services in prison: lessons from two surveys, (3) Minimum standards for medical services in prisons and jails, (4) Standards of medical care and protection in detention camps, (5) Problems arising from biological experimentation in prisons,

(6) Penitentiary medicine in France, (7) Organization of medical care of prisoners and detainees in Poland, (8) The Canadian experience, (9) Medical psychiatric survey in Alabama State Prison, (10) The English Prison Medical Service: its historical background and more recent developments, (11) Violence in prisoners and patients, (12) The interaction between prisoners, victims and their social networks, (13) Management of conflict in correctional institutions. Also included are five appendices as follows: (1) Standard minimum rules for the treatment of prisoners (United Nations), (2) Association of State Correctional Administrators. Policy guidelines: health services, (3) Administrative regulations: State of Illinois Department of Corrections, Adult Division, Sections 836, 837, 817, (4) ACA Manual of Correctional Standards of Health and Medical Service Corrections Evaluation Report, (5) Extract from *The Emerging Rights of the Confined.*

The book will be of value particularly to those who look after prisoners professionally, but others who are concerned about offenders and victims will find the work of interest.

181. Committee for Economic Development. Research and Policy Committee. **Building a National Health-Care System.** New York, Committee for Economic Development, 1973. 105p. charts. $1.75pa. LC 73-75244. ISBN 0-87186-049-X.

This publication presents an official statement of the Committee regarding national health care policy. The present system is outlined, its weaknesses discussed, and specific recommendations made for an improved national system. Cost estimates are given. The statements are supported by statistical data. The members of the Committee are well-known educators, business men, and industrialists. The publication is important because of the timeliness of the subject matter and the plan outlined which appears to be a workable one.

182. Dickerson, O.D. **Health Insurance.** 3d ed. Homewood, Ill., Richard D. Irwin, 1968. 773p. bibliog. index. (Irwin Series in Risk and Insurance). $12.65. LC 68-19499.

This book was written primarily as a college textbook in health insurance and for use in professional educational programs such as those conducted by the American College of Life Underwriters and the American Institute for Property and Liability Underwriters. Also, insurance companies can make use of the material. In addition, administrators, government personnel, and those interested in medical economics and social security can use it as a reference source.

The author's viewpoint is that of a person sympathetic to health insurance and who has considered the interests of insurers of all types, insured persons, the medical profession, and the public. Evaluations of theories, coverages, and practices are included. There are four sections as follows: (1) Health losses and how they are met, (2) Expense coverage, (3) Income coverages, and (4) Health insurer operations. Also included are a great number of charts and tables presenting statistical data. The book is very thorough and comprehensive.

183. Donabedian, Avedis. **Aspects of Medical Care Administration: Specifying Requirements for Health Care.** Cambridge, Mass., Published for the Commonwealth Fund by Harvard University Press, 1973. 649p. bibliog. index. $25.00. LC 72-93948. SBN 674-04980-2.

The object of this book is to bring about a fundamental understanding of and a particular way of thinking about medical care problems which will enhance administrative competence. This volume reviews basic concepts and principles— social, economic, and medical—which must be dealt with. The book is written at a high level, the approach conceptual and abstract. A major feature is the attempt at systematization. Chapter titles are as follows: (1) Social values, (2) Program objectives, (3) The assessment of need, (4) Assessment of supply, and (5) Estimating requirements for services and resources. Students, teachers, researchers in medical care problems, and administrators will find the book valuable.

184. Edwards, Marvin Henry. **Hazardous to Your Health: A New Look at the "Health Care Crisis" in America.** New Rochelle, N.Y., Arlington House, 1972. 318p. index. $9.95. LC 73-183679. ISBN 0-87000-138-8.

This book is the story of the campaign for national health insurance in the United States. The author is against such plans because he feels that the result will be rising costs (through taxation) and lower quality medical care as a kind of impersonal assembly-line care will develop. He says there is no "health care crisis"; the U.S. has one of the world's highest per capita physician populations. Also, the average American spends a small portion of his annual expenditures on medical insurance and health care, and we are enjoying a health-care boom that has resulted in longer, healthier life. His feeling is that the public is being deceived by propaganda advocating government medicine which is costly and inefficient. The author is a journalist, lawyer, and editor of the magazine *Private Practice.* The book has two appendices: (1) A history of the campaign for national health insurance and (2) The Planners' Plans (resumes of some proposed plans).

185. Ehrenreich, Barbara, and John Ehrenreich. **The American Health Empire: Power, Profits, and Politics.** New York, Random House, 1970. 279p. $7.95. LC 79-127539.

The authors feel that although there is no lack of funds, manpower, or facilities, the U.S. health care crisis has been brought about because the priorities of America's sixty-billion-dollar health industry are profit making, research, development and institutional expansion. The authors are a part of a group of young activists called Health Policy Advisory Center (Health-PAC). They are critical of practically every medical institution including voluntary hospitals, private health insurance, medical centers, voluntary health planning agencies, and liberal health programs such as Medicaid and national health insurance. Their only solution to the problem is insurgent movements of health workers and con- sumers to gain community and worker control of health institutions.

186. Elling, Ray H., ed. **National Health Care: Issues and Problems in Socialized Medicine.** Chicago, New York, Aldine-Atherton, 1971. 287p. bibliog. index. $7.95. LC 77-159602. ISBN 0-202-30232-6; 0-202-30233-4pa.

The intention of the editor of this work is to provide for a better understanding of the many complex issues around which the controversy over health care centers. Articles are presented on important issues written by noted authorities. The editor takes the point of view that there is general agreement in the U.S. that some form of national health care is needed. The controversy is over issues that he states in the introduction, which are these: (1) The place of health care in the hierarchy of values, (2) Ways of financing care, (3) Evaluation of care, (4) Preparation of health workers and division of labor, (5) Boundaries of the health worker's role, (6) Alternative ways of rewarding health workers, (7) Appropriate organizational units, (8) Interrelationships among health agencies and programs, (9) Alternative structures and processes in planning and administering health services. The book will be of most interest to students of medical sociology, medical care, public health, and to policymakers who will shape the system for the future.

187. **Evolving Health Care Patterns and Issues.** St. Louis, Catholic Hospital Association, 1969. 112p. $2.00. LC 71-88665.

The papers presented here were taken from the 20th anniversary symposium of the St. Louis University Graduate Program in Hospital Administration, held in October 1968. Titles of the presentations are as follows: (1) Political forces in a community, (2) The politics of health care, (3) Health planning in the voluntary sector, (4) Health planning in a governmental structure, (5) Hospital mergers and affilitations, (6) The concept of the public utility, (7) A changing role for the public hospital, (8) Providing comprehensive health care—a modified utility approach, (9) A proposed national health insurance plan, (10) Catholic hospitals— a look to the future.

188. Fisher, Peter. **Prescription for National Health Insurance: A Proposal for the U.S. Based on Canadian Experience.** Croton-on-Hudson, N.Y., North River Press, Inc., 1972. 96p. $6.00. LC 72-77266.

This book attempts to show that it is possible to set up a non-socialistic national health insurance system that would be quite adequate, better than we now have, and cost less than we are currently spending. The model program for such a plan is the British Columbia system. The author thinks that most of the plans which have been proposed are poor ones. Several such proposals are discussed, including the Nixon Plan, the Health Security Act, the AMA's Medicredit, and others.

189. French, Ruth M. **The Dynamics of Health Care.** New York, Blakiston Division, McGraw-Hill Book Co., 1968. 140p. bibliog. index. $4.95pa. LC 68-24341.

This book was written primarily for students of medical technology, but is also of value for all students in health care fields. The aim is to acquaint the reader with the whole pattern of comprehensive health care. Teachers of courses of this kind will find the book useful. Chapter headings are as follows: (1) Our concern: health, (2) The patient, (3) Agencies for health care, (4) History and development of hospitals, (5) Sociologic aspects of the hospital, (6) Organizational structure of hospitals, (7) Health services personnel, (8) Toward a professional philosophy, (9) Ethical foundations of professional practice, (10) Law and professional practice, (11) Interpersonal relations, (12) Introduction to research.

190. Fry, John. **Medicine in Three Societies: A Comparison of Medical Care in the USSR, USA, and UK.** New York, American Elsevier Pub. Co., Inc., 1970 (c.1969). 249p. index. $7.50. LC 114436. SBN 444-19658-7.

The British physician who is the author of this book compares and contrasts three systems of medical care in the hope that what is gleaned can help achieve better services for all. The material presented is based on information gained when the author made visits to the USA and USSR and from published statistics. Topics treated are: medical care—common goals and common problems, national characteristics, structure and patterns of medical services, first contact care, specialist ambulatory care, hospitals, preventive aspects of medical care, public health and social services, maternity and child care, mental health care, the greater medical profession—medical manpower, education and training, and the present dilemmas of medical care.

191. Fry, John, and W. A. J. Farndale, eds. **International Medical Care: A Comparison and Evaluation of Medical Care Services throughout the World.** Wallingford, Pa., Washington Square East Publishers, 1972. 341p. bibliog. index. $15.00. SBN 852-999-359.

This book provides a guide to the present state of medical care throughout the world. There has been considerable interest shown in this subject, and comparisons are often made between services in the various countries. Since there is little literature available on this subject, the publication makes a notable contribution. The largest part of the volume is devoted to health systems of Western Europe, the United Kingdom, the United States, Canada, the Soviet Union, the developing nations, and Australia. Then follows a more general discussion. The conclusion is made that many of the problems of the world are the same; nobody has devised a perfect medical system; and national systems are inclined to recognize different national differences of development, means, tradition, and attitude. The book will be of value to anyone interested in health care outside his own country.

192. Garb, Solomon, and Evelyn Eng. **Disaster Handbook.** 2d ed. New York, Springer Publishing Co., Inc., 1969. 310p. bibliog. index. $7.00. LC 78-89688.

This book was intended primarily for physicians and nurses, but others interested in disaster casualty prevention and management will find it valuable. It is estimated that 95% of disaster deaths and injuries could have been prevented, so prevention has been emphasized although an equal amount of space has been given to describing ways of helping disaster victims. More detail has been given on disasters that the reader will most likely be involved in, such as fires. Less emphasis has been given to mine disasters, for example. Chapter headings are as follows: basic features of disasters; rescue, first aid, and emergency care; nursing in disasters; major types of disaster, and thermonuclear disaster. 24 kinds of disasters are discussed in Chapter 4.

193. Gatherer, A., and M. D. Warren, eds. **Management and the Health Services.** Oxford, New York, Pergamon Press, 1971. 175p. bibliog. index. $8.00. LC 74-130370.

This publication is a collection of papers which introduce a variety of subjects and point the way to further reading and study on the subject of managing health care services. It is a British publication and is mostly concerned with the management of their own system of national health care. However, many of the papers will be of interest in other countries including the United States. Chapter headings are as follows: (1) Change and the National Health Service, (2) An anatomy of management, (3) The analytical approach to decision-making, (4) The use of statistics in the management of health and welfare services, (5) Planning services, (6) Evaluation of services, (7) Operational research in the health services, (8) Personnel selection, (9) Sociology and medical administration, and (10) Tomorrow's community physician.

194. Gerber, Alex. **The Gerber Report: The Shocking State of American Medical Care and What Must Be Done About It.** New York, David McKay Co., Inc., 1971. 242p. $6.95. LC 78-150066.

The author, who is a physician, is disturbed over the fact that the U.S. is a second-rate nation in many aspects of health care. In this report, the current medical situation is reviewed and analyzed. Some of the things that the author finds the worst are: the doctor shortage, the fading general practitioner, surgery done by unqualified physicians, performance of unnecessary surgery, the unrealities of community control of health centers, the absurdities of a small radical fringe of medical students attempting to take over the running of medical schools, the unrealistic hopes for paramedical personnel, reliance on physicians trained outside the United States, and the birth of unwanted children. The author gives suggestions for improving the situations that exist. He is particularly convinced that poverty brought on by overly large families is responsible for much that is wrong, and strongly advocates birth control. In general, Gerber advocates a pluralistic health-care delivery system. The doctor must be able to choose the way of practice that suits him best, and so must the patient. The report is a thoughtful and realistic presentation.

195. Glaser, William A. **Paying the Doctor: Systems of Remuneration and Their Effects.** Baltimore and London, Johns Hopkins Press, 1970. 323p. bibliog. index. $10.00. LC 72-97054. SBN 8018-1083-3.

This book analyzes the principal methods of paying physicians in several different countries. The question the author hoped to answer is: if doctors are paid by one or another method, what is the difference in how the public is treated? Information is drawn from 16 countries in Europe, including Great Britain, France, Sweden, The Netherlands, and Spain, the Middle East, and the Soviet bloc. Data came from interviews, publications, and institutional records. Chapter headings are as follows: (1) The effects of payment systems, (2) Organized systems of medical care, (3) Types of payment: fee-for-service, (4) Types of payment: salary, (5) Types of payment: capitation, (6) Development of payment systems, (7) Effects of fee-for-service and case payments: service benefits, (8) Effects of fee-for-service: cash benefits, (9) Effects of salaries, (10) Effects of capitation, (11) Designing effective payment systems. The book will be of interest to legislators, medical economists, administrators, and insurers, or anyone who is concerned with the organization, administration, financing, and distribution of physicians' services. The study is well-prepared and presents useful information. No real conclusion is reached, however, about what system might be best.

196. Goodrich, Charles H., Margaret C. Olendzki, and George G. Reader. **Welfare Medical Care: An Experiment.** Cambridge, Mass., Harvard University Press, 1970. 343p. charts. index. $7.00. LC 77-85075. SBN 674-94895-5.

This publication is a report on the New York Hospital-Cornell Project, 1960 to 1965, which was an experiment in the organization of welfare medical care services. The experiment was brought about by the desire of the New York City Departments of Health and Welfare to improve the quality and lessen the fragmentation of the medical care available to welfare patients. The purposes of the project were to determine if it was feasible for a voluntary teaching hospital to provide complete medical care to welfare recipients, and to compare the utilization, cost, and quality of that care with that provided to a control group who received care under the usual system.

Part I covers the genesis of the project and the characteristics of the welfare population who served as subjects for the study. Part II describes the experience of the staff and patients at the hospital. Part III focuses on the whole city and the total study group system of care. Part IV summarizes the findings. The book includes a large number of charts, tables, and graphs of statistical information.

The authors conclude that a hospital such as the one in question can render a full range of medical services to welfare recipients in a community. The success of such an undertaking depends on a number of innovations in customary outpatient practice, however. The most important of these were: (1) Providing a clinical team within the hospital who would come to know the patients and provide continuity of care, (2) Taking the initiative in beginning care, and (3) Guaranteeing availability of services to patients so they did not face repeated screening for eligibility.

197. Government Studies and Systems, Inc. **An Advanced Health Planning System.** A report to the New Jersey Department of Health and New Jersey State Comprehensive Health Planning Agency. Boyd Z. Palmer, Project Director. Distributed by National Technical Information Service, U.S. Dept. of Commerce. 1972. 201p. bibliog. (PB-210 647) $3.00pa.

This monograph describes a method for planning health services. It summarizes a three-year effort to develop workable procedures for comprehensive health planning as authorized by federal legislation in 1966 and 1967. The goal-oriented approach is used. An evolutionary approach is recommended for implementation of the planning system, with sequential introduction of subsystems. Some knowledge of the "systems approach" and terminology is helpful for an understanding of the document.

198. Greenberg, Selig. **The Quality of Mercy: A Report on the Critical Condition of Hospital and Medical Care in America.** New York, Atheneum, 1971. 385p. index. $6.95. LC 79-135571.

This book, written by a journalist, is another expose of the poor hospital conditions and inadequate care received in the U.S. today. Many readers will agree with a good deal of what is said—that there are too few doctors, nurses, and support staff, too few hospitals and clinics, and too large a bill to pay when the battle with disease is over. Also, the reader may agree that doctors are too concerned about their patients' pathology and not enough with them as human beings. However, this reviewer finds it hard to accept the author's view that too much of our medical outlay goes to research.

The book is interesting and well-written, and has been widely read and reviewed. However, it does not really offer many constructive ideas that will being about reform. The author is optimistic, though, that public attitudes will bring about the necessary reform.

199. Havighurst, Clark C., and John C. Weistart, eds. **Health Care.** Dobbs Ferry, N.Y., Oceana Publications, Inc., 1972. 452p. (Library of law and contemporary problems, no. 15). $16.50. LC 72-37739. ISBN 0-379-11515-8.

This material was originally published as the Spring 1970 and Autumn 1970 issues of *Law and Contemporary Problems,* volume 35, numbers 2 and 4. The book is a collection of papers which should offer some perspective on the national health care program that will best suit the nation's needs. It develops some of the social and economic aspects of health care with the intention of showing how the present system's deficiencies came about and suggests some alternatives. Also emphasized is the matter of maintaining high standards. The book is divided into two parts; the first gives political background primarily and the second develops specific issues in the ongoing policy debate. The real issue, according to the editor, is whether health care should become the next great "regulated industry," the first one brought under comprehensive economic regulation since the 1930s. He feels there would be no turning back if such an all-out regulatory course was pursued in regard to health care. The papers presented in the publication cover the subject thoroughly. Many footnote references are included, particularly to laws and decisions.

200. Hyman, Herbert Harvey, ed. **The Politics of Health Care: Nine Case Studies of Innovative Planning in New York City.** New York, Praeger Publishers, 1973. 208p. bibliog. (Praeger Special Studies in U.S. Economic, Social, and Political Issues). $16.50. LC 72-12971.

This book is a study of how change takes place over a period of time in the field of health care. A number of case studies are analyzed. The nine studies presented are divided into three sections: financing health care, meeting health needs, and planning health care services. Under financing health care, there are studies of ghetto medicine and Medicaid. Under meeting health needs are studies of family planning, abortion, pest control, the Health and Hospital Corporation (HHC), and comprehensive health care centers. Under planning health care services are the regional medical programs and comprehensive health planning. The last chapter analyzes the materials previously presented. The author draws a number of conclusions, among them that most of the innovative attempts to improve health services have not been achieved.

201. Institute of Life Insurance and the Health Insurance Institute. **List of Worthwhile Life and Health Insurance Books.** 1972 ed. New York, Institute of Life Insurance, 1972. 78p. index. free.

The booklet lists current publications under various subject headings. Each title is briefly annotated. The material listed appeals to the general reader, student of insurance, and individuals in the insurance business. The list may serve as a buying aid and a reading list. Also included is a list of periodicals on the subject of insurance, publishers' addresses, and indexes of author and titles. The booklet is frequently revised.

202. Institute of Medicine. National Academy of Sciences. **A Strategy for Evaluating Health Services.** David M. Kessner, Project Director. Washington, National Academy of Sciences, 1973. 219p. bibliog. (Contrasts in Health Status, vol. 2). LC 73-3494. ISBN 0-309-02104-9.

In an attempt to develop a method for evaluating health care status, it was assumed that a number of specific health problems could be chosen and focused on to view the system. In effect, a set of problems could become "tracers" that allow an investigator or evaluator to examine selected parts or the entire matrix of a health system. This publication reports the development of the tracer methodology for evaluating ambulatory health services. Also, it examines application of the tracer method in evaluating a hypothetical health delivery system.

In addition to the section on the tracer method, there are chapters on middle ear infection and associated hearing loss, visual disorders, iron-deficiency anemia, essential hypertension, urinary tract infections, and cervical cancer.

203. Kane, Robert L., and Rosalie A. Kane. **Federal Health Care (With Reservations!).** New York, Springer Publishing Co., Inc. 1972. 180p. bibliog. index. $6.95. LC 76-175906. SBN 0-8261-1252-8.

This book relates day-to-day realities of life on an Indian reservation with respect to health care. The authors, one of whom was Director of the Indian Health Service's Navajo Unit at Shiprock, probe the effects that a hierarchial service organization has on patients and personnel, its capacity for responding to local needs, and the conflicts that erupt when providers and consumers are of different cultural backgrounds. The analysis the authors have made has relevance for the debate now taking place on the adoption of national health care insurance.

204. J. K. Lasser Tax Institute. **Your Social Security and Medicare Guide.** Editor, Bernard Greisman. New York, Simon and Schuster, 1968. 160p. index. $5.95.

This book covers almost every aspect of the Social Security law. It is of value to the layman and the professional. With this guide, the layman can determine the extent of protection he has and what steps should be taken to supplement and increase his family's security. The advice given is good. The professional will find the book of value in explaining the technical aspects of the law. Chapter headings are as follows: (1) Your benefits under the hospital insurance program, (2) Supplementary plan for medical expenses, (3) Your Social Security benefits, (4) How to figure the amount of your benefits, (5) Benefits paid by Social Security, (6) How Social Security helps the disabled, (7) Will you lose benefits by

working after retirement? (8) How to collect your Social Security benefits,
(9) How employees get Social Security coverage, (10) How you are covered by
Social Security if you are self-employed, (11) How to get Social Security if you
are a farmer, (12) How ministers are covered under Social Security, (13) How to
get Social Security if you work for a nonprofit organization, (14) Special Social
Security provisions for veterans and their families, (15) How to appeal if you
believe you are not getting all your benefits, (16) How to get a refund of Social
Security taxes, (17) Your Social Security card and your account, (18) Investing
for retirement, (19) How the income tax law helps retired persons.

205. Levey, Samuel, and N. Paul Loomba. **Health Care Administration: A Mana-**
     gerial Perspective. Philadelphia, Toronto, J. B. Lippincott, 1973. 603p.
     bibliog. index. $17.00. LC 72-10830. ISBN 0-397-52059-X.
The primary objective of this book is to present health care administrators with
management concepts, tools, and techniques which will assist them in the
management of health organizations. Both theoretical foundations and practical
applications of modern management are presented. The book is comprehensive
and readable. It is made up of articles reprinted from other sources and also contains considerable text material by the editors. There are fourteen chapters
grouped under five headings as follows: (1) The framework of health care systems, (2) Decision-making, (3) Planning, (4) Evaluation and control, and
(5) Management science models: Evolution and application.

The book gives clear and simple explanations of such terms as systems analysis,
organization theory, decision theory, cost-effectiveness, health information systems, linear programming, and simulation models. A great many modern management concepts are related to health care administration in the hope of helping to
solve health care delivery problems. The book will be of most value to administrators of nursing homes, hospitals, and extended care facilities. In addition, it will
be useful to public health administrators and to graduate and undergraduate students in schools of public health and health administration.

206. Levey, Samuel, and N. Paul Loomba. **Health Care Administration: A**
     Selected Bibliography. Philadelphia, Toronto, J. B. Lippincott, 1973. 149p.
     $4.00pa. LC 72-11486.
This bibliography of approximately 1,500 references is a companion volume to
the authors' book entitled *Health Care Administration: A Managerial Perspective.*
The objective of the main book is to provide pragmatic approaches to the resolu-
tion of managerial problems in health organizations. The bibliography provides
an additional effort for achieving the same objective. The bibliography is divided
into 14 parts (by broad subject) which correspond to the 14 chapters of the main
book. Reference materials for further study and research are presented. As the
theory and practice of management have evolved so rapidly, most of the references are no more than 10 years old. The plan is to update the bibliography every
two years and perhaps to expand its scope. The subject matter of this work is of
particular importance at the present time as legislation for a national health program is slowly being brought about, and it undoubtedly will change the methods
by which health care is delivered. The book is perhaps of greatest value for students in programs of health care and hospital administration and community

medicine and to those who manage institutional and noninstitutional health care services.

207. Levin, Arthur. **The Satisficers.** New York, McCall Publishing Co., 1970. 187p. $5.95. LC 74-137678. SBN 8415-0054-1.

This book is a personal record of the author's experience as an officer in the U.S. Public Health Service. It is an indictment of the agency which is most responsible for health care in the United States. The term "satisfice" is a word Washington officials use to describe the bureaucratic art of just getting by, doing a job that is barely adequate to both satisfy and suffice. The book is about how government officials face, or fail to face, social problems and problems concerned with health care, their fumbling and bungling. The book is for individuals who think about the social tasks of our nation.

208. Marmor, Theodore R., with the assistance of Jan S. Marmor. **The Politics of Medicare.** Chicago, Aldine Publishing Co., 1973. 150p. bibliog. index. $5.95. LC 76-169517. ISBN 0-202-24036-3; 0-202-24037-1pa.

This small book is a report of the political strategies and maneuvering that resulted in Medicare. It tells about how the U.S. adopted a government health insurance for the elderly in the 1960s and about the controversy and problems involved in carrying out the program. It is a case study and an attempt to contribute more broadly to the knowledge of U.S. politics and public policy. Chapter headings are as follows: (1) The origins of the Medicare strategy, (2) The politics of legislative impossibility, (3) The politics of legislative possibility, (4) The politics of legislative certainty, (5) Epilogue, and (6) Medicare and the analysis of social policy in American politics. Sociologists, economists, political scientists, government officials, and those interested in social policy development will be interested in the book.

209. Mechanic, David. **Public Expectations and Health Care: Essays on the Changing Organization of Health Services.** New York, Wiley-Interscience, 1972. 314p. bibliog. index. $12.95. LC 72-4398. ISBN 0-471-59003-7.

This book is a collection of papers published by the author in recent years in journals of sociology, medicine, and law. Also, a few new essays have been added. All the papers deal with the changing organization of medical practice in the United States and England. Major attention is given to the health care system as a whole and to the sociocultural, organizational, and technical forces that have molded it. The author hopes that the essays will contribute to a constructive discussion of the future of health care in the United States. The book is divided into five sections as follows: (1) The context of health care. This part includes materials on goals in health care, an overview of the health care system, and the changing structure of medical practice. (2) The character and distribution of health services. This part includes chapters on human problems and the organization of health care, inequality and the delivery of health services, and a note on the concept of "health maintenance organizations." (3) The United States and England: Some comparisons. This part presents original data concerning the strength and limitation of medical care in the United States and England. (4) Special issues in health care. This part deals with such things as the use of medical facilities, mental health care, the relationships between social and psychological factors, and how physicians might be trained to respond to such factors. (5) Directions in the future of health care. This section offers recommendations for improving health services in the United States.

210. Medical Economics. **1978: 110 Handpicked Medical Thinkers Tell You What Will Happen Over the Next Five Years.** special Issue, October 29, 1972. Oradell, N.J., Medical Economics Co., 1973. 226p. $2.00.

For this special issue commemorating the 50th anniversary of *Medical Economics,* 110 informed medical thinkers were asked to express their opinions and predict the future on such matters as fee for service vs. salaried practice, physician vs. hospital control, universal national health insurance, and the malpractice crisis. Minority opinions as well as majority are included. Section headings are as follows: (1) Art vs. science, (2) Solo vs. group, (3) Office vs. hospital, (4) Salary vs. fees, (5) Liability vs. protection (3 parts), (6) Supply vs. demand, (7) Work vs. leisure, and (8) U.S. vs. you.

211. Munts, Raymond. **Bargaining for Health: Labor Unions, Health Insurance, and Medical Care.** Madison, Wisconsin, University of Wisconsin Press, 1967. 320p. bibliog. index. $7.50. LC 67-13555.

Negotiating health insurance has been a complex problem for labor and management, much more complicated than was originally supposed. At least one reason for this is that the standards for good medicine and its financing are not readily recognizable to the consumer. The author, who is an economist with a good deal of experience in union bargaining, tells of the development and evolution of health bargaining as he has seen it.

The book is divided into three parts. The first provides a background and setting where the efforts of some of the more militant and established unions are examined. These include the auto and steel workers, the garment workers, and the miners. In part two, community health bargaining is explored. The relationship between the employers, physicians, the insurance business, hospitals, etc. and workers are taken up. The merits of various plans are discussed. In part three, the stages of health bargaining are defined, the contributions of labor summarized, the lessons learned discussed, and some conclusions for public policy suggested.

212. Myers, Robert J. **Medicare.** Published for the McCahan Foundation, Bryn Mawr, Pa. Homewood, Ill., Richard D. Irwin, Inc., 1970. 352p. bibliog. index. $9.50. LC 73-105914.

The author of this volume is one of the foremost authorities on social insurance. He is Chief Actuary of the Social Security Administration and has, since 1934, been involved with the country's social insurance system. The book provides an analysis and review of Medicare and Medicaid from the viewpoint of legislative evolvement, program analysis, and financial experience and implications. It should answer questions for those who are interested about what we have, how we got it, and what may evolve in the future. The principal question now in the Medicare area is whether the program will be extended to younger persons, and if so, what categories will be included. The first part of the book is about the development of Medicare, the second about the Medicare program, the third about the Medicaid program, and the fourth about related current developments and possible trends.

213. National Health Council, Inc. **Meeting the Crisis in Health Care Services in Our Communities.** Report of the 1970 National Health Forum, Washington, February 23-25. Editor: Harry Milt. New York, National Health Council, Inc., 1970. 249p.

The purpose of this forum was to bring together concerned persons from the health professions and related fields with representatives of all types of consumers of health services and with government, to examine solutions proposed for meeting the supposed crisis in health care services in the U.S. today. This publication records the proceedings of the meeting. First, the problem of health care was stated from the viewpoint of a consumer spokesman and then from the viewpoint of a provider spokesman. Then, six proposals for solution to the problem were presented. Comments on the proposals were then presented by experts. A summary of discussions is included as well as an appraisal of the meeting, resolutions and statements by various interested groups, and a list of participants.

214. Norman, John C., ed. **Medicine in the Ghetto.** Editorial assistant, Beverley Bennett. New York, Appleton-Century-Crofts, Educational Division, Meredith Corporation, 1969. 333p. $7.30. LC 75-105061. ISBN 0-390-67360-0.

This publication is a collection of papers presented at a conference sponsored by the Harvard Medical School, the Boston Globe, and the National Center for Health Services Research and Development. The format of the conference was a series of six panels as follows: (1) Community expectations and separatism, (2) The nation's experiences to date, (3) The role of the ghetto physician, (4) The economic issues of medical care in the ghetto, (5) Organization for health care, and (6) Community control, voice, and participation. The panel presentations were expanded for the book, and also included is a summary of the discussions. One of the most recurring themes was the extent to which racism can be blamed as the cause and the continuation of the plight of the ghetto residents. The last chapter relates the essence of a series of impromptu sessions held during the conference which were a form of "protest" against alleged inaction.

215. Oakes, Charles G. **The Walking Patient and the Health Crisis.** With a foreword by Louis Block, Columbia, South Carolina, University of South Carolina Press, 1973. 432p. bibliog. index. $9.95. LC 73-6667. ISBN 0-87249-272-9.

The author of this publication explores the contemporary developments in medical care which have had a direct bearing on the delivery of health services. The current factors which affect policy making, planning, the organization and financing of ambulatory programs, both on a community and regional basis are discussed. The approach taken is to define the problems that require solution rather than to supply answers. Chapter titles are as follows: (1) The nature of policy for ambulatory care, (2) Planning ambulatory care programs, (3) Community and regional authorization of ambulatory services, (4) The organization of ambulatory care programs, (5) Medical records, evaluation, and research, (6) Continuity of care, and (7) The Delphic Oracle's miscellany.

216. **One Life—One Physician: An Inquiry Into the Medical Profession's Performance in Self-Regulation.** A report to the Center for Study of Responsive
Law. By Robert S. McCleery and others. Washington, Public Affairs Press,
1971. 167p. bibliog. $5.00. LC 76-155138.

This book is a report of a Ralph Nader task force. It concentrates on a single
facet of medical care, the quality of care given by the individual physician. It
does not go into the economics of health care delivery. Chapter headings are as
follows: (1) Overview, (2) General quality of physician performance, (3) Influence
of education on quality of physician performance, (4) Impact of law on physician
performance, (5) Impact of organized medical societies on physician performance,
(6) Impact of present self-regulatory systems on hospital practice, (7) Impact of
self-regulatory systems on office practice. (8) Conclusions, (9) Recommendations.
The conclusions chapter is a summary of the book and could stand alone as it
presents its own evidence. Some of the recommendations are substantial, others
naive. The book is too superficial for a professional reader, but does provide the
layman with a view of a difficult and complex subject.

217. Panzetta, Anthony F., **Community Mental Health: Myth and Reality.** Foreword by C. Knight Aldrich. Philadelphia, Lea and Febiger, 1971. 197p.
index. $6.95. LC 71-152029. ISBN 0-8121-0358-0.

This book evaluates the community mental health center program. The author,
who is a psychiatrist, neither attacks nor defends the movement, but gives an
appraisal. Basically, however, he believes in it. The book is intended for those who
are experts in or plan to have careers in community public health, but others may
find it of value. The topic of this work is a timely one because of the interest of
the federal government in setting up these centers.

218. Pauly, Mark V. **Medical Care at Public Expense: A Study in Applied Welfare
Economics.** New York, Praeger Publishers, 1971. 160p. bibliog. index.
$12.50. (Praeger Special Studies in U.S. Economic and Social Development).
LC 72-142445.

This book, written by an economist, explores the economic efficiency of public
policy with regard to the provision of medical care at public expense. The study
on which the book was based was a doctoral dissertation, but the author has
made changes and revisions to make the work more readable and understandable.
Readers do not require formal training in economics. Mathematical treatment of
the theory, however, has been supplied in appendixes for those who are interested. Chapter headings are as follows: (1) The meaning of efficiency in the public provision of medical care, (2) An approach to optimality in the public provision of medical care, (3) Optimal insurance against the cost of medical care,
(4) Efficient national health insurance, (5) Medicare—public provision regardless
of wealth, (6) Medicaid—public provision without controls, and (7) Conclusions.

The author concludes that it is not, of course, possible in practice to obtain the
theoretically optimal provision of medical care. But he hopes that knowledge
about the shape of an optimal program will help to form rational public policy
in this area.

219. Pharmaceutical Manufacturers Association. **Pharmaceutical Payment Programs—an Overview: The Financing of Prescription Medicines Through Third Party Programs.** Washington, Pharmaceutical Manufacturers Association, 1973. 144p. (PMA Report).

This publication outlines individual existing and proposed third party payment plans and analyzes the future impact of Medicare, Medicaid, health maintenance organizations, and national health insurance upon the manufacture and distribution of pharmaceuticals, and also upon total health care. Also included are substantial statistical reports on national health care trends and the growth of private health insurance. In addition, an economic profile of prescription drug supply and demand is given. It is predicted that health insurance programs, both public and private, will increasingly include out-patient drug coverage, and the probability of national health insurance and an increase in health maintenance organizations will add to the proportion of pharmaceutical expenditures covered by third party plans.

Legislative proposals on national health insurance are compared, and existing drug payment programs outlined.

220. Placere, Morris N., and Charles S. Marwick. **How You Can Get Better Medical Care for Less Money.** New York, Walker and Co., 1973. 192p. bibliog. index. $7.95. LC 70-188476. ISBN 0-8027-0387-9.

This book warns the public that although medical costs are skyrocketing, health care is increasingly shoddy. It presents a number of case histories and gives advice on how one can get the best from the physician, clinic, hospital, and pharmacist at a fair price. The authors further warn that there is a medical Parkinson's Law at work: the amount of surgery expands to fill the number of available beds, the operating rooms, and the surgeon's time.

Also, the authors are not impressed with the comprehensive insurance plans that are being proposed, including national health insurance. They only attack the problem by altering the system of payment, the authors say, when what they should be tackling is the problem of quality. If public financing replaces private financing, it will merely encourage health professionals to continue on their present course. There is a need for more equitable allocation and more intelligent use of medical resources. The poor are not served adequately or not at all, and the middle and upper classes are overdoctored, medically and surgically.

The authors feel that the enlightened citizen can learn to outflank the medical and health bureaucracy, can select the best doctors and facilities, and can demand and receive better care. They have attempted to guide the reader in this respect. The material of the book is well-presented, fair, and sensible. The public could gain a good deal by reading it.

221. Power, Lawrence, Doris L. Bakker, and Marilyn I. Cooper. **Diabetes Outpatient Care Through Physician Assistants: A Model for Health Maintenance Organizations.** Springfield, Ill., Charles C. Thomas, 1973. 101p. illus. bibliog. index. $6.95. LC 72-88452. ISBN 0-398-02676-9

The authors of this work propose that a new kind of health care provider, in a new kind of delivery system, can best serve the patient who must live many years with a disability such as diabetes. The new health care provider would be able to teach patients the nature of their disability and how to manage it, adjust medication, etc. The provider would not be a physician, nurse, or dietitian, but something of each. The role of physician assistants is being defined in many centers, but educational programs for them are few, and their legal status unclear. There is a feeling, however, that because of the shortage of physicians and the need for the existing ones to delegate responsibility that such programs may be developed in the near future.

The book contains much information about the disease diabetes mellitus, but the approach could also be used in dealing with other long-term illnesses such as hypertension, obesity, or coronary artery disease. Chapter headings are as follows: (1) Emerging patterns of health care, (2) What is a health care team? (3) Diabetes now, (4) The diabetes outpatient load, (5) Diabetes care: the team approach, (6) Diabetes care: diet, (7) Diabetes care: medication, (8) Diabetes care: the younger diabetic, (11) Diabetes as a social disease, (12) Acute complications of diabetes, (13) Chronic complications, (14) Organizing for health maintenance.

222. Purtilo, Ruth. **The Allied Health Professional and the Patient: Techniques of Effective Interaction.** Philadelphia, W. B. Saunders, 1973. 229p. illus. bibliog. index. $5.95pa. LC 72-90725. ISBN 0-7216-7408-9.
This book is written for the student in the allied health professions. The author attempts to bridge the gap between theory and practice of effective interaction with the patient and the health professional. The book explains the basis for and the methods of achieving effective interaction by helping the student understand himself, understand the dynamics of the health professional-patient relationship, and develop his awareness of the complementary roles of other health professionals. The book addresses itself to a wide variety of situations, and gives practical suggestions for solving specific problems. Also, the reader will be stimulated to explore the topics further. The work is divided into six sections as follows: (1) The allied health professional, (2) The patient, (3) Determinants of effective interaction between allied health professional and patient, (4) The allied health professional-patient relationship, (5) Effective interaction with the elderly patient, and (6) Effective interaction with the patient who has a terminal illness. The book is unusual; particularly of note are the last two chapters on "Dying in the 1970's" and "The Process of Dying." There is much material for thought in these chapters on dealing with the dying patient and his family.

223. Rapoport, Roger. "It's Enough to Make You Sick." **Playboy,** vol. 20, no. 3 (September, 1973), pp. 112-262.
This article is an expose of the deplorable situation that exists in many instances in the U.S. regarding health care. The Cook County Hospital in Chicago is pointed out as a particularly bad example where management is poor, confusion reigns, and the patient is left helpless. The medical profession, particularly the physician, with his out-of-line high income is blamed. Modern medical technology, the author says, is simply not being effectively applied where it is most desperately needed. Neither the rich nor the poor get the balanced care they need.

224. Reynolds, Alan. "The High Cost of Health." **National Review,** vol. 25, no. 29 (July 20 1973) pp. 780-784, 802-803

This article analyzes the reasons that medical care, particularly hospitalization, is so expensive. Suggestions are made about what can be done to alleviate the problem and useful statistics are given in tabular format. In brief, the author's contention is that although the health care situation is very bad, socialized medicine is no solution to escalating costs as many believe. Consumers need more choice of doctors, hospitals, insurers, and drugs. Socialized medicine offers less choice. Consumers need more information about the prices of medical services. Socialized medicine obscures these. The monopoly that exists should be broken by competition. The article is worthwhile and presents a different point of view from those so often expressed.

225. Ribicoff, Abraham, with Paul Danaceau. **The American Medical Machine.** New York, Saturday Review Press, 1972. 212p. index. $6.95. LC 74-154257.

The author, who is a U.S. senator and a former Secretary of Health, Education and Welfare, describes the present health care system and points out its weaknesses. He also indicates ways of improving the system. Some of the problems and some of the causes of them are well outlined. He shows how the high cost of medical school and soaring rates for malpractice insurance contribute to higher fees, and how complex machinery and tests raise hospital costs. Some other probable causes are not so well analyzed. The senator feels that a federally financed program of national health insurance is the only solution to these problems. While it is doubtful that such a plan would reduce costs, it is a solution most often mentioned. Adequate health care does not seem to be available otherwise. The book is written in readable, popular (and a bit dramatic) fashion, and may oversimplify this complex subject.

226. Roy, William R. **The Proposed Health Maintenance Organization Act of 1972.** Washington, Science and Health Communications Group, 1972. 285p. (Sourcebook Series, vol. 2). $13.50. LC 72-76357.

This work was prepared by U.S. Congressman Roy who is also a physician, lawyer, a member of the Subcommittee on Public Health and Environment, and the author of the health legislation presented. The book is intended as a source document for one part of the debate in the area of health care delivery, health maintenance organizations. The book is designed so the reader can study and consider the views of prominent individuals and organizations who will have weight in the development of policy in the area under discussion. The book is in two parts: the first is the author's analysis of health problems of the nation, the difficulties to be found in solving the problems, the author's solutions, and a section-by-section analysis of his bill on health maintenance organizations. The second half of the book consists of congressional and administrative documents of importance, along with exact reprinting of the views of others. Some of the latter are as follows: the Nixon administration's proposed health maintenance assistance act, Senator Edward Kennedy's proposal, the American Medical Association position, the American Hospital Association program, AFL-CIO position, American Public Health Association's position, and several others.

227. Ruchlin, Hirsch S., and Daniel C. Rogers. **Economics and Health Care.**
Springfield, Ill., Charles C. Thomas, 1973. 317p. bibliog. index. $14.95.
LC 72-88468. ISBN 0-398-02712-9.

The purpose of this book is to acquaint the reader with basic economic concepts
as they relate to the health care field. No previous knowledge of economics is
presumed. Health administrators and planners and students will be particularly
interested in the work. Chapter headings are as follows: (1) Health economics
and economic analysis: an introduction, (2) National income and health care,
(3) The medical care price index, (4) Demand, (5) Demand studies, (6) Production and cost, (7) Production and cost studies, (8) Investment, (9) Investment
studies, (10) Economic growth and health, (11) Financing health care. Much
tabular data is presented, and mathematical and statistical appendices are
included which illustrate quantitative concepts and tools which are frequently
used in health economics literature. Previously published studies in the areas of
demand, production, and investment are reproduced in the chapters covering
these topics.

228. Rushmer, Robert F. **Medical Engineering: Projections for Health Care
Delivery.** New York, Academic Press, 1972. illus. bibliog. index. 391p.
$19.50. LC 77-182648.

This is a timely book as there is now an increased demand for more and better
health care. It offers a plan for improving the distribution of health care and the
technology of medical diagnosis and therapy over the next decade or so. It is
based on careful projections of the needs of the nation. The current crisis in
health care in this country is examined with the author's experience in other
countries as background. The situation is presented in terms of manpower, health
care facilities, and the distribution of health care. Since much data is available
now because of the new types of information sources and automated techniques,
these developments are summarized. Utilization of simulation and modeling systems are discussed. Research in biomedical engineering, for example, basic
research in biomechanics and biomaterials, is considered. New training requirements for health manpower are discussed. Descriptions of technological devices
in common use in medical centers today are presented. The book ends with the
forecasting of future technology. The material presented will be of interest to
everyone involved in planning for future health care needs. This includes physicians, public health officers, hospital administrators, biomedical engineers, and
those responsible for policy-making in health services.

229. Schwartz, Harry. **The Case for American Medicine: A Realistic Look At
Our Health Care System.** New York, David McKay Co., Inc., 1972. 240p.
bibliog. index. $6.95. LC 72-90173.

This book attempts to place the American medical care "crisis" in its proper perspective. The author allows that there is room for improvement in the system,
but that it does not need to be overthrown completely. He proposes that we
focus on particular troubled areas and try to improve them. He examines the
areas of most criticism such as high costs, unavailability of medical care in some
areas, and the shortage of physicians. He is, however, against nationalizing and
bureaucratizing American medicine as an answer to these problems, particularly

since big government has disenchanted so many in other areas, such as government-dominated education and welfare. The author is an authority on the Russian economy and points out that they have not adequately met their health care crisis either. He says, "there are no utopias in real life." The British and Swedish systems of socialized medicine have proved inadequate also, but this is rarely mentioned by critics of the American system. The book makes a contribution by presenting the other side and a more balanced view of the debate on health care policy.

230. Schwartz, Jerome L. **Medical Plans and Health Care: Consumer Participation in Policy Making With a Special Section on Medicare.** Springfield, Ill., Charles C. Thomas, 1968. 349p. bibliog. index. $16.75. LC 67-12707.

This book reports on doctoral dissertation research toward defining the "consumer role" in health care. Programs and benefits of health plans in which consumers share in making policy decisions were compared with health plans in which they do not. In the second type, physicians determine policy. Six plans of each type were studied in the locations of Washington, California, Oklahoma, Minnesota, and Washington, D.C. Also, a short section on Medicare is included.

The reports on the plans are interesting, but the conclusions are not very enlightening. Both type plans had common problems and pressures influencing policies, and their boards frequently made similar decisions. There was so little consumer participation in some of the former type plans as to make an evaluation inconclusive. The study did show that professionals and executives have a higher degree of participation than persons from lower socioeconomic classes. In spite of these findings, the author feels that consumer participation in future developments in plans may provide the key to building an informed, responsive and responsible public.

231. Skidmore, Max J. **Medicare and the American Rhetoric of Reconciliation.** University of Alabama, University of Alabama Press, 1970. 198p. bibliog. index. $6.75. LC 67-16144. SBN 8173-4718-6.

This publication is a legislative history of governmental health care in the U.S. It should assist in a better understanding of the obstacles facing social reforms along these lines. The author analyzes the situation thus: proponents and opponents of major changes of any kind are found to share most of the same "ideological symbols," as well as most of the same basic ideas, prejudices, and yearnings, which comprise the "American ideology." Therefore, advocates of social reforms have to argue for change in terms that seem to imply that no significant changes are possible or even desirable. Programs that have been established, such as social security, generally have found ready acceptance by the people without greatly altering the main currents of an ideology that would seem to require their rejection. The author believes that the major reconciliation of opposites that permits the American to live at peace with practices directly contrary to his ideology, is largely rhetorical.

Chapter headings are as follows: (1) The American ideology, (2) The American process of rhetorical reconciliation, (3) The Social Security Act and the insurance-company model, (4) The struggle for Medicare, (5) The rhetorical battle, (6) Rhetorical reconciliation in the Senate, (7) Rhetorical reconciliation and American leadership.

232. Somers, Anne R. **Health Care in Transition: Directions for the Future.** Chicago, Hospital Research and Educational Trust, 1971. 176p. bibliog. index. $3.95. LC 77-160033.
This report was written because there is a current need for informed opinion on health care delivery. The book sets forth the issues and the alternatives. The bases of the health care problem are seen as complexities and inequities, rising costs, and disparities in quality and distribution. Part one presents four paradoxes: the physician, the patient, the hospital, and recent developments in financing. Part two sets forth goals and guidelines and develops these topics: (1) A national program of consumer health education, (2) Redefinition of professional roles to assure personalized care, (3) Rationalization of community health services and the role of the hospital, (4) National health insurance: major proposals, issues and goals.

233. Stevens, Rosemary. **American Medicine and the Public Interest.** New Haven and London, Yale University Press, 1971. 572p. bibliog. index. $18.50. LC 77-151592. ISBN 0-300-01419-8.
This book is the second volume of a trilogy designed to explore patterns of medical practice in the U.S. and England. The author is particularly concerned with the effects of medical specialization and its implications for the cost and organization of medical care and the training of physicians. Much historical background material is presented and developments then traced to the present time. Major influences and questions to be dealt with in planning new legislation are considered. There are five parts to the work as follows: (1) The professional setting, (2) Formal recognition of the specialties, 1900 to 1930, (3) The specialties come of age, 1930 to 1950, (4) Professional structures reexamined, and (5) The medical profession and medical care. Also, a statistical appendix has been included. The work is very well documented.

234. Strauss, Marvin, and Leah Arnonoff. **Bibliography of Periodicals for the Health Planner.** Monticello, Ill., Council of Planning Librarians, 1969. 9p. (Council of Planning Librarians. Exchange Bibliography 102). $1.50pa.
While this bibliography contains only 86 entries, it should prove useful as many of the titles are annotated, and it contains some not-so-well-known titles. The subject matter dealt with largely falls in the area of health care economics.

235. Strauss, Marvin. **Policy Formulation in Comprehensive Health Planning.** Monticello, Ill., Council of Planning Librarians, 1969. 6p. (Council of Planning Librarians. Exchange Bibliography 95). $1.50.
This bibliography was prepared for a workshop on "Policy Formulation in Comprehensive Health Planning" held June 17-20, 1969 in Cincinnati and conducted by the Graduate Department of Community Planning, University of Cincinnati with the assistance of a grant from the U.S. Public Health Service. Books, periodical articles, and government documents are included in the listing which is a good selection.

236. Strickland, Stephen P. **U.S. Health Care: What's Wrong and What's Right.**
     A Potomac Associates book. New York, Universe Books, 1972. 127p.
     $2.45. LC 72-85247. ISBN 0-87663-176-6.

Health care delivery is frequently spoken of as being in a "crisis" state in the U.S.
This book reports on an opinion poll taken of doctors and laymen on this matter
of basic health care. Opinions were gathered on such questions as confidence in
our present system, perception of the most acute problems, and receptivity to a
national health insurance plan. The results may be surprising. Both physicians
and the public expressed striking confidence in the ability of the American medical system to provide good treatment, but they also acknowledged serious short-
comings in the care available. Both groups think the federal role will grow, probably through a national health insurance plan. The physicians did not feel this
would necessarily help matters, however. There were a great many differences of
opinion about the priority of health problems.

237. Texas Instruments Incorporated. **Development of an Implementation Plan
     for the Establishment of a Health Maintenance Organization.** Washington,
     GPO, 1971. lv. (various paging). $5.75pa. DHEW Publication No. (HSM)
     73-13005.

This report was prepared under HEW Contract HSM 110-71-276. The objective
was to develop a health maintenance organization implementation plan and supply fiscal data as they relate to the cost of initiating the plan. Seven main tasks
were undertaken: consumer identification, market planning, benefits determination, legal analysis, system design, medical group organization, and financial analysis; and, in addition, some special activities were conducted.

The report is of note because of the attention being given experimentation with
new and innovative health care systems. It is felt that many diverse plans will be
developed and evaluated in the next decade or so.

238. Tushnet, Leonard. **The Medicine Men: The Myth of Quality Medical Care
     in America Today.** New York, St. Martin's Press, 1971. 217p. $7.95.
     LC 78-166194.

The purpose of this book is to explode the myth of quality medical care in the
U.S. The author is a retired physician. He feels that many of the modern treatments are dangerous and not fully understood by the medical profession. He
does not indict all doctors, but does alert the patient to the unnecessary and perhaps harmful treatment sometimes used. The book is interesting and instructive,
and much of the criticism of the profession is probably justified. However, the
reviewer feels that a great deal of it is not, or that the author has not made his
point clear. In several cases related, there seemed to be no reasonable alternative
to the treatment given, or the patient himself was responsible for the failure.

239. U.S. Health Services and Mental Health Administration. Regional Med-
     ical Programs Service. **Quality Assurance of Medical Care. Monograph.**
     Washington, GPO, February, 1973. 483p. bibliog. DHEW Publication
     No. (HSM) 73-7021.

This publication contains all the papers presented by experts who participated in
a National Conference on Quality Assurance of Medical Care held January 23-24,
1973, in St. Louis, Missouri. Every major aspect of the subject was covered;

however, the speakers were asked to discuss the following subjects specifically:
the many aspects of criteria, medical records systems, assessment, response to
assessment, and present and future needs of quality assurance.

240. U.S. Health Services and Mental Health Administration. **Towards a Systematic Analysis of Health Care in the United States: A Report to Congress.**
Washington, GPO, 1972. 49p. DHEW Publication No. (HSM) 73-25. $.80.
This report summarizes efforts in support of a systems anslysis of national health
care plans which was requested of the Secretary of Health, Education, and Welfare by Public Law 91-515. It examines the system in terms of four components:
providers, consumers, financing, and regulations, the major factors within these
components, and selected alternative elements. The report cites important
studies and their findings. This short presentation does not attempt to be a final
work on all aspects of health care in the country; it is only a beginning. There
are several sections of the report as follows: broad alternatives, providers and
supply factors, consumer demand and health insurance, financing health care and
incidence of costs, and the role of regulations.

241. U.S. Social Security Administration. **Compendium of National Health
Expenditures Data.** Compiled by Barbara S. Cooper, Nancy L. Worthington,
and Mary F. McGee. Washington, GPO, 1973. 89p. DHEW Publication No.
(SSA) 73-11903. $1.50pa. LC 72-600302. 1770-00104.
Data on health expenditures of various sorts is published regularly in several
places, particularly in the *Social Security Administration Bulletin.* This publication collects all available data on health expenditures in one easy-to-use place.
Much attention has been given to rising health care costs recently, and this material is presented in order to provide the bases for further analysis and interpretation. No attempt is made at analysis in the publication. Material (mostly tabular)
is presented on trends and expenditures, total and broken down under public
programs, private health insurance, and by age groups.

242. U.S. Social Security Administration. **Directory, Medicare Providers and
Suppliers of Services.** 7th ed. Washington, GPO, Nov. 1972. 284p. $3.00pa.
1770-00103.
This directory is based on Social Security Administration records. It is a compilation of the names and addresses of all medical facilities which are participating
as providers and/or suppliers of services in the Health Insurance for the Aged Program. It includes hospitals, extended care facilities, home health agencies, outpatient physical therapists, independent laboratories, and portable x-ray units.
The purpose of the listing is to furnish identifying information to possible users.
The arrangement is alphabetical by state, by city within the state, and by the
name of the facility for each type of provider/supplier.

243. U.S. Social Security Administration. Office of Research and Statistics.
The Impact of Medicare: An Annotated Bibliography of Selected Sources.
Washington, GPO, 1970. 69p. index. $.40. LC 70-604540. SS PUB 69-67
(12-69).
This publication is a collection of selected references from periodicals, reports,
and books. Annotations of some length are included. The dates covered are 1965

to 1968. In addition, a list of medical reports of the Social Security's Office of Research and Statistics are listed at the end without annotation. The entries are grouped into nine broad subject categories as follows: administration and planning; hospital reimbursement; home health, extended care, and psychiatric services; physicians' services; private health insurance; public policy and issues; standards; use and financing of medical care services; utilization review. An author index has been provided.

244. U.S. Social Security Administration. Office of Research and Statistics. **Medical Care Costs and Prices: Background Book.** Washington, GPO, 1972. 148p. DHEW (SSA) 72-11908. $1.25. Stock No.: 1770-0192.

This report is of particular interest because medical care prices have risen at a much faster rate than most other costs, and have attracted much attention. It presents in summary fashion comprehensive data on medical care costs and prices. The following topics are covered: (1) Medical care price trends, (2) Hospital prices and costs, (3) Physicians' fees and income, (4) Dentists' fees and income, (5) Drug prices and expenditures, (6) Skilled nursing home charges, (7) Medical care expenditures, (8) Private health insurance, (9) Medical pricing policies, and (10) Reimbursement under public programs.

245. Willard, Harold N., and Stanislav V. Kasl. **Continuing Care in a Community Hospital.** A Commonwealth Fund Book. Cambridge, Mass., Harvard University Press, 1972. 192p. bibliog. index. $8.00. LC 75-186676. SBN 674-16775-9.

This book was written with the hope that it would stimulate practicing physicians to take more interest in the problems of chronic illness. The authors feel that at the present time such an interest is sadly lacking. The book will also be of interest to students, the staffs of health care institutions, and those interested in public health. The point of view of the senior author is that the community hospital should be the center for developing methods for health maintenance and care of the chronically ill. The model for continuing care which is presented in the book was established in a small community hospital in a town of only 19,000 persons. A similar program has been successfully set up in the teaching center at the School of Medicine at Yale University.

The joint author presents two chapters which provide a theoretical background for continuing care, discuss the importance of the contributions made by the behavioral sciences in continuing care programs, and suggest how to evaluate the effectiveness of patient care. The authors stress two areas: services for the evaluation of treatment of patients and evaluation and treatment of individual patients. The "total patient" must be considered. The time is approaching when guidelines for quality in continuing care will be required; therefore, this book is of current interest.

246. Witkin, Erwin. **The Impact of Medicare.** Springfield, Illinois, Charles C. Thomas, 1971. 286p. bibliog. index. $12.50. LC 72-119990.

The author of this book was formerly Chief Medical Consultant to the Bureau of Health Insurance, that part of the Social Security Administration which is responsible for the administration of the Medicare program. He held that post from the inception of the program in 1966 until about 1969. The following topics are discussed: (1) History, (2) Health plans in existence before Medicare,

(3) The law, (4) The size of the program, (5) The hospital and the Medicare program, (6) The consumer and the Medicare program, (7) Medicare and the medical profession, (8) Medicare and the insurance world, (9) Medicare and medical fees, (10) The extended care facility, (11) Durable Medicare equipment, (12) Home health agencies and independent laboratories, (13) Utilization review, (14) The cost of medical care, and (15) The lessons learned—the impact of Medicare on tomorrow. Also, several appendices are included such as speeches presented by the author, Title XVII of the Social Security Act, a Medicare Handbook, and tables and charts. The author's point of view is that the Medicare program has been a magnificent health experience, principally because one can look at what has been done and use the facts in planning for the future.

247. Wolstenholme, Gordon, and Maeve O'Connor, eds. **Teamwork for World Health.** A Ciba Foundation Symposium in honor of Professor S. Artunkal. London, J. & A. Churchill, 1971. 241p. illus. bibliog. index. £3.00. ISBN 0-7000-1497-7.

This book records the speeches presented at a meeting. The greatest concern of the speakers was the problem of inequities of health care about the world and how teamwork might alleviate some of it. There are sixteen papers as follows: (1) Florence Nightingale—handmaid of civilization, (2) Response to emergencies, national and international, (3) The new priorities in tropical medicine, (4) The health corps in Iran: An approach to the better distribution of health resources in remote areas, (5) An example of an integrated approach to health care: The Turkish National Health Services, (6) Experiments in expanding the rural health service in people's China, (7) Backcloth to the National Health Service in England and Wales, (8) The family care team: Philosophy, problems, possibilities, (9) Paediatrics and the community, (10) Paramedical paradoxes—challenges and opportunity, (11) New concepts in medical education, (12) Philosophy of management: The place of the professional administrator, (13) Teamwork at ministry level, (14) Mental health care: A growing concern to communities, (15) Volunteers—their use and misuse, (16) Teamwork for world health: Personal conclusions and recommendations. The book shows that there is a very large amount of work to be done. General readers, all those interested in medical care, psychologists, and sociologists will find the book pertinent.

248. Yost, Edward. **The U.S. Health Industry: The Costs of Acceptable Medical Care by 1975.** New York, Praeger, 1969. 138p. (Praeger Special Studies in U.S. Economic and Social Development). $10.00. 69-19352.

This book reports on a study which examined the health care industry in the U.S., using industrial engineering techniques to establish the capital and operating investment in people, facilities, and money to bring the output of the services to meet a particular level of performance. The assumption was made in extrapolating the investment required by 1975 that the social and technological arrangements for rendering health care would not change greatly in the intervening years. A large amount of tabular statistical data has been included in the publication. Subject areas covered in the text are: (1) The state of the nation's health, (2) Manpower and wages in the health industry, (3) Health facilities and construction costs, (4) Technological innovation and manpower requirements, (5) Estimate of health facility operating costs, (6) Minimal health needs—1975, (7) Improved health services by 1975.

2. PUBLIC HEALTH

249. Alexander, Raphael, ed. **Sources of Medical Information.** New York, Exceptional Books, 1969. 84p. $4.50. LC 78-77323.

This booklet is a "guide to organizations and government agencies which are sources of information in the fields of medicine, health, disease, drugs, mental health, and related areas, and to currently available pamphlets, reprints and selected scientific papers." The topics, which mostly fall in the public health category, are arranged alphabetically with the publications listed beneath. Prices are indicated, although a good many are free. Also, under many topics, the names of pertinent associations and agencies are listed with addresses and brief information about the purpose of the organization. Some of the more important subjects treated are: abortion, aging, alcoholism, drugs, epilepsy, heart disease, suicide, and weight control.

250. Corey, Lawrence, Steven E. Saltman, and Michael F. Epstein, eds. **Medicine in a Changing Society.** St. Louis, C. V. Mosby Co., 1972. 228p. bibliog. $4.95. LC 72-86528. ISBN 0-8016-1049-4.

This book is a collection of presentations made in a course at the University of Michigan Medical School in the field of public health. The material is divided into two parts: (1) The need for change, and (2) Medicine in transition. The editors, who were interns at the time the book was compiled, were evidently students who helped in the development of the course when it was first presented in 1969. Some of the papers were written by well-known figures in education, politics, and labor and include the late Walter Reuther and Senator Edward M. Kennedy.

251. Hobson, W., ed. **The Theory and Practice of Public Health.** 3d ed. London, New York, Oxford University Press, 1969. 520p. illus. bibliog. index. $29.50.

This book, which was prepared by a large group of experts (mostly British), is a comprehensive textbook covering the community aspects of medicine and which can be used by those engaged in health work in different parts of the world and by graduate students in public health. Throughout the book, the "epidemiological approach" has been kept in mind to assist in solving the problems of controlling disease and finding the most efficient ways of organizing health services (operations research). This edition of the work has some new chapters which are as follows: evaluation as a tool in health planning and management; planning of health services and the health team; use of computers in public health; systems of medical care: some international comparisons; economic aspects of health planning; and problems and trends in health evaluation and screening procedures. As can be seen, this edition emphasizes the increasing complexity of the planning, administration, and evaluation of health services. Also, it is interesting to note that economists, behavioral scientists, mathematicians, and computer scientists are becoming members of the health team.

252. La Rocco, August, and Barbara Jones. "A Bookshelf in Public Health, Medical Care, and Allied Fields." **Bulletin of the Medical Library Association.** vol. 60, no. 1 (January 1972) pp. 32-101.

This excellent annotated bibliography consists of a listing of 610 nonserial publications. It will serve as a guide for libraries that are attempting to build collections in the indicated fields, and will also assist researchers and educators. Most of the titles are relatively new, from 1960 on. The arrangement is by topic or subject. An index is included.

253. Marshall, Carter L., and David Pearson. **Dynamics of Health and Disease.** New York, Appleton-Century-Crofts, Educational Division/Meredith Corporation, 1972. 458p. illus. bibliog. index. $8.50. LC 72-78478.

This text was written particularly for students in the allied health professions who have had little or no previous exposure to the health field. It can be used by groups such as nursing students, laboratory technicians, public health students, and physical therapists. It will provide a general background to help the reader understand more advanced and specialized literature, and also, it will serve as a general reference text which consolidates and summarizes material from a number of sources. The book is divided into two main sections: the nature of health and disease and the delivery of health care. Chapter titles are as follows: (1) Some basic concepts of health and disease, (2) Some background determinants of health and disease, (3) The analysis and measurement of disease, (4) Infectious diseases, (5) Chronic diseases and their management, (6) Health problems of mothers, children, and the elderly, (7) Mental illness, (8) The social environment, (9) The physical environment, (10) Trends affecting health care, (11) Resources for health care, and (12) The provision of medical care services: organization, financing and utilization.

254. Rosen, George. **A History of Public Health.** Foreword by Felix Marti-Ibanez. New York, MD Publications, Inc., 1958. 551p. bibliog. index. (MD Monographs on Medical History No. 1). LC 58-8307.

The aim of this history is to tell the story of community health action. It begins with early civilizations and ends with the state of development of the advanced countries of the world at about the time the book was written. Therefore, it centers on the U.S., Great Britain, France, and Germany. Laymen, as well as professional health workers, will be interested in the work which is authoritative and scholarly. The book is divided into sections as follows: (1) The origins of public health, (2) Health and the community in the Greco-Roman world, (3) Public health in the Middle Ages, (4) Mercantilism, absolutism and the health of the people (1500-1750), (5) Health in a period of enlightenment and revolution (1750-1830), (6) Industrialism and the sanitary movement (1830-1875), (7) The bacteriological era and its aftermath (1875-1950), (8) The bacteriological era and its aftermath (concluded). In addition, there are some interesting lists: Memorable Figures in the History of Public Health, A Selected List of Periodicals (old, but includes some unusual foreign titles), Public Health Societies and Associations, and Schools of Public Health.

255. Sartwell, Philip E., ed. **Maxcy-Rosenau Preventive Medicine and Public
Health.** 9th ed. New York, Appleton-Century-Crofts, 1965. 1970p. illus.
bibliog. index. LC 64-21339.

This volume is a comprehensive widely used text book in the field of public
health. It has gone through a number of revisions, and many changes have taken
place since the 8th edition came out, reflecting the changes in the field and new
knowledge. For instance, material on dental public health, medical genetics, and
cancer have been added, and the chronic disease section has been expanded.
There are nine sections as follows: (1) Methods in public health and preventive
medicine, (2) Infectious diseases, (3) Nutrition and deficiency diseases,
(4) Chronic illness, (5) Maternal and child health, (6) Environmental and occupational health, (7) Milk and food sanitation, (8) Water supply and waste disposal,
and (9) Public health organization and activities.

256. Smolensky, Jack, and Franklin B. Haar. **Principles of Community Health.**
3d ed. Philadelphia, W. B. Saunders, 1972. 441p. illus. bibliog. index.
$10.50. LC 70-168600. ISBN 0-7216-9369-5.

This kind of book is important because a primary concern of the decade is the
quality of human life. We are attempting to achieve environmental quality without sacrificing our way of life, an increasingly difficult task. Social action and
social change as they affect health programs are stressed in the work. This edition
of the text has been revised and rewritten to include new concepts and practices
such as more planning by community agencies, more efficient utilization of present health professionals, recruitment and training of paramedical personnel, and
coordination among health and welfare agencies. Also, such complex problems as
medical care and poverty, malnutrition, minority health problems, ecology, population control, genetic counseling, legislation, and international health are discussed. The book is college and university level and was written for those planning to assume some degree of responsibility in community health programs.
Chapter headings are as follows: (1) Basic health problems, (2) Historical aspects
of community health in the United States, (3) Sociological aspects of community
health, (4) Solving community health problems, (5) Community health education, (6) Organization and administration of official and voluntary health agencies, (7) Chronic disease, (8) Communicable disease, (9) Mental health, (10) Safety
education, (11) Environmental sanitation. Also, several useful and unusual appendices have been included: (1) Your career in public health, (2) What doctors
think of their patients, (3) Planning a program for nutritional health, (4) What
bylaws should contain, (5) Preventing food poisoning, (6) State health department inspection forms, (7) Student semester project, and (8) Career information.

257. Steele, James H. "A Bookshelf on Veterinary Public Health." **American
Journal of Public Health.** vol. 63, no. 4 (April 1973). pp. 291-311.

This publication is a comprehensive bibliography which covers about 100 years
of literature in the field. The emphasis is on transmission of diseases from animals
to man. The text of the article discusses the 156 publications which are listed as
"References." The author takes the historical approach, discussing early literature first, then proceeding to the current. In addition to the references, about
two pages of other publications are listed under "Bibliography." "Laboratory
Animal Medicine Reference Material," and "Publications for Sale" (by the

National Academy of Science). The list is of particular interest to veterinarians, epidemiologists, veterinary schools, and schools of public health.

258. U.S. National Institutes of Health. **A Bibliography of Chinese Sources on Medicine and Public Health in the People's Republic of China: 1960-1970.** A publication of Geographic Health Studies by the John E. Fogarty International Center for Advanced Study in the Health Sciences. Prepared under an interagency agreement with the Library of Congress. Washington, GPO, 1973. 486p. DHEW Publication No. (NIH) 73-439. $5.55. Stock No. 1753-00013.

This impressive bibliography was prepared to bring to interested persons a better awareness of medicine and health in another country so our own might be better assessed. The bibliography covers sources translated by the Joint Publications Research Service and are available at the Library of Congress. Some of the unusual areas covered are herbal medicine and acupuncture.

The work is in two parts: the first, and largest, covers articles from medical journals and more popular magazines and newspapers; and the second includes titles of books, monographs, and pamphlets. The first part has been subdivided into clinical subjects and health related subjects. This comprehensive work should help dispel the mystery about Chinese medicine.

259. U.S. National Institutes of Health. **Medicine and Public Health in the People's Republic of China.** Publication of the Geographic Health Studies, John E. Fogarty International Center for Advanced Study in the Health Sciences. Joseph R. Quinn, editor. Washington, GPO, 1973. 333p. bibliog. index. DHEW Publication No. (NIH) 73-67.

This book is one of a series commissioned by the Fogarty International Center. It is based largely on bibliographical searches, although some of the contributors have visited China. There are three main sections: (1) Chinese medicine through the ages, (2) Health care organization and administration, and (3) Health problems. There are chapters on such topics as acupuncture, pharmacology, medical personnel training, overpopulation (the country's major health problem), and parasitic diseases, to name a few. The book is quite interesting reading, although it leaves a good deal to conjecture. It is of particular value for those who want to assess the reports on Chinese health that come from within the People's Republic.

260. U.S. National Library of Medicine. **A Profile of the United States Public Health Service, 1798-1948.** By Bess Furman in consultation with Ralph C. Williams. Washington, GPO, 1973. 487p. illus. bibliog. index. DHEW Publication No. (NIH) 73-369. $4.35. Stock No. 1752-00140.

This history, or rather as the author calls it, "a profile" is written in the style of newspaper reporting. The work is interesting, and perhaps will reveal to the reader that the American public can be proud of the accomplishments of the Public Health Service. Particularly, the text shows how the history of the PHS is interwoven with other government agencies, the medical profession, voluntary agencies, and individuals.

261. Wilner, Daniel M., Rosabelle Price Walkey, and Lenor S. Goerke. **Introduction to Public Health.** 6th ed. New York, Macmillan; London, Collier Macmillan, 1973. 470p. illus. bibliog. index. $9.00. LC 73-5281. ISBN 0-02-428200-6.

The earlier editions of this well-known textbook were written by Harry S. Mustard and various co-authors. The book is designed to offer the student a broad view of the health care field at the present time, and is oriented to professional schools and training programs in such fields as nursing, nutrition, dietetics, pharmacy, medical technology, x-ray technology, optometry, podiatry, and the like. Public health students will find it of some value, but they will receive more in-depth training than this book presents. This edition of the text is primarily concerned with four things: objectives of the major health and health-related programs in the U.S.; their general sponsorship and financial backing; their personnel requirements, qualifications, and opportunities; and certain health trends such as health manpower, health care delivery, mental health care, and environmental health. There are four sections of the book as follows: (1) The framework of public health, (2) Medical care, mental health, and environmental health, (3) Health and disease of population groups, (4) Selected public health supportive services.

262. World Health Organization. **World Directory of Schools of Public Health. 1971.** Geneva, World Health Organization, 1972. 277p.

This second edition of the directory lists about 120 schools of public health in 44 countries, and gives pertinent data about each institution. The countries are listed alphabetically, and there is a chapter on each giving the following information: general information, courses offered, conditions of admission, curriculum, examinations, and qualifications. At the end of each chapter, the schools are listed alphabetically in a table with the following information included: name, address, year the public health course started, number of teaching staff, number of students in all courses, and number in the public health course.

3. HEALTH SCIENCE CAREERS, MANPOWER, AND EDUCATION

263. **Allied Medical Education Directory, 1973.** 4th ed. Chicago, Council on
Medical Education of the American Medical Association, 1973. 423p.
bibliog. $2.00.

This directory, published annually, provides information on allied medical education. There are four sections. Section I is a report on the 25 organizations that
cooperate for allied medical education and the review committees they sponsor.
Such organizations as the American Academy of Pediatrics and the Society of
Nuclear Medicine are involved. Other miscellaneous information about the organizations, committee, and councils is included. Section II is on the process of
approval of the education programs. Section III, the consolidated listing, is a
state by state listing of the sponsors of the AMA-approved educational programs.
Section IV contains chapters on each of the 22 allied medical occupations.
Included is a description of the occupation, explanation of the approval process,
essentials, and listing of individual programs with information on each. Section V
consists of a statistical breakdown of programs by state, data on enrollment,
capacity and graduates of each program, and studies on licensure of health occupations and accreditation. Section VI outlines some other AMA services available
for allied medical education, and Section VII is a bibliography.

264. American Medical Association. **Horizons Unlimited: A Handbook Describing Rewarding Career Opportunities in Medicine and Allied Fields.** 8th ed.
Chicago, American Medical Association, 1970. 134p. illus.

The book is designed primarily for high school students and beginning college
students to help acquaint them with career pursuits and opportunities in the
health field. There are two sections presented, the first on medicine as a career
and the second on careers allied to medicine. Much practical information is
included, such as choosing a college, getting into medical school, financing, and
internship training. The information on training for medicine is more complete
than that given for the allied fields.

265. Association of American Medical Colleges. **Medical School Admission
Requirements, U.S.A. and Canada, 1974-75.** 24th ed. Washington,
Association of American Medical Colleges, 1973. 345p. bibliog. $4.00pa.

This publication, which is revised annually, provides current, official information
on premedical preparation and admission to medical schools which will be of
help to prospective students and counselors. Nine chapters are presented on
various topics such as premedical planning, choosing a school, admission processes, financial information, etc. Chapter 10, which takes up the bulk of the
book, contains short monographs of about two pages on each of the schools in
the U.S. (arranged by state), Puerto Rico, and the American University of Beirut.
Chapter 11 gives information on affiliate medical schools of Canada and the

Philippines. The publication is of particular value since competition among qualified applicants to medical schools has been so great recently.

266. Burton, Lloyd Edward, and Hugh Hollingsworth Smith. **Public Health and Community Medicine for the Allied Medical Professions.** Baltimore, Williams and Wilkins, 1970. 561p. illus. bibliog. index. $14.50. LC 76-96772. SBN 683-01233-9.

This book was written primarily for undergraduate students with an interest in health careers such as pharmacy, nursing, medical technology, medical social work, and the like. An effort has been made to describe the converging interests of public health and private medicine. The relationships and interdependencies of community activities in maintaining the health of individuals at a high level are stressed. Chapter titles are as follows: (1) Historical introduction, (2) Organization and administration of health agencies, (3) Convergence of private medicine and public health, (4) The methodology of public health, (5) Factors contributing to ill health, (6) Some characteristic diseases of man, (7) Methods of disease control, (8) Mental health, (9) Socioeconomic health problems, (10) Health problems of a modern age, (11) Protective and preventive health measures, (12) The health team approach to combating disease, (13) Limitations to progress and opportunities for action.

267. **Conference on Meeting Medical Manpower Needs: The Fuller Utilizaticn of the Woman Physician. Report.** Sponsored by American Medical Women's Association, the President's Study Group on Careers for Women, and Women's Bureau, U.S. Department of Labor. Jan. 12-13 1968. New York, American Medical Women's Association, 1968. 104p. illus. $1.25.

The purpose of this Conference was to consider how the skills of women could be drawn upon more fully as larger numbers of young people are recruited for medical training. Also of concern was the contribution of women physicians already trained. The Conference papers presented give greater visibility to the potential for the better use of womanpower in the medical field.

268. Derbyshire, Robert C. **Medical Licensure and Discipline in the United States.** Baltimore and London, Johns Hopkins Press, 1968. 183p. bibliog. index. $9.00. LC 79-84589. SBN 8018-1082-5.

This volume is designed to take up where another left off. The first book of note on medical licensing in America, written by Richard Harrison Shryock, was entitled *Medical Licensing in America, 1650-1965,* (Johns Hopkins Press). Medical licensure is important at the present time because the apparent shortage and/or faulty distribution of physicians has brought about demands for more physicians, and licensing authorities find themselves under pressure to lower standards. Also, there is some feeling that licensing by boards is not necessary at all, as all schools of medicine are accredited. The author brings up problems such as the diverse laws regulating licensure and discipline in the various states, medical imposters, legal background for disciplinary actions by licensing boards, types of disciplinary actions taken by boards, and the causes for such actions. Many of the offenses of physicians involve narcotics. The author also discusses professional incompetence, the problem of foreign medical graduates, and lack of uniformity of standards of licensing throughout the states. The need for a new approach and suggestions for improvement are presented.

269. Greenfield, Harry I., with the assistance of Carol A. Brown. **Allied Health Manpower: Trends and Prospects.** Foreword by Eli Ginzberg. New York, Columbia University Press, 1969. 195p. index. $8.00. LC 75-76249.
This publication provides a view of the health manpower available today in the United States. The book is not concerned with physicians or other health professionals, but with the 1.7 million health workers who are sometimes called "paramedicals" or "allied health manpower." In general, these people have less than a full college education. Specifically, the authors consider five categories of technicians: x-ray, medical records, occupational and physical therapy, medical and dental, and three large categories of assistants: licensed practical nurses, nurse's aides, and psychiatric aides. The majority of these workers (about four out of five) are women.

The authors feel that improvement in recruitment, education and training and utilization of this allied manpower should be brought about through innovative action. Opportunity for advancement presently discourages many workers. The authors also feel that government programs affecting allied health programs should be extended and strengthened, and improvement in wages, working conditions, and management be made. It is evident that large numbers of these people will continue to be required, and that the health services industry will need to attract and hold these workers.

Chapter headings are: (1) Manpower dynamics of the health services industry, (2) Allied health personnel in the health manpower spectrum, (3) Sources of supply, (4) Education and training, (5) Structure and function of allied health labor markets, (6) Facets of utilization, (7) Federal programs, and (8) Overview and recommendations.

270. Hospital Research and Educational Trust. **Training and Continuing Education: A Handbook for Health Care Institutions.** Chicago, Hospital Research and Educational Trust, 1970. 261p. index. illus. bibliog.
The handbook is the first basic comprehensive work on the subject of personnel development through training and continuing education in the field of institutional health care. The topics covered are similar to those in general continuing education guides. The book describes the techniques involved in the process of developing educational programs and presents a variety of sample teaching materials.

The publication of the handbook was carried out by the Hospital Continuing Education Project of the Hospital Research and Educational Trust, an affiliate of the American Hospital Association. The purpose of the project was to improve and expand continuing education opportunities for hospital personnel through a partnership between hospitals, hospital associations, and universities. Chapters of the book were used in regional conferences on hospital training and education.

The work is of particular importance because of the nationwide attention that has been focused on health care institutions and their problems.

271. Moore, Wilbert E. **The Professions: Roles and Rules.** In collaboration with
    Gerald W. Rosenblum. New York, Russell Sage Foundation, 1970. 303p.
    bibliog. index. $8.95. LC 78-104184. SBN 87154-604-3.

This book, written by a sociologist, attempts to define the characteristics of the
professional and to describe the attributes that give professionals their basis for
status and esteem. The author indicates that the possession of particular knowledge or skills is an attribute, but also that the modern scale of professionalism
demands other criteria such as practicing a full-time occupation, commitment to
a calling, authenticated membership in a formalized organization, advanced education, service orientation, and autonomy restrained by responsibility. The
author also discusses the professional person's roles on various levels, with
clients, peers, employers, colleagues in complementary professions, and the public. Physicians and related medical professionals are used as examples and referred
to frequently in the text. The work is well written, interesting, and well worth
reading by anyone interested in professions and their part in modern society.

272. Odgers, Ruth F., and Burness G. Wenberg. **Introduction to Health Profes-
    sions.** St. Louis, C. V. Mosby Co., 1972. $4.95. ISBN 0-8016-3698-1.

This book provides education and occupational information for a wide variety of
health careers. It describes each career, tells what education and training is
required, and what opportunities for employment are available. It can be used as
a textbook in a survey course of the medical and allied professions or as a
resource for vocational guidance and counseling. Each chapter is written by a
different author, most of them members of the faculty at the Ohio State University. The following fields are covered: medicine, dentistry, optometry, veterinary
medicine, nursing and related programs, pharmacy, physical therapy, dental
hygiene, dietetics, inhalation therapy, medical record administration, medical
technology, occupational therapy, radiologic technology, speech and hearing
science, medical social work, hospital and health services administration, medical
communications, medical illustration, environmental sanitation, and emerging
health professions.

273. Shryock, Richard Harrison. **Medical Licensing in America, 1650-1965.**
    Baltimore, Johns Hopkins Press, 1967. 124p. bibliog. index. $5.00.
    LC 67-16045.

This work is a history of medical licensing in the United States. The development
of standards for medical practice are traced and linked with developments in
medical education. The American history is presented with comparisons to European, particularly in Great Britain, France, and Germany as these countries
exerted considerable influence on American thinking along these lines. Also, a
comparison is made with medical licensing and licensing to practice law. The
book covers only the licensing of physicians, not dentists, pharmacists, or other
medical practitioners. The presentation is in three parts as follows: (1) Early
licensing and subsequent decadence, 1650-1875, (2) Medical reform: Achieve-
ments and limitations, 1875-1965, (3) Problems and procedures in licensing,
1900-1965.

274. U.S. Department of Labor, Manpower Administration and U.S. Department of Health, Education and Welfare, National Institutes of Health. **Health Careers Guidebook.** 3d ed. Washington, GPO, 1972. 166p. illus. index. $2.25. 2900-0158.

This guidebook is valuable for high school students, counselors, and management and personnel workers seeking information on careers in the health field. Information is given on performance requirements for the occupations, sources of financial aid, and community health training information. There are a number of newer health science occupations which have recently evolved that are included, such as biomedical engineering and voluntary health agency administration. Also included is a salary chart and a referral list of organizations which can supply information on a particular career.

275. U.S. Health Resources Administration. **Proceedings, the First National MEDIHC Conference** (Military Experience Directed into Health Careers). Washington, March 21-23, 1973. 66p. DHEW Publication No. (HRA) 74-4.

This publication presents the proceedings of the first MEDIHC conference held about four years after the establishment of the organization. The MEDIHC program is implemented at the State level to reach veterans who need job counseling and to minimize the wastage of allied health manpower being separated from the Armed Services. The Department of Defense identifies all persons with medical ratings prior to their separation date and refers them to state centers where they are matched with jobs or with educational opportunities as civilians. A list of state MEDIHC agencies and a list of regional MEDIHC coordinators have been included.

276. U.S. National Institutes of Health. Bureau of Health Manpower Education. Division of Manpower Intelligence. **Foreign Trained Physicians and American Medicine.** By Rosemary Stevens and Joan Vermeulen. Washington, GPO, 1972. 170p. bibliographic supplement. DHEW Publication No. (NIH) 73-325. $2.35. Stock No. 1741-00051.

The purpose of this publication is to bring together materials on the location, activity, and function of the more than 63,000 foreign trained physicians in the United States; to review the political, economic, and organizational factors which have led to the current manpower situation; and to analyze the data in terms of physician manpower policies and research. The study describes the current situation in the U.S. and reviews the implications of this for future policy development. One of every six physicians now practicing in the country is a graduate of a medical school outside the U.S. and Canada.

In addition to the discussion presented, there is an appendix of statistical tables and a supplementary bibliography.

4. FAMILY HEALTH AND PERSONAL CARE

277. Allen, Linda, ed. **The Look You Like.** Chicago, American Medical Association, 1966. 129p. illus. $1.70.

This book was prepared in consultation with members of the AMA Committee on Cutaneous Health and Cosmetics. It consists of selected questions and answers about skin care, problems, and cosmetics that have appeared in a column in *Today's Health.* Although the book was published a number of years ago, it is still a very good authoritative common-sense source of information. The following topics are discussed: cosmetic creams, rejuvenating creams, other cosmetic preparations, reactions to cosmetics, hair dyeing and bleaching preparations, hair waving and straightening, miscellaneous hair preparations, excess hair (hirsutism), hair loss (alopecia), other hair problems, acne, aging and wrinkles, birthmarks, dry skin, oily skin, hand and nail problems, perspiration and body odor, soaps and bathing, sunlight and the skin, other skin problems, and cosmetic surgery.

278. Bauer, W. W., ed. **Today's Health Guide: A Manual of Health Information and Guidance for the American Family.** Chicago, American Medical Association, 1965. 624p. illus. index. $5.95. LC 64-8095.

This guide brings together an enormous mass of information about health, topics which are most helpful to the family in making the best use of sources of health information, preventive medical services, treatment of illness, and the meeting of emergencies. More than 200 physicians, scientists, and others have contributed to the work. There are fifteen parts as follows: (1) The home as a health center, (2) Health and your family, (3) The wonderful human body, (4) Safeguarding your health, (5) Mental and emotional health, (6) Recreation and relaxation, (7) Safety, (8) Medical services for the family, (9) When you need a doctor, (10) Dangerous and disabling diseases, (11) Surgery today, (12) The proper use of drugs, (13) Physical handicaps, (14) Community health, and (15) Keeping posted.

279. Brown, J. A. C. **The Stein and Day International Medical Encyclopedia.** Rev. by A. M. Hastin Bennett, with drawings by Margot Cooper. New York, Stein and Day, 1971. Originally pub. in England under title **Pears Medical Encyclopedia,** Illustrated. 464p. illus.(part col.) $17.50. LC 165481.

This work is designed primarily for the layman, but it should also be useful to students, nurses, and other professionals who are seeking to refresh their memories. The text is supported by a large number of illustrations, some in color, and including a series of anatomical transparent overlay diagrams. The coverage is rather comprehensive; the articles are short, concise, and readable. Since the approach is international, many of the articles are concerned with disease conditions rarely found in the U.S. or with treatments seldom used. For this reason, there may be better home medical guides available. However, the work appears to be an accurate source of medical and scientific information.

280. Brown, Warren J. **Patients' Guide to Medicine, from the Drugstore through the Hospital.** Largo, Florida, Aero-Medical Consultants, Inc., 1969. 236p. illus. index. $4.95. LC 72-112417.

This book, written for the layman by a physician, attempts to bridge the communication gap existing between the average patient and the physician. The first chapters take up common problems of health and hygiene including mental health. Later follows rather extensive sections on pharmaceuticals including both over-the-counter and prescription drugs. There are short chapters on choosing a doctor, medical terminology, common diagnostic tests, and the hospital. The work is illustrated with a large number of line drawing, diagrams, and charts. Also, a number of useful tables are included giving information on such things as immunization, desirable weights, and calorie counting. Good text material is included throughout although it is concise.

The book is quite well-done and written at the proper non-technical level for the layman. It also has a good deal of reference value as it will answer many questions asked by a layman. It is recommended for most libraries as well as for use in the home. One criticism of it is that it may be difficult to locate the answers to specific questions as the arrangement is rather odd ("Help from the Drugstore" is Chapter IV, but "Prescription Drugs" does not come until Chapter VII), and the index is brief. Also, the Table of Contents does not give page numbers, and there is no list of the figures included.

281. Clark, Randolph Lee, and Russell W. Cumley, comps, and eds. **The Book of Health: A Medical Encyclopedia for Everyone.** 3d ed. New York, Van Nostrand Reinhold, 1973. 975p. illus. index. $24.95. LC 72-12256. ISBN 0-442-01606-9.

This impressive encyclopedia was designed primarily to enlighten the layman although health professionals will find it of interest also. A large number of well-known experts contributed to the volume, and the quality of the work is high. The reader is not told how to treat diseases, but they are described, and he is assisted in knowing when to seek medical advice. The layman will be better informed by consulting the volume, and it will allow him to communicate better with his physician. The arrangement is by topic. Physiology is stressed as is historical development. Interwoven is the story of the great contributions to medical knowledge, and biographical sketches and portraits are scattered throughout the text. The third edition has added new material in each chapter. Much of this is an outgrowth of the space age and advances in technological procedures. There is a new chapter on space medicine.

282. **The Concise Home Medical Guide.** New York, Grosset and Dunlap, 1972. 630p. illus. index. $9.95. ISBN 0-448-01949-3.

This guide is designed to inform the family on basic medical procedures and practices and includes a wide variety of topics. Function and care of the body, hygiene, information on illness and accidents, and treatments that may be given at home are stressed. Mental health is also discussed. The book is said to be compiled by a distinguished group of physicians and medical writers. Although they are not named, the text material seems to be reliable. An interesting feature is that topics of recent interest have been included such as "Father and the Family." "Unarmed Combat," "Social Security and Medicare," and "The Family Pet."

283. Davis, Adelle. **Let's Have Healthy Children**. New and expanded ed. New
   York, Harcourt Brace Jovanovich, 1972. 486p. illus. index. $6.95.
   LC 77-160400. ISBN 0-15-150440-7.
This book is a guide, primarily for mothers and expectant mothers, concerning
nutrition. There are chapters dealing with prenatal care, the feeding of children,
and good nutrition in preventing disease. In general, the advice given is probably
good, but many of the claims made for vitamins and "proper" diets seem to be
exaggerated, or at least overemphasized. There is a growing awareness among
experts that many Americans are over-dosing themselves with vitamins and
minerals, that this is harmful (as well as expensive) as toxic symptoms develop.
It is felt that a doctor's advice should be sought before using them. The author
puts a great deal of emphasis on the value of Vitamin E. However, many reputable nutritionists question that it has a necessary role at all in ordinary nutrition.
The author has a reasonably good scientific background, but the reviewer notes
that many other scientists do not agree with her on several other matters, for
instance, the importance placed on "organically" grown food and her criticisms
of the use of pesticides in agriculture. Numerous references are made in the text
to scientific studies, but no literature references are included. However, the
author has written other books on nutrition where much scientific documentation
was included. This book was obviously intended for a lower level layman audience,
and perhaps this is where the fault lies. There is an oversimplification of the
material.

The book contains useful tables of recommended daily dietary allowances and of
food composition.

284. Eichenlaub, John E. **A Minnesota Doctor's Home Remedies for Common
   and Uncommon Ailments**. 2d ed. Englewood Cliffs, N.J., Prentice-Hall,
   1972. 264p. index. $6.95. LC 75-179448.
This book gives approved remedies and treatments for some 200 rather common
ailments and injuries. Many of the treatments might be called folk remedies, but
the author also discusses modern medication as well. Treatment is outlined for
such conditions as backache, rheumatism, gastrointestinal ailments, colds, head-
ache, allergies, etc. Chapters are also included on family planning, pregnancy, and
on preventing cancer. The book is written for the layman in simple fashion. It
will be most useful in home libraries as it is perhaps too elementary for institutional libraries.

285. Fishbein, Morris, ed. **Modern Home Medical Adviser**. Rev. ed. Garden City,
   N. Y., Doubleday, 1969. 997p. illus. index. $8.95. LC 69-10978.
This convenient reference book was edited by a well-known physician who is
also the author and/or editor of a number of popular medical works for the layman. 22 medical specialists are contributors. The emphasis is on hygiene and prevention of disease. First aid, prenatal care, child care, sex hygiene, diet, mental
health, and old age are some of the considerations. For the most part, only common ailments are discussed. There is a brief chapter on drugs and their uses, and
also a chapter on the family medicine chest.

286. Glasscote, Raymond M., and others. **The Community Mental Health Center: An Interim Appraisal.** Washington, Joint Information Service of the American Psychiatric Association and the National Association for Mental Health, 1969. 156p. $6.00; $4.00pa. LC 77-75807.

This publication reports on a field study undertaken under a contract with the National Institute of Mental Health. There is an emphasis on inpatient service in community mental health centers, although all aspects of the operation of the centers are considered. There is an attempt to identify successes as well as problems and solutions. Several centers were studied, but two seemed to be farther ahead than the others, so these are described in detail. These two are the Community Mental Health Center of Denver General Hospital and the Mid-Houston Community Mental Health Center located in St. Joseph Hospital in Houston. The publication also contains a record of a Conference on Community Mental Health Centers held in November 1967 in which representatives from the centers, members of the Joint Information Service survey team, staff of the American Psychiatric Association and the National Association for Mental Health, and representatives of the National Institute of Mental Health participated.

287. Gomez, Joan. **A Dictionary of Symptoms: A Medical Dictionary to Help Sufferers, by Easier Self-Diagnosis, to Eliminate Groundless Fears and Know When to Consult Their Doctor.** Edited and with an introduction by Dr. Marvin J. Gersh. New York, Stein and Day, 1968; repr. New York, Bantam Books, 1972. 398p. illus. index. $1.95pa.

The main purpose of this dictionary is to give the layman a basic knowledge of physiology, to outline what is normal and abnormal, to allow the reader to discover for himself the probable cause of his symptoms, to suggest what action he should take, to allay unnecessary fears, and to indicate when medical advice should be sought. The book fulfills its purpose very well and is certainly worth the small price. The dictionary is easy to use. There is a table of symptoms on colored pages in the center of the volume. Here the symptoms are arranged alphabetically and page references given where information is found. The information is concise but accurate and probably complete enough for the layman. There are several special sections that should prove valuable. They are as follows: children, the first year; from 1-13 years; adolescents; men; and women. A glossary of technical terms has also been included. The book should prove useful in libraries, and be of particular value for home use.

288. Hymovich, Debra, and Martha Underwood Barnard. **Family Health Care.** New York, McGraw-Hill Book Co., a Blakiston Publication, 1973. 462p. bibliog. index. $5.95. LC 72-12743. ISBN 0-07-031656-2.

This book brings together selected papers from various areas which are applicable to the delivery of nursing care to members of family units. There are three parts presented: (1) The family: general considerations, (2) The expanding and contracting family, and (3) The family in crisis. The object of the book is to inform nurses and others of how nursing can be practiced by considering the family unit.

289. Institute of Medicine. National Academy of Sciences. **Infant Death: An Analysis by Maternal Risk and Health Care.** David M. Kessner, Project Director. Washington, National Academy of Sciences, 1973. 203p. bibliog. (Contrasts in Health Status, vol. 1). LC 73-8821. ISBN 0-309-02119-7.

This report is a serious effort by medical researchers to determine the relationship between pregnancy and the availability and receipt of maternal health services. The results show that women who are pregnant and do not take advantage of contemporary medical knowledge have a far greater likelihood of losing their children than those who visit physicians during pregnancy. The report contains much statistical data, much of it in tabular form. The data analyzed was from 140,000 births in New York City for 1968. It should be noted that 1968 was two years before the state's abortion laws were liberalized. The author points out that since the law was enacted, there has been some evidence to show that infant death rate has been significantly reduced. The report includes suggestions for further research in the area of maternal and infant health services.

290. Ross, Milton S. **Skin Health and Beauty.** New York, Funk and Wagnalls, 1969. 260p. index. $6.95. LC 68-29079.

This book, written by a dermatologist, is an easy to understand, sound, and sensible guide to skin care and treatment. There is a section on the normal skin, one on principles of skin therapy, and a longer section on skin problems and their treatment. This section includes material on such problems as warts, acne, ear piercing, fungus infections, psoriasis, poison ivy, hives, insect bites, virus skin infections, bacterial skin infections, venereal disease, side reactions of drugs, eczema, age spots, skin cancer, sun tanning, and hair and nails. The book is of interest to laymen and physicians, and is suitable for home libraries.

5. ETHICS

291. Barber, Bernard, John J. Lally, Julia Loughlin Makarushka, and Daniel Sullivan. **Research on Human Subjects: Problems of Social Control in Medical Experimentation.** New York, Russell Sage Foundation, 1973. 263p. index. $10.50. LC 72-83831. SBN 87154-090-8.

The book is based on two studies, one a nationally representative sample of biomedical research institutions, the second a sample of 350 researchers who use human subjects. The work was done by professional sociologists, and the book is intended for sociologists and others who are primarily interested in the ethical problems connected with the use of human subjects in biomedical experimentation. The chapter headings are as follows: (1) Research design and methodology: the two studies, (2) Is there a problem? Current patterns of ethical standards and practices, (3) The dilemma of science and therapy: the effects of competition in the science community, (4) The dilemma of science and therapy: the effects of competition in the local institution, (5) Social control: some patterns and consequences of socialization, (6) Social control: Some patterns and consequences of socialization, (6) Social control: some patterns and consequences of collaboration groups and informal interaction structures, (7) Six case studies, (8) Social control: the structures, processes, and efficacy of peer group review, (9) Social control: have medical schools been ethical leaders? (10) The social responsibilities of a powerful profession: some suggestions for policy change and reform. Also included are two appendices, the National Survey Questionnaire and the Intensive Two-Institution Interview Schedule. The authors feel that biomedical researchers get inadequate training in the ethics of research on human subjects, that schools pay relatively more attention to scientific training of their students. However, it seems that local peer review groups that screen research on human subjects do a fairly good job. The authors make a plea for more contributions by sociologists in the quest for better information and analysis in this field.

292. Mendelsohn, Everett, Judith P. Swazey, and Irene Taviss, eds. **Human Aspects of Biomedical Innovation.** Cambridge, Mass., Harvard University Press, 1971. 234p. bibliog. index. $9.95. LC 74-160027. SBN 674-41331-8.

Dramatic events like human heart transplants and breakthroughs in genetic research have increased recognition of the importance and difficulty of the social and ethical problems involved. The issues discussed in this book have to do with the social control of new biomedical technologies and with problems in the organization and delivery of medical care that have arisen as a result of technological and social change. The essays presented in this book are divided into three classifications: (1) Introduction, (2) Toward a social policy for biomedical science and technology, and (3) Science, technology, and the practice of medicine. Titles of the individual contributions are as follows: (1) Problems in the social control of biomedical science and technology, (2) PKU: a study of biomedical legislation, (3) Physicians, patients, and society: some new tensions in medical ethics, (4) Some ethical problems in clinical investigation, (5) The Harvard Conference on Behavior Control Technologies, (6) New technologies and the practice of medicine, (7) The health care system of industrial society: the disappearance of the general practitioner and some implications, (8) Notes on medical manpower: quantity, quality, and medicine's current efforts.

The significant viewpoint expressed in the volume seems to be that we are beginning a new cycle in medicine which will see equal attention paid to the social problems of medicine as well as to the technological.

293. Ramsey, Paul. **The Patient as Person: Explorations in Medical Ethics.** New Haven and London, Yale University Press, 1970. 283p. index. $10.00. LC 77-118737. ISBN 0-300-01357-4.

This book, which is written by a Christian ethicist, is a book about ethics which examines some of the problems that are especially urgent at the present time because of the options for saving lives which are available such as transplanting organs and human experimentation. The work is based on the 1969 Lyman Beecher Lectures at the Divinity School and the School of Medicine at Yale University. The chapter headings are as follows: (1) Consent as a canon of loyalty with special reference to children in medical investigations, (2) On updating procedures for stating that a man has died, (3) On (only) caring for the dying, (4) The self-giving of vital organs: a case study in comparative ethics, (5) Giving or taking cadaver organs for transplant, (6) A caveat on heart transplants, (7) Choosing how to choose: patients and sparse medical resources.

294. Symposium on Legal and Other Aspects of Artificial Insemination by Donor (AID) and Embryo Transfer. **Law and Ethics of A.I.D. and Embryo Transfer.** Amsterdam, Elsevier-Excerpta Medica-North Holland, Associated Scientific Publishers, 1973. 110p. bibliog. index. Ciba Foundation Symposium 17 (new series). LC 73-80904. ISBN Excerpta Medica 90-219-4018-3; American Elsevier 0-444-15014-5.

The participants of this international symposium examine the legal, social and psychological problems affecting children born of artificial insemination by donor or by embryo transfer. Also, the problems of the parents and the physicians involved are considered. The feeling expressed in the book is that the legality of A.I.D., which is ordinarily used only to cure infertility, and of embryo transfer, and the civil status of children born by these means, need clarification. Moral and ethical issues also are of concern. The book is of general interest as well as of value to those in such fields as reproductive biology, genetics, obstetrics and gynecology, sociology, philosophy, religion, theology, and law.

295. Torrey, E. Fuller, ed. **Ethical Issues in Medicine: The Role of the Physician in Today's Society.** By 20 authors. Boston, Little, Brown and Co., 1968. 433p. bibliog. index. $7.50. LC 68-23936.

This book explores ethical issues in medicine with the hope of developing insights in the reader. Physicians at the present time are confronted with many difficult decisions that must be made on an ethical or moral basis. The chapter headings will make it clear what some of these problem areas are: (1) The third revolution: prelude and polemic, (2) Contraception, (3) Artificial insemination, (4) Abortion: a non-Catholic view, (5) Abortion: a Catholic view, (6) Sterilization, (7) Elective death, (8) Truth and the physician, (9) Professional secrecy,

(10) Ethical problems in human experimentation, (11) The medical profession and the drug industry, (12) Ethical problems with artificial and transplanted organs: an approach by experimental ethics, (13) Problems facing psychiatry: the psychiatrist as party to conflict, (14) Problems facing psychiatry: medical and educational, (15) The doctors' right to strike, (16) The physician and war, (17) Medicine and poverty, (18) Ethical issues in medicine: the future, and (19) Toward solutions. Many of the topics are obviously controversial, but in some instances opposing viewpoints are presented. This is an excellent book. In addition to physicians, others such as clergymen, social workers, educators, and allied health scientists will also be much interested in it. The questions posed are for society as a whole, really, as well as for the specialized groups mentioned.

6. MEDICAL SOCIOLOGY

296. Coe, Rodney M. **Sociology of Medicine.** New York, McGraw-Hill, 1970. 388p. bibliog. index. $9.95. LC 67-24947.
This book was designed primarily as a textbook for use in courses which require a comprehensive presentation of a sociological interpretation in the field of medicine. Such courses are increasing in number in colleges and universities. Historical and current problems are discussed and analyzed, ranging from primitive and folk medicine to the modern. Social interactions and relationships are analyzed as are the institutions designed to assure the continuation of medical care. Some of the recent developments discussed are education and training of medical and paramedical personnel, public health department activities, and the cost of medical care. Three chapters on the hospital are presented: (1) The development, (2) Social structure, and (3) The meaning of hospitalization. The author, who is a sociologist, attempts a sociological interpretation of medicine and medical institutions. However, much of the material presented should be of interest to non-sociologists in the health field.

297. Freeman, Howard E., Sol Levine, and Leo G. Reeder, eds. **Handbook of Medical Sociology.** 2d ed. Englewood Cliffs, N. J., Prentice-Hall, Inc., 1972. 598p. bibliog. index. $12.95. LC 78-152864. ISBN 0-13-380311-2.
This book is made up of a collection of original articles by well-known authorities. The first edition of this title was the first book of its kind. The beginning chapters introduce the subject by outlining the contributions of sociology to medicine and the evolution of social medicine. The rest of the book is divided into four parts: (1) The sociology of illness, (2) Practitioners, patients, and medical settings, (3) Sociology of medical care, and (4) The strategy, method, and status of medical sociology. The editors have provided a good assessment of the subject as it stands. The emphasis is on bringing medical education back into the university where the other university disciplines, particularly the social sciences, can be used as research tools in medicine and be available for the development of the individual medical student to add to his perspective.

A comprehensive bibliography is included of the literature on social research in health and medicine. The handbook is especially important for physicians, nurses, social workers, community organizers, and social scientists interested in health.

298. Freidson, Eliot. **Profession of Medicine: A Study of the Sociology of Applied Knowledge.** New York, Dodd, Mead, 1970. 409p. index. $12.50. LC 72-108049.
The intent of this book is to contribute to an understanding of professions by making a close analysis of the medical profession. The nature of professional knowledge and the justification for professional autonomy in present-day society is evaluated. The author is a sociologist, and the subject is presented from a sociological viewpoint rather than from a medical or professional one.

299. Jaco, E. Gartley, ed. **Patients, Physicians and Illness: A Sourcebook in Behavioral Science and Health.** 2d ed. New York, Free Press; London, Collier-Macmillan Ltd., 1972. 413p. bibliog. index. $12.95. LC 70-143526.

This anthology in the field of medical sociology contains some reprinted material, but about forty percent of the contents are original articles. The contributors are well-known experts in their fields. The book is arranged in three main sections: (1) Society and disease, (2) Societal coping with illness and injury, and (3) Society and health care administration. Each section has an introduction by the editor. This field is rapidly growing and changing, and considerable advancement is being made. Only two articles from the first edition of this work have been included in the second edition.

300. Susser, M. W., and W. Watson. **Sociology in Medicine.** 2d ed. London and New York, Oxford University Press, 1971. 468p. bibliog. index. $10.50. ISBN 0-19-264911-6; 19-264912-4pa.

The first edition of this work, which was published in 1962, dealt with the cultures of Great Britain and Africa. This material has been retained in the second edition, but the authors have added material about the United States. Matters such as theories and indices of social classes; the status, roles, networks, and mobility of community members; and the administration and organization of the medical profession are dealt with in some detail. There are chapters on the following topics: (1) Economy, population and health, (2) Culture and health, (3) Theories and indices of social class, (4) Social class and disorders of health, (5) Community: status, roles, networks, mobility, (6) Social mobility and disorders of health, (7) Medicine and bureaucracy, (8) The cycle of family development, (9) Mating and marriage, (10) Infant to adult, and (11) Old age: the phase of replacement.

7. HOSPITALS AND NURSING HOMES

301. American Hospital Association. **Disaster Management: A Planning Guide for Hospital Administrators.** Chicago, American Hospital Association, 1971. 14p. bibliog. $1.00.

The purpose of this pamphlet publication is to give the hospital administrator a view of the factors to be considered in coping with a possible disaster and to outline his role in the management of such. The text is brief and sketchy; it is not intended as a detailed planning guide. The hospital administrator has an obligation to develop a program of action for disaster with the help of the community, and it is hoped that this pamphlet will encourage comprehensive planning.

302. American Hospital Association. **The Extended Care Unit in a General Hospital: A Guide to Planning, Organization, and Management.** Chicago, American Hospital Association, 1973. 52p. bibliog. $2.50. LC 73-80342. ISBN 0-87258-131-4.

Most general hospitals of necessity have a considerable long-stay population. Some operate extended care units of various kinds, others have units in the building or planning state, and some are just beginning to consider the feasibility of establishing such units. This guide will help all general hospitals in developing and planning these facilities. The contents of the booklet are as follows: Chapter 1, Introduction; Chapter 2, Determining need for and type of service; Chapter 3, Planning the extended care unit; Chapter 4, Operating the extended care unit.

303. American Hospital Association. **Outpatient Health Care—the Role of Hospitals.** Report and recommendations of a conference on hospital outpatient care conducted Mar. 11-13 and a follow-up meeting of a working party on June 13-15, 1968. Chicago, American Hospital Association, 1969. 58p. bibliog. $3.75.

This report sets forth general principles, goals, and recommendations which will assist in achieving satisfactory outpatient care in hospitals. Detailed guidelines are not set up. The largest part of the report is discussion and recommendations. There is a short section on the changing use of hospital outpatient services, and a bibliography of 60 references is included. This topic is important because demand for outpatient services has grown at a rapid rate. The publication will be of most interest to hospitals, physicians, other health care professionals, planning agencies and financers of health services.

304. American Hospital Association. **Quality Assurance Program for Medical Care in the Hospital.** Chicago, American Hospital Association, 1972. 72p. (looseleaf). $12.00.

This publication was prepared primarily as a guide for hospital trustees, administrators, and the medical staff. A hospital quality assurance program is a program designed to improve and standardize the quality of care, brought about primarily through continuing education. This document presents guidelines developed by an advisory panel of experts of the American Hospital Association's Division of

Hospital Medical Staffs with consultation with representatives of other organizations concerned with quality assurance programs. There are 11 sections presented, each concerned with a specific aspect of the program. Sections 2 and 3 answer the questions where and what. The program is described in Section 4. Utilization review is taken up in Section 5 and medical audit in Section 6. The linkage of the program to external peer review mechanisms is described in Section 7, linkage of the program with claims processing in Section 8, and linkage with office practice review for physicians in Section 9. Section 10 takes up motivation for commitment to the program, and patient education is discussed in Section 11. There are several appendices which contain pamphlet publications explaining things such as requirements for Medicare and other federal programs. The publication is of looseleaf format which allows the insertion of additional materials. Inserts are to be furnished.

The publication is of value because of the increased interest in peer review and quality assurance in the health science professions.

305. American Hospital Association. **Survey of Hospital Charges as of January 1, 1973.** Chicago, American Hospital Association, 1973. 262p. $6.00. LC 72-620995. ISBN 0-87258-130-6.

The data presented in the survey was collected through use of a questionnaire sent to all U.S. community hospitals registered by the American Hospital Association. Two sets of tables are presented, Section A for nongovernmental not-for-profit and for-profit hospitals, and Section B for nonfederal governmental hospitals. The data gathered was tabulated to determine the average charges and the range of charges according to geographic area, hospital size, and controlling organization of hospital. Average charges were also tabulated for intensive and cardiac care beds, extended care beds, and selected ancillary services. The American Hospital Association has collected similar data for more than 25 years, although surveys prior to 1966 presented somewhat different coverage. This information is all useful to hospital administrators, third-party payers, and various governmental agencies in studying the changes in the cost of hospital care.

306. Annual Symposium on Hospital Affairs, 14th, held May 1972. Proceedings. **Public Control and Hospital Operations.** Conducted by the Graduate Program in Hospital Administration and Center for Health Administration Studies, Graduate School of Business, University of Chicago, 1972. 81p. $6.50.

This publication presents the papers and discussion of the Symposium. The material is pertinent to the ongoing discussion and evolution of controls in the health care field. The following topics were discussed: reimbursement, prospective budgeting, who shall judge the adequacy and the cost of health care, health care facility franchising, and implications for hospitals of currently proposed health insurance legislation.

307. Association of Hospital and Institution Libraries. Hospital Library Standards Committee. **Standards for Library Services in Health Care Institutions.** Chicago, American Library Association, 1970. 25p. bibliog. $1.75. LC 74-124576. ISBN 0-8389-3115-4.

It is expected that this document will be revised frequently because of rapidly changing patterns of health care with their impact on library service and those who are served. The present statement recommends one set of standards which cover two types of libraries in health care institutions, the health science library and the patients' library. Several sections are included in the booklet as follows: (1) Introduction, (2) Management of library services, (3) The health science library, (4) The patients' library. Also included is an appendix with standard specifications, a glossary, and selected references.

308. Berki, Sylvester E. **Hospital Economics.** Lexington, Mass., D. C. Heath and Co., Lexington Books, 1972. 270p. bibliog. index. $13.50. LC 72-165462. ISBN 0-669-75366-1.

The purpose of this book is to show how the hospital, which is the central part of our medical care system, can be understood. The author feels that an understanding of the hospital's objectives, function, contributions, and its economic bases of operations is a prerequisite to the formulation of policies that will assure all people the best medical services. Chapter headings are as follows: The framework of analysis, hospital objectives, the hospital's outputs, productivity and efficiency, the cost of hospital operations, demand and utilization, pricing and reimbursement strategies for hospitals, the municipal hospital, and conclusions. The book is of most value to hospital administrators, medical care specialists, economists, planners, and policy analysts.

309. Bond, Richard G., George S. Michaelsen, and Roger L. De Roos, eds. **Environmental Health and Safety in Health Care Facilities.** New York, Macmillan; London, Collier Macmillan, 1973. 368p. illus. bibliog. index. $16.50. LC 72-91267. ISBN 0-02-311970-5.

This book is important because little attention has been given to environmental health and safety requirements of hospitals, nursing homes, and other health care facilities. The aim of the publication is to educate hospital and nursing home administrators, environmental practitioners, medical staff, nurses, dieticians, engineers, laboratory personnel, and others concerning the basic principles of environmental health and safety that can be applied to the health care facility. Unit I of the book deals with historic and administrative matters. Unit II takes up environmental microbiology, sterilization, and cleaning techniques. Unit III covers ventilation, toxic agents, noise, and radiation protection. Unit IV discusses safety, including that of patient and personnel, and laboratory and fire safety. Unit V deals with sanitation and includes such aspects as food hygiene, solid and liquid wastes, and water supply. Unit VI covers miscellaneous matters such as insect and rodent control, laundries, and emergency and disaster planning.

310. Braverman, Jordan. **Nursing Home Standards: A Tragic Dilemma in American Health.** Washington, American Pharmaceutical Association, 1970. 75p. $2.50pa. LC 75-123216.

This publication analyses, by state, nursing home standards under federal Medicare and state licensure programs. Administrative, patient care, environmental health, fire safety, and construction standards are examined. It is hoped that the publication will bring attention to current regulative deficiencies which will result in improved standards, and ultimately, in nursing home care of the highest quality.

A large amount of tabular data has been included in appendices which made comparisons by state and region possible. Also included is a list of references to nursing home licensure documents.

While the title of this report suggests that standards for nursing homes are very low, this does not necessarily appear to be the case.

311. Feldstein, Martin S. **The Rising Cost of Hospital Care.** Washington, Information Resources Press, 1971. 88p. bibliog. $4.25. LC 72-171922. ISBN 0-87815-004-8.

Because the cost of hospital care has risen so sharply (in 1970, five times as much as in 1950), the author, who is an economist, attempts to explain the reasons. He says there are two main ones: (1) A day of hospital care is a different product than it used to be; more expensive technology has been introduced. (2) Hospital wages have risen more rapidly than the general level of wages. Also, there has been an increased demand by patients for hospital services, and our current methods of hospital insurance have encouraged increases. However, the author feels that there has been a tendency for hospitals to produce more expensive care than the public really wants.

The essay is addressed to anyone interested in the problem of high hospital costs.

312. Georgopoulos, Basil S., ed. **Organizational Research on Health Institutions.** Ann Arbor, Institute for Social Research, the University of Michigan, 1972. 418p. bibliog. $12.00. LC 72-619554. ISBN 0-87944-125-9.

This book is a collection of articles concerned with health organizations, particularly the general hospital. The contributors, a group of researchers, were invited to "examine the state of organizational research in the hospital field, to review the product of such research during the decade of the 1960's, and to present their current thinking on research needs for the 1970's." This has resulted in a particularly good review of the literature which will be useful for teachers and potential researchers. Also, a rather good summary of the research is presented. The bibliographies are extensive.

The book is divided into six parts, as follows: (1) The hospital as an organization and problem-solving system, (2) Social control of general hospitals and structural comparative studies of hospitals, (3) Professionals in hospitals: technology and the organization of work, (4) Hospital organization from the viewpoint of patient-centered goals and ecological aspects of patient care and organization, (5) The role of the doctor in institutional management, and (6) The hospital administrator.

313. Greenfield, Harry I. **Hospital Efficiency and Public Policy**. New York, Praeger Publishers, 1973. Published in cooperation with the Center for Policy Research, Inc. 80p. bibliog. index. (Praeger Special Studies in U.S. Economic, Social, and Political Issues). $11.00. LC 72-14205.

The focus of this study is on hospital efficiency, or the efficient utilization of resources in the hospital. An attempt is made to analyze major promoting and inhibiting factors affecting efficiency, to evaluate major empirical studies of hsopital efficiency, to present current data from a sample of hospitals that illustrate some elements of efficiency, and to point out ways to promote efficiency. The work touches on both economic analysis and organization theory or management, with the emphasis on the former. The study moves from the basic unit of health care to the study of health care systems, from microeconomics to macroeconomics. Chapter headings are as follows: (1) Hospitals as firms, (2) Costs and efficiency, (3) The elusive output and other measurement problems, (4) Moving the hospital, (5) Moving the hospital system, and (6) Summary and conclusions. The book will be of interest to both economists and hospital administrators.

314. Griffith, John R. **Quantitative Techniques for Hospital Planning and Control**. Lexington, Mass., Lexington Books, D. C. Heath and Co., 1972. 403p. bibliog. index. $16.00. LC 72-3550. ISBN 0-669-84087-4.

This book provides conceptual understanding of a variety of techniques useful in hospital decisions. Particularly emphasized are planning, forecasting, scheduling, cost control, quality control. Also a detailed discussion of the practicalities of applying the techniques is presented. Measurement, data collection, utility of solutions, dangers implicit in common assumptions, and examples of promising applications are discussed in depth. Technology has been simplified and advanced mathematics, including calculus, has been avoided. Some elementary statistics and probability concepts are required, however. The book is intended for managers of hospitals and other health care institutions, and for operations research specialists interested in hospital applications. Students in these fields will also find it of value. The book is divided into three parts: (1) Forecasting demand, (2) Models for resource allocation, and (3) Control systems. The chapter titles are as follows: (1) Introduction, (2) The forecasting problems and simple time series analysis, (3) Forecasting by multivariate analysis and techniques for forecasting variation, (4) Determining population service areas and calculating use rates, (5) Demand forecasts in specialized situations, (6) Total value analysis, (7) Queueing and simulation models for resource allocation, (8) PERT and mathematical programming models, (9) Evaluating capital investment opportunities, (10) Nature and application of control systems in hospitals, (11) Examples of hospital control systems, (12) Measuring the quality of the medical care process, (13) Advanced information systems for hospital planning and control.

315. Health Law Center. **Problems in Hospital Law**. Pittsburgh, Aspen Corporation, 1968. 203p. $10.00. LC 68-26662.

This is a timely book because the operations of health care institutions are subject to increasing scrutiny by the public, government, and business. Legal aspects of hospital operations are of particular concern. The book is written primarily for hospital administrative staff, but is also of value to other staff and may be used as a text in courses on hospital law. There are 16 chapters as follows: (1) Administrator, (2) Admitting and discharge, (3) Consent to medical and surgical procedures, (4) Medical-moral problems, (5) Dead bodies, (6) Governing board, (7) Hospital auxiliaries and volunteer activities, (8) Labor, (9) Principles of hospital liability, (10) Liability of nurses, (11) Immunity of hospitals, (12) Medical staff, (13) Medical records, (14) Pharmacy, (15) Federal taxation, (16) State and local property taxation.

316. Joint Commission on Accreditation of Hospitals. **Accreditation Manual for Hospitals, 1970. Updated 1973. Hospital Accreditation Program.** Chicago, Joint Commission on Accreditation of Hospitals, 1973. 186p. $3.50pa.
The Joint Commission on Accreditation of Hospitals was incorporated in 1952 to establish standards for the operation of hospitals and other health care facilities and to conduct survey and accreditation programs. This publication contains information and standards that hospitals require to meet standards for accreditation by the Joint Commission. There is a section on each service of the hospital in addition to sections on general administrative policies and procedures, governing body and management, and medical staff. Also included is a glossary of terms, an appendix on accreditation procedures and appeal, and an appendix on medical care evaluation and utilization review.

317. Joint Commission on Accreditation of Hospitals. **Accredited Hospitals.** Chicago, Joint Commission on Accreditation of Hospitals, 1972. 52p.
The hospitals listed are those accredited by the Commission. They are arranged by state and secondarily by city. Supplements are issued from time to time to indicate additions or other changes.

318. Joint Commission on Accreditation of Hospitals. **Accredited Long-Term Care Facilities.** Chicago, Joint Commission on Accreditation of Hospitals, 1972. 32p.
Quarterly supplements to this list are issued to keep it up-to-date by showing additions, deletions, and changes. There are three separate listings presented by state with addresses: (1) Extended care facilities, (2) Nursing care facilities, and (3) Resident care facilities. Those facilities operated by an accredited hospital are marked with an asterisk.

319. Kademani, Guru B. **Hospital Management Bibliography.** Athens, Ga., Center for Management Systems Development and Analysis, University of Georgia, 1971. 27p. (TIPS Report No. 71-1). $1.00.
The articles for this annotated bibliography were chosen from sources published from January 1967 to August 1970. It is not an exhaustive listing, but the articles were considered highly relevant to ongoing projects. The publications are classified under the following subject areas: hospital data processing; financial management; hospital administration; labor relations; management concepts, tools and methods; personnel management; purchase management; medical records; systems designing and development.

320. Kurtz, Harold P. **Public Relations for Hospitals: A Practical Handbook.**
Springfield, Ill., Charles C. Thomas, 1969. 150p. bibliog. index. $8.00.
LC 69-12063.

This is a handbook of practical hints for the conduct of a public relations program in a hospital, particularly a small voluntary one. It is a timely book because
voluntary hospitals have been under a good deal of public scrutiny by a number
of groups. These include individuals who are irritated about rising costs, politicians who seek public favor, and individuals who would substitute the voluntary
pattern with a governmental system. Subjects covered include: the scope of hospital public relations, what the job is, getting along in the hospital family, telling
the hospital story, working with the news media, relating to fund raising, working
with volunteers, working with the printer, working with the photographer, serving the community, evaluating public relations, and where to get help.

321. Mathieu, Robert P. **Hospital and Nursing Home Management: An Instructional and Administrative Manual.** Philadelphia, W. B. Saunders, 1971.
280p. illus. index. $9.75. LC 76-158401. SBN 0-7216-6188-2.

This manual is designed to guide the health care facility administrator in the discharge of his duties. All aspects of the subject are covered, although some rather
generally because of differing regulations from state to state, and differences in
facilities and patient needs. However, the book should be of a good deal of help
in day-to-day administration of the facility. Several sections deal with policies,
procedures, and practices necessary to operation of such facilities. Chapter headings are as follows: general requirements for the extended care facility; personnel
policies; patient care policies; policies on physicians' services; nursing service policies; dietary services; restorative services; pharmaceuticals—dispensing procedures;
diagnostic, dental and podiatric services; social services; patient activities; clinical
records; transfer agreements; physical environment; housekeeping services; disaster plan; accident prevention; fire safety; barber and beautician services; utilization review plan; business services; and accreditation. It is evident that the field
is covered rather extensively.

322. Rakish, Jonathan S., ed. **Hospital Organization and Management: A Book
of Readings.** St. Louis, Catholic Hospital Association, 1972. 300p. bibliog.
index. LC 79-190548. ISBN 0-87125-001-2.

This publication is a collection of readings and abstracted material, taken from
hospital periodicals, which treats hospital organization from a managerial point
of view. Controversial points of view are included as well as current and classical
articles. The subject material has been divided into five parts: (1) The hospital as
an organization, (2) The management of personnel in hospitals, (3) Labor relations
in hospitals, (4) Quantitative decision making, and (5) Health care policy and
trends. There are several articles in each part. The work is oriented toward the
voluntary hospital system, and emphasis is given to administration, organization,
personnel management, labor relations, decision making, planning, and social
responsibility.

323. **A Reference Handbook and Dictionary of Nursing: Olson's Nurses' Handbook.** 10th ed. and **Dorland's Pocket Medical Dictionary.** 21st ed. Philadelphia, W. B. Saunders, 1968. 1v.(various paging). illus. index. $8.50. LC 70-104663.

This volume includes the content of the 21st edition of Dorland's "Pocket Medical Dictionary" (1968) and that of the 10th edition of Olson's "A Nurses' Handbook for Hospital, School and Home" (1960). The dictionary section provides spelling, pronunciation, and the meaning of words in the field of health and medical sciences, and other miscellaneous information in tabular form such as tables of veins, muscles, and nerves.

The handbook section is organized in several parts, giving the work encyclopedic range. There is a section on the nursing profession, the nursing arts, descriptions of diseases, first aid, diet, pediatrics, obstetrics, the operating room, pharmacology, psychiatry, and many other topics.

The material presented is of general interest to students and practitioners of the allied medical sciences, teachers, and students of home nursing, and to the homemaker.

324. Roemer, Milton I., and Jay W. Friedman. **Doctors in Hospitals, Medical Staff Organization and Hospital Performance.** Baltimore and London, Johns Hopkins Press, 1971. 322p. index. $12.50. LC 79-109096. ISBN 0-8018-1239-9.

This book is devoted to the study of the relationship of the pattern of medical staff organization in general hospitals to the performance of those hospitals. The hypothesis of the study is that, in general, higher levels of hospital efficiency, effectiveness, or performance, are achieved in conjunction with more firmly disciplined medical staff organization. Performance and medical staff organization and all their components are analyzed. Chapter headings are as follows:
(1) Doctor-hospital relations and the current American hospital scene, (2) Historic development of medical staff organization in hospitals, (3) The world scene in doctor-hospital relations, (4) Contractual physicians and their influence, (5) Medical staff organization: a typology for analysis, (6) A voluntary hospital with moderately structured medical staff organization, (7) Nine hospitals on the scale of medical staff organization, (8) Medical staff patterns—interhospital comparisons, (9) Inpatient hospital care in relation to medical staff organization, (10) The wider community role of hospitals in relation to medical staff organization, (11) Medical staff organization and hospital performance: conclusions and implications. An appendix on methodology is also included.

The authors conclude that the more highly structured medical staff patterns go along with a higher level of performance. They suggest that the future trend will be toward greater structuring in all hospitals, coupled with increased control of hospital costs, improved care, and more regional planning of health services.

325. Rosengren, William R., and Mark Lefton. **Hospitals and Patients.** New York, Atherton Press, 1969. 225p. bibliog. index. $8.95. LC 75-90768.

This publication is concerned with four tasks. The first is to draw together a summary of the sociological literature dealing with the structure and operation of hospitals. The second is to draw attention to the newer ways of delivering medical services. The third is to organize these materials in terms of prevailing models for organizational analysis which are used by sociologists in studying hospitals, and the fourth is to set forth an analytic model of organizations in the hope of yielding a better understanding of the forms of medical organization. The literature referred to in the book deals only with the patient as a person and the hospital as an organizational system. The literature of medical sociology in its entirety is not reviewed. The chapter titles are as follows: (1) Hospitals and patients: an overview of issues, (2) New forms and trends in medical care, (3) Hospitals as bureaucracies, (4) The hospital and its patients, (5) The hospital and its environment, (6) Hospitals and the biographical career of the patient, (7) The patient in the context of the hospital, (8) Orientation toward clients and interorganizational relationships. There is an Epilogue which deals with the future of medical care organization, especially as it may be affected by the intervention of public sectors, particularly the federal government, into the private sphere of medicine.

326. Spencer, James H. **The Hospital Emergency Department.** Springfield, Ill., Charles C. Thomas, 1972. 360p. illus. index. $18.75. LC 71-190337. ISBN 0-398-02482-0.

The emergency department of hospitals has grown enormously in the past few decades and has frequently been a problem area in hospitals. This book was prepared for the purpose of improving the quality of care of patients with medical emergencies. Emphasis is given to the fact that allowing the department to become a general medical clinic will result in lowering the quality of emergency care. A good deal of emphasis is also given to the physical layout of the emergency area. Descriptions, illustrations of good planning, and the like are supplied. Also, construction and supplies and equipment are discussed. Staffing is considered, as is the importance of adequate record keeping, economic problems, and public relations. The psychiatric patient is considered. The book should be valuable for hospital trustees and administrators, physicians, nurses, architects, and engineers.

327. U.S. Comptroller General. **Report to the Congress: Study of Health Facilities Construction Costs.** Washington, GPO, 1973. 888p.

This document is a report on a study of health facilities construction costs undertaken pursuant to section 204 of the Comprehensive Health Manpower Training Act of 1971. (85 Stat. 462). The study is broad based, and it considers the costs of operating hospitals in addition to initial construction costs. Also, the study group identified and evaluated ways in which the demand for facilities could be reduced or eliminated. Also, comments from various federal agencies and private organizations have been incorporated into the text in appropriate places. The study is very detailed, but a digest of the findings and conclusions is included.

328. U.S. Department of Health, Education, and Welfare. Health Services and Mental Health Administration. National Center for Health Services, Research, and Development. **Quantitative Methods for Evaluating Hospital Design.** By Gerald L. Delon and Harold E. Smalley. Washington, GPO, 1970. 239p. bibliog. (Report NCHS-RD-70-1)

This report is a final one on a project supported by a grant (HM 00529) from the National Center for Health Services and Development. The specific aim of the project was to provide a quantitative basis for decisions evaluating the relative location of certain functions, and hence certain facilities, within the individual hospital. The topics presented are as follows: a methodology for nursing unit design, applications of the nursing unit methodology, a methodology for total hospital design, and application of the methodology for total hospital design.

329. U.S. Department of Labor. Manpower Administration. Training and Employment Service. **Job Descriptions and Organizational Analysis for Hospitals and Related Health Services.** Prepared in cooperation with the American Hospital Association. Rev. ed. 1970. Washington, GPO, 1971. 732p. index. $4.25.

This publication was prepared for use by public employment offices as a source of occupational information for hospital personnel administrators. Descriptions are given for every kind of position that exists in hospitals. Each occupation is described in a generalized composite form. Under each job title, a department narrative is presented, then an organization chart showing how the position is placed in the hierarchy is given, and lastly, the description appears. Hospitals, schools, colleges and universities, employment officers, librarians, and related groups will find the work of value. It is hoped that the compilation will help bring about uniformity and some standardization in hospital positions.

330. U.S. Social Security Administration. Office of Research and Statistics. **Hospital Utilization Review and Medicare: A Survey.** By Rona Beth Schumer. Washington, GPO, 1973. 119p. bibliog. index. (Its Staff Paper No. 8). $2.00. LC 72-600354. Stock No. 1770-00105.

Utilization review is a national requirement for hospitals participating in the Medicare program. This publication presents a general orientation to the subject. It presents survey material relating to utilization review projects, contracts, and other activities. It describes the nature of these activities, their scope, methodology, and limitations.

8. FAMILY PLANNING AND POPULATION CONTROL

331. Barber, Hugh R. K., Edward A. Graber, and James J. O'Rourke. **Are the Pills Safe?** Springfield, Ill., Charles C. Thomas, 1969. 103p. bibliog. $6.75. LC 73-83830.

This book was written primarily for physicians, but is reasonably simple, straightforward and easy to understand. The purposes of the work are to present a review of the current literature on oral contraceptives, show their effects, evaluate reports of untoward effects, review the reports of various evaluation committees, and recommend a responsible course of action for the physician to follow. The changes that occur in the various organ systems of the body when the pill is used are summarized system by system. The book is subdivided as follows: (1) Effect on the organs of female reproduction, (2) Endocrine and metabolic effects, (3) Carcinogenic potential, (4) Thromboembolic diseases, (5) Effect on miscellaneous systems, (6) Side effects and adverse reactions. An outstanding feature of the book is that about half of it is a bibliography which covers the literature through March 1968.

332. Calderone, Mary Steichen, ed. **Manual of Family Planning and Contraceptive Practice.** 2d ed. Balitmore, Williams and Wilkins, 1970. 475p. illus. index. $9.95. LC 76-113624. SBN 683-01310-6.

This excellent manual was prepared by a large group of experts. The scope of the work is greater than that of the first edition which was called *A Manual of Contraceptive Practice.* Medical, social, legal, and psychological factors are considered. The book is divided into three broad topics: family planning, contraception, and areas of research in the physiological control of fertility. Chapter headings are as follows: (1) Indications: establishing priorities for intensive contraceptive care, (2) Practice, (3) The roles of government agencies, (4) The roles of voluntary organizations, (5) Legal status of contraception in the United States, (6) Teaching, (7) Sociocultural attitudes affecting practice, (8) Factors in failure, (9) Evaluation, (10) The methods. Two useful appendices are also included, one a list of contraceptive products and manufacturers.

333. Drill, Victor A. **Oral Contraceptives.** New York, McGraw-Hill Book Co., Blakiston Division, 1966, 211p. bibliog. index. $10.00. LC 66-21864.

This book, written by a well-known pharmacologist and researcher, provides a compendium of chemical, biological, and clinical material pertaining to oral contraceptives. It is one of the classic works on the subject. The presentation is rather technical, but can be understood reasonably well by laymen. Chapter headings are as follows: (1) Chemistry, available preparations, (2) Biologic properties, (3) Mechanism of action, (4) Directions for use, (5) Clincal effectiveness, (6) Effects on uterus, vagina, and ovary, (7) Menstrual cycle phenomena, (8) Associated endocrine effects, (9) Discontinuance of contraceptives, (10) Metabolic effects and metabolism, (11) Side effects and safety.

The author, at the time the book was written, at least, found no reliable evidence of anything more than uncommon and mild side effects from use of the products. A plea is made for an understanding of the magnitude of the overpopulation problem.

334. Elliott, Katherine, ed. **The Family and Its Future.** A Ciba Foundation Symposium. London, J. and A. Churchill, 1970. 230p. £3.00. ISBN 0-7000-1462-4.

This book is a collection of papers presented at a Symposium on The Family and Its Future held March 10-12, 1970. Most of the participants were concerned with the family and the Western world although a little material was presented on Asia, Africa, Peru, and the West Indies. Representatives from a large number of disciplines took part from several countries. Women were rather well represented, and the future of women was of primary concern because of the recent changes that have been brought about by the social acceptance of birth control. Titles of the papers are as follows: (1) Comparative family patterns, (2) The Analysis of family roles, (3) Parental responsibility for adolescent maturity, (4) Future family patterns and society, (5) Marriage and the family in the near future, (6) Environmental planning and its influence on the family, (7) The family and the law in 1970, (8) Biological regulation of reproduction, (9) The development of contraception: psychodynamic considerations, (10) Changes in concepts of parenthood, (11) Changing trends in child development, (12) The making of the modern family.

335. Haller, Jurgen. **Hormonal Contraception.** Translated from the 2nd German edition by Herbert Gottfried. Los Altos, California, Geron-X, 1969. 288p. bibliog. index. $12.00. LC 73-98141. SBN 87672-001-7.

This book was written because it was felt necessary to review and evaluate the field of hormonal contraceptives and issue a warning about their use where necessary. The book is fairly technical, and will be of considerable interest to physicians and researchers, but much of it is understandable and of interest to laymen, particularly since the lay press and popular magazines have published many reports on the subject.

The author presents a detailed discussion of the causes and diagnosis of ovulation occurring in rhythmic fashion in women. Also, the different possibilities for the suppression or the inhibition of follicular rupture by hormone applications are discussed. A considerable portion of the work is dedicated to the different types of hormone combinations available. Then there is a presentation and survey of uses of the hormones for such purposes as (1) stimulating fertility, (2) the treatment of various abnormal conditions, (3) the prevention of conception. Also, the question of the possibility of producing cancer is discussed. The last chapter is a question and answer presentation to assist the physician in becoming knowledgeable on all aspects of this therapy. An extensive bibliography is included with many highly technical and German language articles cited. The book is particularly valuable and useful in assisting with a better understanding of the mechanisms of action of hormonal contraceptives.

336. Johnson, George. **The Pill Conspiracy.** Los Angeles, Sherbourne Press, Inc., 1967. 244p. bibliog. index. $4.95. LC 66-22234.

The author of this book, who is a journalist, discusses drug companies, governmental agencies, and the medical profession in relation to medicines and their use by the public. He gives details on such specific matters as honesty in packaging, honesty in advertising claims, fairness of price, malpractice, etc. While the writer makes it clear that today's powerful complicated drugs are more likely to cure disease than those used in the past, they are also more likely to produce massive, troublesome, and sometimes dangerous side effects. The public is often unaware of this. The conclusions of the book are that although some blame can be placed on pharmaceutical companies, the federal government (because of inadequate laws), and the medical profession, the culprit is really the individual who continues to take drugs that he really does not need.

337. Kistner, Robert W. **The Pill: Facts and Fallacies about Today's Oral Contraceptives.** New York, Delacorte Press, 1969. 329p. bibliog. index. $5.95. LC 72-85473.

The book provides full, accurate information about oral contraceptives. The author felt that too little factual information and too much incorrectly interpreted information has appeared in the news media and that such a reference source was needed. Approximately 13 million women use this medication as an aid to family planning and another million use it for various physical disorders. The book should help these users decide about their continuing the "Pill" since so many questions regarding it have come up. The author, who is a distinguished gynecologist, gives the information on the Pill in nontechnical language, tells how it works, possible side effects and complications, and its many uses other than for contraception. He believes the Pill may be the most effective instrument for future survival on earth because overpopulation is overtaking us. The book is divided into sections as follows: (1) Contraception, (2) Effects of the Pill, (3) The Pill and women's disorders, (4) Psychological, social, and moral effects of the Pill, (5) Questions women ask most about the Pill.

338. Potts, Malcolm, and Clive Wood, eds. **New Concepts in Contraception.** Baltimore, University Park Press, 1972. 231p. bibliog. index. $14.50. LC 72-4327. ISBN 0-8391-0740-4.

This book contains 12 chapters by contributors from a number of different countries, including the United States and some emerging nations. Several of the chapters are concerned with the medical and technical innovations associated with contraception. There is no look into the future as to what new developments might come to fruition; all the methods discussed are in use now or could be used. In addition, several chapters deal with the attitudes of populations towards contraception, the organization of institutions currently disseminating advice and supplies, and commercial distribution of contraceptives. The editors present a multi-disciplinary overview of the problem. The book should have rather wide appeal. Besides physicians and other medical personnel, it should interest sociologists, social psychologists, population experts, family planners, and marketing specialists.

339. Potts, Malcolm, and John Peel. **Textbook of Contraceptive Practice.**
    Cambridge, Cambridge University Press, 1969, 297p. bibliog. index.
    $8.50. LC 69-19380. SBN 521-07515-7.
This book first presents the history of contraception, then the patterns of family
planning that exist about the world. The need for the control of population is
emphasized, and the fact that no perfect contraceptive has been found is pointed
out. The largest part of the text is made up of descriptions of the contraceptive
methods available accompanied by discussion of their effectiveness and a detailed
explanation of the physiological mechanisms involved. Possible side effects are
mentioned. Sociological, legal, and medical aspects of the subject are considered.
There are several appendices, one a list of contraceptive products available in
England and the U.S., and another a list of organizations specializing in the field
of conception control. The work will be of interest to physicians, nurses, students, social workers, social science students, and laymen. It is an excellent book,
well written, easy to read, scientifically accurate, and presents a realistic view of
a serious problem.

340. Seaman, Barbara. **The Doctors' Case Against the Pill.** New York, Peter H.
    Wyden, Inc., 1969. index. $5.95. LC 75-96788.
The author of this book presents a case against the use of the oral contraceptives
because she feels that they are not safe. Case histories from Pill users were
obtained from interviews. There is little real scientific evidence of any kind presented in the book; there are mostly just opinions of the users. However, in spite
of the lack of references to scientific studies, it does appear that many side
effects do occur and that the Pill is not a perfect contraceptive device by any
means.

341. Sheps, Mindel C., and Jeanne Clare Ridley, eds. **Public Health and Popula-
    tion Change: Current Research Issues.** Pittsburgh, University of Pittsburgh
    Press, 1965. 557p. index. $10.00.
The papers published in this volume were presented at a Symposium on Research
Issues in Public Health and Population Change sponsored by the Graduate
School of Public Health at the University of Pittsburgh in June 1964. The purposes of the Conference were: (1) To review the present state of knowledge and
research with respect to population change, with special reference to natality,
(2) To identify future research needs in the areas of natality and population
growth, (3) To promote understanding and communication among workers in the
fields of public health, medicine, biology, demography, and the social sciences
regarding their mutual interests in the determinants and consequences of population growth, and (4) To further the development of teaching and research programs in problems of health and population change. The publication resulting
from this conference should be of interest to individuals from disciplines concerned with population change. The papers are authored by demographers, social
and behavioral scientists, biologists, physicians, statisticians, and public health
workers.

The book is divided into seven parts as follows: (1) Demographic history and
population policy, (2) Natality patterns and programs for effecting change,
(3) Measurement and evaluation, (4) Biological aspects of natality and its control,

(5) Methods of controlling reproduction, (6) Report on the symposium, and (7) Public health and population. Also included is a glossary of terms.

342. Tyler, Edward T., ed. **Progress in Conception Control, 1969.** Fifth Physician's Conference. A Report of a scientific discussion held in Miami at the time of the Seventeenth Annual Meeting of the American College of Obstetricians and Gynecologists, April 1969. Philadelphia and Toronto, J. B. Lippincott Co., 1969. 133p. illus. bibliog. index. $5.00. LC 77-84654.

This book presents papers given by physicians participating in the Conference. They include presentations on the more complicated biochemical and physiological aspects of the subject, clinical features of the new contraceptive methods, and speculation about the future. Also included are discussions.

343. U.S. Food and Drug Administration. Advisory Committee on Obstetrics and Gynecology. **Second Report on the Oral Contraceptives.** Washington, GPO, 1969. 88p. bibliog. $1.00.

This report was prepared with consultation with numerous scientists in order to make the medical profession and public accurately informed. The first report, published in 1966, reported reservations about the safety of oral contraceptives. Adverse reactions are still reported in the scientific literature and lay press. This publication makes accurate information available and presents it dispassionately. The task is said to be to balance the risk against the benefit to society and the individual.

The publication presents a number of task force reports and includes recommendations such as making available support for further studies, support to develop new methods of contraception, and continued surveillance by the FDA. The committee's conclusion is that the ratio of benefit to risk is sufficiently high to justify the designation of "safe" for oral contraceptives.

344. U.S. National Institutes of Health. **The Family in Transition.** A round table conference sponsored by the John E. Fogarty International Center for Advanced Study in the Health Sciences, National Institutes of Health, November 3-6, 1969. Washington, GPO, 1971. 342p. bibliog. (Fogarty International Center Proceedings No. 3). $3.00.

This book is based on the papers presented at the Conference on "The Family in Transition" and on the discussions they stimulated. The aim of this conference was mainly to encourage the development of a stronger research base from which to initiate policies and launch programs that will hasten the trend toward smaller families in the world. Many gaps in knowledge are noted throughout the work, and stress is placed on the research needed to fill these gaps. The papers presented at the conference are arranged under the following chapter heads: (1) The family and population change, (2) Changing family structures, (3) Family and fertility, (4) Changing positions of women, (5) Migration, urbanization, and fertility, (6) Needed research. Each chapter examines the relationship between family and population from a different perspective. Also included is an introduction summarizing the major points made by each of the conference participants. Much material is presented about foreign countries as well as the United States.

345. Vaughan, Paul. **The Pill on Trial.** New York, Coward-McCann, 1970. 244p.
     index. $5.95. LC 73-127950.
The author, who is a British medical journalist, attempts to evaluate the question
of oral contraceptives, particularly their safety. The book is based on interviews
with researchers, doctors, sociologists, and family planning counselors. The arguments for and against the use of the drugs are given. The report is a reliable,
unbiased account, but does not add much to what is commonly known and
written about in countless articles in the popular periodicals. The conclusions
are that there may be some danger in the continued use of the oral contraceptives, but they are widely used anyway in spite of full knowledge of the possible
hazards.

9. PHARMACY AND PHARMACEUTICALS

346. American Chemical Society. **Drug Discovery: Science and Development in a Changing Society.** Two symposia sponsored by the Division of Medicinal Chemistry at the 160th Meeting of the American Chemical Society, Chicago, Ill. Sept. 15-16, 1970. Washington, American Chemical Society, 1971. 294p. illus. bibliog. index. (Advances in Chemistry Series 108). $10.00. LC 70-184206. ISBN 8412-0136-6.

This publication is a collection of papers from two symposia "The Science of Drug Discovery" and "Drug Discovery and Development in a Changing Society." These papers attempt to assess how the fundamental changes taking place in society will affect the coalition of industry, universities, and government involved in the drug discovery process. In the first part of the book, changes in the science of drug discovery itself are discussed, for instance, the use of computers and analytical instruments and the probing of biological processes at the molecular level. In the second part of the book, the articles deal with the changes in society. For instance, concern is expressed over the development of a national policy of health care, government regulation of the drug industry, and the possibility that the research and development process is reaching the point where it will no longer pay for itself. The current problems in the discovery and development of drugs are well presented.

347. American Pharmaceutical Association. **A Ph A Directory of Pharmacists.** Washington. American Pharmaceutical Association, 1964. 1741p. index. $16.00pa.

This publication is the first listing of the pharmacist population in the United States. Future revisions are planned. The book is divided into sections; the first is a geographical listing (including only name and address) alphabetically by state. Within each state, cities are listed alphabetically with the pharmacists' names also alphabetically arranged. Section 2 is an alphabetical listing with the city of practice or residence given and the state of registration appearing with the name. The directory is too old to be of great value, but is the only such listing available.

348. American Pharmaceutical Association. **Pharmacy and the Poor: A Report on the First Two Years of a Project by the American Pharmaceutical Association to Assist the Office of Economic Opportunity with the Pharmacy Services for Their Neighborhood Health Centers.** Washington, American Pharmaceutical Association, 1971. 541p. illus. bibliog. LC 73-171223.

This report covers the first two years' activities on the project and the findings. It will be of most interest to those involved with the problems of delivering ambulatory health care. The first activity of the project was a literature search, and the bibliography is included. It is rather short; not much literature existed.

The report contains the following parts: (1) Opinion summary, (2) Descriptive survey, (3) Conclusions—opinion and descriptive surveys, (4) Models, (5) Other major activities, and (6) Conclusions, summary and recommendations. The conclusions of the study are many; perhaps the most surprising is that there were few differences between the services available to the poor versus the nonpoor living in the same neighborhood. Also, this was true of the opinions of the patients. In addition, the opinion survey revealed several things about how the pharmacist as a professional is viewed by the public which will be of interest to individuals in that field.

349. Arnow, L. Earle. **Health in a Bottle: Searching for Drugs that Help.** Philadelphia and Toronto, J. B. Lippincott, 1970. 272p. illus. index. $5.95. LC 76-85423.

This book tells of the search for new drugs in the laboratories of the U.S. pharmaceutical industries. The author, who is Senior Scientific Consultant at the Warner-Lambert Research Institute, points out that the odds for success in the discovery of new drugs are unbelievably small. In spite of this, spectacular advances have been made in the last third of a century. He tells how drugs are discovered and tested, in animals and in human beings, gives short sketches on synthetic drugs, and tells how the Food and Drug Administration, patents, and trademarks work. The book is fascinating and worth reading. The primary message the author has for the reader is that we do not yet have curative drugs for major killers, coronary disease and cancer. He thinks it will be a long time before we do have and stresses the need for basic research and the development of new, clinical meaningful procedures.

350. Bobst, Elmer Holmes. **Bobst: The Autobiography of a Pharmaceutical Pioneer.** New York, David McKay Co., 1973. 360p. illus. $7.95. LC 72-93992.

This book is an autobiography of a self-made pharmaceutical industrialist who made a large fortune. He was associated with Hoffman-La Roche Laboratories and other pharmaceutical houses who held to high standards. Bobst was a leader in public service and philanthropy. He was associated with the American Cancer Society and endowed the Elmer Holmes Bobst Library and Study Center of New York University.

The story is interesting because of the way the author's independent personality comes through and because of his association with well-known figures such as U.S. presidents and ambassadors, and leaders in education, medicine and industry. Also, some insight is shown into the operation of the pharmaceutical industry.

351. Breckton, William. **The Drug Makers.** London, Eyre Methuen, 1972. 222p. index. $8.50. ISBN 413-27260-5.

This book is mainly concerned with the British pharmaceutical industry, but much of what is said applies to the world and the U.S. industry as well. The drug industry is frequently under attack because its critics claim that it sells its products too well, advertises too intensely, and makes too great a profit. Yet, no other industry can claim so great a contribution to the welfare of mankind. The aim of the book is to explore the underlying reasons for the criticism and to outline their historical background. The situation in Great Britain is somewhat different from that of most countries, including the U.S., as the British National Health Service is the monopoly purchaser of pharmaceutical products, although the industry that supplies the products is a good example of successful capitalism in action.

The book is divided into three parts: the facts, the arguments, and the outcome. Chapter headings are as follows: (1) Historical background, (2) Organization, (3) How a drug is made, (4) Prices and profits, (5) Advertising and promotion, (6) Safety, (7) Doctors and drugs, (8) Government and drugs, (9) The future. The book is a very good guide to the intricacies of the debate over the manufacture, sale, and use of drugs. In the last chapter, the author makes his own conclusions clear. Some of them are as follows: that there is danger in over-control, that the criticism against the drug industry is, to a certain extent, an attempt to find a scapegoat for inevitable soaring costs, and that an international drug regulating agency should be set up.

352. Burack, Richard. **The New Handbook of Prescription Drugs: Official Names, Prices, and Sources for Patient and Doctor.** New York, Pantheon Books, 1970. 362p. index. $7.95. LC 67-13318.

This is the kind of book which irritates a great number of professionals in the health sciences, particularly the pharmaceutical scientist. The book is based on the premise that all drugs with the same official (generic) name are identical, a premise that many hold to be false. Variations in such factors as strength, purity, stability, solubility, and ease of administration are quite possible. The author, who is a physician, in the beginning section of the book encourages other physicians to prescribe cheaper medicines and to prescribe by generic name rather than by trade name (as is usually done) since the well-known trade named products usually cost more. The largest part of the book is a "Prescription Drug List," an alphabetical list of common drugs, some listed by trade name and some by generic name, with a short monograph on each included. These monographs give minimal information about the products and make price comparisons. An additional price list is also included.

The information presented in this publication is all better available elsewhere, as far as the health professional is concerned, in the standard drug compendia. However, this publication is designed for use by the patient as most compendia are not.

It is generally presumed that prices charged for drugs is the province of the individual pharmacy, but suggested retail prices are given in two useful annual compendia, the *Drug Topics Red Book* and the *American Druggist Blue Book*. It is the feeling of many that most physicians and patients would prefer that drugs be prescribed on the basis of merit rather than cost. This handbook has limited value.

353. Clarke, Frank H., ed. **How Modern Drugs are Discovered.** Mount Kisco, N.Y., Futura Publishing Co., 1973. 177p. illus. bibliog. index. $10.00. LC 73-80696. ISBN 0-87993-027-6.

This book, written by medicinal researchers, tells how modern medicines are discovered and developed. It is interesting to note that pharmaceutical companies expend huge sums for research and development in this field—nearly 4.4 billion dollars in the U.S. from 1962-1971, but in this period of 10 years, only 170 new synthetic drugs were marketed. In addition, millions of dollars are spent annually for medicinal research in universities and research institutes. Hundreds of drugs are prepared in a single laboratory before one promising one is found. Even then, many prove to be too toxic for use. The book is written from the viewpoint of the medicinal chemist and is addressed primarily to those who have some understanding of biology and chemistry and who want to obtain a broad view of drug research and development. Students contemplating careers in the field will be especially interested. Chapter titles are as follows: (1) How modern medicines are discovered, (2) Natural antibiotics, (3) The control of pain, (4) The sulfa drugs and their legacy, (5) To tranquilizers and antidepressants from antimalarials and antihistamines, (6) Hormones and control of body functions, (7) Chemical transmitters and the control of blood pressure, (8) Biochemical approaches to medicinal research and development.

354. Cooper, Joseph D., ed. **The Quality of Advice.** Published by the Interdisciplinary Communication Associates, Inc. for the Interdisciplinary Communications Program, Smithsonian Institution, Washington, 1971. 335p. bibliog. (Philosophy and Technology of Drug Assessment, vol. 2). $5.50. LC 71-187534.
This volume is basically the verbatim transcript of the second Conference on the Philosophy and Technology of Drug Assessment. There are few formal papers; the text is mostly an interchange of ideas. The main problem concentrated on was the bringing of outside advice to bear successfully on official decisions of the U.S. Food and Drug Administration. Such matters were discussed as selection, organization, support, and utilization of advisory groups. Also, the conference gave some attention to the need for scientific appeals mechanisms to assure that redress would be possible in the face of scientific disagreement. In addition, it was the consensus of the conference that scientific and other bases for decision-making by the FDA should be open to inspection by those affected and by the scientific community. The belief was that this would improve decision-making and the dissemination of scientific information about drug effects. 16 well-known scientists, industrialists, educators, and government representatives participated in the conference.

Topics discussed were: (1) Defining the problem, (2) The credibility of advice, (3) Predictability of success, (4) Inputs for decision-making, (5) Inputs as outputs, (6) Appeals and executive strategies, and (7) Executive response to advice. In addition, there is quite a bit of appended material such as some prepared papers and reports.

355. Damerow, Ronald D. **The Right to Live.** New York, Vantage Press, 1971. 174p. $4.95.
The author's point of view is that the government (particularly the Food and Drug Administration) has gone so far in protecting the citizen against possibly harmful medicines that he is being deprived of drugs that might help him or even

save his life. Americans who can afford to are flying to foreign countries for the treatment of diseases, and our country is no longer known as the prime developer of new drugs. There are many, particularly in the scientific community, who share this view.

356. De Felice, Stephen L. **Drug Discovery: The Pending Crisis.** New York, Medcom Learning Systems, 1972. 93p. illus. bibliog. $9.95. LC 72-87152.
The author, who is a physician and has had wide experience in academic, governmental, and pharmaceutical chemistry research, deals with the key issues in clinical drug development. His most important message is that the non-clinical aspects of drug development are stressed too much and that the early and adequate study of potentially useful drugs in man are not stressed enough. While caution may prevent some harm to the public from untoward effects of drugs, valuable substances are not being tested and used because of possible risks. The author points out that drug effects on animals are not necessarily the same as in man and that many substances are put aside and not tested on man at all if they are found to be toxic or ineffective in animals. Since the thalidomide episode and the passage of the 1962 Kefauver-Harris amendments, the U.S. has been extremely slow to accept new pharmaceuticals. We were the 41st country to approve lithium as a psychopharmacologic agent and the 51st to approve the important antitubercular drug, rifampin. The author is upset that, not only have we had a decline in the discovery and development of new drugs since 1962 (most new developments and discoveries come from abroad now), there is much complacency regarding this fact. This book deals with an important subject about which the public is largely unaware.

357. Di Cyan, Erwin, and Lawrence Hessman. **Without Prescription: A Guide to the Selection and Use of Medicines You Can Get Over-the-Counter Without Prescription, for Self-Medication.** New York, Simon and Schuster, 1972. index. $7.95. LC 77-171603. SBN 671-21137-4.
This book, which is the first of its kind, is a guide to medicines which may be obtained in the drugstore without prescription. It is an authentic, readable, and interesting account. While self-medication obviously has its dangers, almost everyone does it, and a public well-informed about drugs and their ingredients is certainly desirable. In addition to the drug information, there are also articles about health and disease. The following topics are presented: the common cold; drugs for children; stomach and abdominal discomforts; pain; eye, ear, nose, throat—and mouth; feminine hygiene; insomnia and fatigue; allergy; skin; and general articles on topics of health and disease. Also included is an appendix of synonymous names of drugs and a listing of drugs with side effects indicated. This guide is particularly valuable for the home library.

358. Dowling, Harry F. **Medicines for Man: The Development, Regulation, and Use of Prescription Drugs.** Alfred A. Knopf, 1970. 347p. bibliog. index. $7.95. LC 73-98665.
The author has attempted to give a balanced appraisal of the conflicting ideas and attitudes concerning the development, manufacture, sale, regulation, and use of drugs. He is well qualified to do so as he is a physician and former chairman of the American Medical Association Council on Drugs. He traces the commercial,

medical, and governmental development of the pharmaceutical industry and points out the dangers of our present system. He is particularly concerned that physicians rely upon nonmedical sources (the pharmaceutical industry) for vital information aobut new drugs. However, he does point out that many industries employ large numbers of physicians and Ph.D. scientists.

Some of the ideas expressed are a bit out of date, and probably were at the time the book was written. There are frequent references to the current "drug explosion." Drugs have not been developed at a rapid rate in the U.S. for a number of years.

The book is written for the layman, but health professionals will find it of interest.

359. Dunnell, Karen, and Ann Cartwright. **Medicine Takers, Prescribers and Hoarders.** London and Boston, Routledge and Kegan Paul, 1972. 182p. bibliog. index. $10.50. LC 72-85957. ISBN 0-7100-7351-8.
This book is a report of a study done in Great Britain, but it is likely that similar results would have been obtained in the U.S., and in any case, some useful insights can be gained. An effort was made to find the answer to three questions: (1) The distribution and nature of medicine taking: who takes which kinds of medicine and for what conditions, (2) The role of the medical profession, (3) The storage of medicines in people's homes was studied—what medicines were kept, where, and for how long? The real basic aim, however, was to illuminate the relationship between physicians and patients and to find out more about the functioning of the national health service and ultimately to add to the understanding of health behavior. The following paragraph sums up the findings: "Medicine taking is a common activity, frequently indulged in, often over long periods. It serves a variety of needs, many of them social and psychological rather than purely pharmacological. The most powerful and harmful drugs can only be obtained on prescription and much prescribing is done on a repeat basis over long periods. Some of the demand for drugs probably arises because of inadequacies in the doctor-patient relationship, some is a reflection of the impotence of the medical profession and medical science to cure or relieve many common ailments."

360. Fisher, Richard B., and George A. Christie. **A Dictionary of Drugs: The Medicines You Use.** New York, Schocken Books, 1972. 252p. index. $6.95; $2.25pa. LC 72-80037.
Fifty-six drugs, therapeutically useful chemicals, are described in detail. The use and operating mechanisms are described as well as effects, chemical make-up, and side effects. In addition to the 56 entries, some 300 chemically related agents are named, enlarging the scope of the work. Also, seven general classes of drugs are discussed: antibiotics, diuretics, hormones, monamine oxidase inhibitors, prostaglandins, sulphonamides, and vitamins. There are three indexes, one by trade name, one by chemical name, and the third by diseases treated. The dictionary is intended for the layman but is not a guide to self-dosage, nor does it stress price. The main concern is to let the reader know what a drug does and why. A detailed list of side effects are given, even if they rarely occur, because so much concern has been given to them in the mass media. The text is rather technically written, but the book should prove useful to most audiences anyway and is

certainly more authentic and informative than many of the books on drugs written for the layman today.

361. Gulick, William. **Rx Consumers' Guide to Prescription Prices: A Money Saving Guide.** Syracuse, N.Y., Consumer Age Press, 1973. 95p. $3.95.

This book attempts to teach the patient how to read a doctor's prescription and also indicates the average retail price of prescription drugs. The aim of the publication is to make it possible to "shop as wisely for prescription drugs as you do for any other consumer product."

Possibly, the guide will be of assistance to the patient, but the concept of treating medicines as any other consumer product may not be a sensible one. The patient is usually best advised to follow his physician's instruction. Also, there are other things to consider in the purchase of drugs than price alone. There is the quality of the drug, the pharmacist's professional competence, and the extent of services offered, such as the maintenance of patient records. In addition, it is not advisable to use several different drug stores as sources for medicines. One place should have the complete patient record in order to make it possible to determine the possibility of the different drugs an individual uses interacting adversely.

As for the price schedules included, much more complete lists are available (although the public does not always have easy access to them), such as the annual publications *American Druggist Blue Book* and *Drug Topics Red Book.* Any price list becomes outdated very rapidly, and frequent updating is necessary to keep a list current. No indication is made that updatings are planned for the publication in question.

It is probably true that the public should be better informed about medicines than they are, but it is doubtful that many of the suggestions made in this book will be of benefit.

362. **Handbook of Non-Prescription Drugs.** 1973 ed. George B. Griffenhagen and Linda L. Hawkins, co-editors. Washington, American Pharmaceutical Association, 1973. 232p. bibliog. index. $7.50.

This is the 4th edition of this handbook, the first being published in 1967. Although of interest to others, the publication is intended primarily for pharmacists to assist them in giving the best advice on over-the-counter drug products. The handbook is important because manufacturers do not always disclose the ingredients in their products on the package, and this information is not readily available elsewhere, not even to members of the medical and allied professions.

The book contains 33 chapters, each written by a well qualified individual, mostly professors of pharmacy. Each chapter takes up a different kind of product, for instance, antacids, cold medicines, burn remedies, ophthalmic products, etc. Some cosmetic products also are included, such as hair preparations.

Text material is presented and, in addition, the chapters include tables listing products by trade name with such information as manufacturer, application form, and most importantly, ingredients. This is a very valuable publication.

363. **Hayes Druggist Directory.** 1973 ed. Newport Beach, California, Edward N. Hayes, 1973. 647p. $27.00pa.

This directory, which is revised annually, lists alphabetically by state, and secondarily by city, retail drug stores. With each listing is the address, estimated financial strength, and credit rating. This listing seems to be accurate and reliable. The directory has been published each year since 1912.

364. Honigfeld, Gilbert, and Alfreda Howard. **Psychiatric Drugs: A Desk Reference.** New York and London, Academic, 1973. 227p. bibliog. index. $8.95. LC 72-88360.

This small volume was written for psychologists, social workers, occupational therapists, psychiatric nurses, and other mental health professionals. There is no other work similar to this available, although there are comprehensive texts that are written for physicians and pharmacologists. It is important that the non-medical mental health professional has information about psychiatric drugs available as these people are assuming more responsibility for the care of mental patients. The material is presented in a concise, nontheoretical manner. Chapter headings are as follows: (1) Introduction, (2) Antidepressant drugs, (3) Antipsychotic agents, (4) Antianxiety agents and sedatives, (5) Lithium, (6) Stimulants, (7) Electroconvulsive treatment (ECT), (8) Side effects, (9) Discontinuation, maintenance, and prophylaxis, (10) Drug treatment of drug addiction and alcoholism, (11) Current developments, (12) Handling drug emergencies, (13) Diagnosis and somatic treatment, (14) Evaluating your psychiatric colleagues, and (15) Training implications. Also included are seven appendices which include trade and generic drug name lists, and drug identification tables.

365. Kaluzny, Eugene L. **Pharmacy Law Digest.** Milwaukee, Douglas-McKay, Inc., 1971. 505p. looseleaf. index. $14.95. LC 70-19057.

This is a much needed compilation as practicing pharmacists are constantly plagued with new, changing, and complicated government regulations. The book is looseleaf so revisions may be made from time to time from supplements made available. The book consists mainly of text material (in the form of questions and answers or explanations) and reproduction of applicable sections of laws or regulations. The publication is intended to inform rather than to advise. There are eight sections as follows: (1) U.S. Constitution, (2) Alphabetical index, (3) Federal-controlled Substances Act (narcotics and dangerous drugs), (4) Federal Food, Drug and Cosmetics Act and other applicable federal laws, (5) Pharmacists and civil liability, (6) Pharmacists and business law, (7) State pharmacy law analysis, and (8) Pharmacy court cases. The author is a pharmacist and lawyer.

366. Kendall, Edward C. **Cortisone.** New York, Charles Scribner's Sons, 1971. 175p. illus. index. $7.95. LC 72-123853.

This autobiography is a rather personal narrative by a 1950 Nobel Prizewinner biochemist. It tells of the research on hormones which led to the discovery of Cortisone, one of the great breakthroughs of medical history. A good deal of background is given on the author's family; his colleagues and co-winners of the Nobel Prize, Dr. Philip Hench and Prof. Tadeus Reichstein; the Mayo Clinic where the work was done; and some of his experience in the pharmaceutical industry. The climax of the story is the awarding of the prize in Sweden. It is a warm, human story without a great deal of scientific detail.

367. Kern, Kenneth R., ed. **Executive Directory of the U.S. Pharmaceutical Industry.** 2d ed. Princeton, N.J., Chemical Economics Services, 1972. 123p. $21.00pa. LC 66-26782. ISBN 0-912060-13-1.
The directory lists 626 companies and includes the names of approximately 4,000 executives with the listings. There is no separate list by the names of the individuals. For each company, the following information is usually supplied: address of company, ownership (if a subsidiary or division of another company), board of directors, division and plants, annual sales, number of employees, and products (by therapeutic classification).

The editor feels that as medical care becomes more socialized with increasing FDA regulations and controls, and congressional investigations along with consumer recalcitrance continues—companies will need greater strength to meet the challenges and opportunities. It is hoped that this directory will serve as a communication aid and research tool to meet the changes that are called for.

368. Krieg, Margaret. **Black Market Medicine.** Englewood Cliffs, N.J., Prentice-Hall, Inc., 1967. 304p. illus. $5.95. LC 67-18920.
This is a factual account based on the author's undercover invesigations conducted by the U.S. Food and Drug Administration inspectors into the counterfeit drug problem. She reveals the mass market traffic in bogus and bootleg pharmaceuticals. Unscrupulous counterfeiters make a wide variety of capsules and tablets that look exactly like authentic trade-marked products and sell them to unsuspecting patients through various channels. These drugs are dangerous because they are often substandard, adulterated, and contaminated by other drugs and filth. The author's report is authentic; it is corroborated by files made available to the author by the FDA and other federal agencies, investigators, police, and pharmaceutical manufacturers. A great deal of the text of the book is based on taped recordings made on the scenes. The publication is an important contribution as it exposes and documents a very real but little-known problem.

369. National Association of Boards of Pharmacy. **NABP Directory of Licensed Pharmacies.** November 1971. Chicago, National Association of Boards of Pharmacy, 1971. 581p.
The purpose of this directory is to provide to those who distribute drugs in interstate commerce a reliable source of information concerning the outlets that may legally receive and possess drugs. The pharmacies are arranged alphabetically by city within each state. The entries are listed alphabetically under city showing the name of the outlet, its address, city, and zip code. Also included with the entries is the registration number of the facility which has been assigned by the Bureau of Narcotics and Dangerous Drugs of the Department of Justice. The directory is updated frequently with supplements, and new data is being added.

370. National Association of Chain Drug Stores, Inc. **NACDS Membership Directory**. 1972 ed. Arlington, Virginia, National Association of Chain Drug Stores, 1971. 1v.(various paging).

The association represents the management of about 216 chain drug corporations in the U.S., Canada, Mexico, Puerto Rico, and Venezuela. There are also about 400 associate members which are suppliers of goods and services to the chain drug industry. The directory is made up of nine sections, printed on different colored pages, as follows: (1) Alphabetical listing of chain drug company headquarters, including names of executives and buyers, (2) Names of chains and officers that buy pharmaceuticals, (3) Names of chains that buy cosmetics, (4) Geographical listing of chains' headquarters, (5) Geographical listing of stores, (6) Other chain drug associations, (7) Other associations in the drug trade field, (8) Companies that are associate members, (9) A classified list by products.

A good deal of information about chain drug companies can be obtained through these various listings.

371. National Wholesale Druggists' Association. **Membership and Executive Directory**. New York, National Wholesale Druggists' Association, 1973. 74p. $5.40 to members; $100.00 to nonmembers.

This directory lists several groups, arranged first by state and secondarily alphabetically. These groups include active members, associate members, international members, the drug trade press, colleges of pharmacy, and national drug industry associations. Also included are names of officers for the year, members of the Board of Directors, and headquarters staff.

372. Pearson, Michael. **The Million-Dollar Bugs**. New York, G. P. Putnam's Sons, 1969. 291p. index. $6.95. LC 69-11464.

This book, written by an English journalist, tells the story of the drug industry, with emphasis on the progress made in the U.S. with wonder drugs, competition to get new drugs on the market that would pay large profits, and the subsequent federal investigation of the industry (the Kefauver investigation). The report is probably a fair one as the pros and cons of the case are both given. The author's conclusion is that the industry that had done so much to benefit the millions of people throughout the world had been condemned by the society it had aided. The drug makers' crime was that they had profited too much from the good they had done. The result of restrictive laws, the author predicts, will be that there will not be really big profits in the drug industry in the future. Also, there will be few new miracle drugs. Without the big speculators, the rate of drug discovery will be low. This indeed is the case at the present time.

373. Pharmaceutical Manufacturers Association. **Prescription Drug Industry Fact Book**. Washington, Pharmaceutical Manufacturers Association, 1973. 101p. illus. bibliog. free.

This useful publication, which is revised frequently, is designed as a reference guide for those interested in the social and economic aspects of prescription pharmaceutical manufacture and distribution. Statistics used were those available in late 1972. There is a wide variety of information included, such as information on sales, price levels and research and development, facts on the industry structure, employment, quality control, safety and availability of prescription drug products, international operations, and the health care industry in general. The book contains data in text, chart, graph, and tabular form. There is also a glossary, appendix, and a bibliography of sources used.

374. Smith, Mickey C., and David A. Knapp. **Pharmacy, Drugs and Medical Care.** Baltimore, Williams and Wilkins, 1972. 278p. bibliog. index. $9.50pa. LC 76-185028. SBN 683-07758-9.

Although this work is intended primarily as a school of pharmacy textbook, others will find it of interest and value. It provides an orientation to the field of pharmacy presented in the context of the system in which it is practiced. There are discussions on the delivery of health care, the various professions and occupations which provide care, and the agencies which administer the system.

375. Sperber, Perry A. **Drugs, Demons, Doctors, and Disease.** St. Louis, Warren H. Green, Inc., 1973. 294p. $15.50. LC 70-111808.

The purpose of this book is to give laymen an insight into the world of drugs along with some historical background. The material is presented in readable interesting style and seems to be authentic as well, although no formal literature references are cited. Many authorities are quoted indirectly, however. The author is a physician.

The first few chapters are historical; then the next 11 chapters take up the various types of drugs one by one. The last three chapters are on drug interactions, drugs and the biological time clock, and pollution, respectively. The book was meant to be read and is of limited value as a reference tool on drugs because there is no index. Since there are few books on drugs for laymen, this title is of interest in spite of its limitations.

376. **"Take as Directed": Our Modern Medicines.** Cleveland, CRC Press, a division of the Chemical Rubber Co., 1967. 457p. illus. bibliog. index. $14.95.

This book was written for the general public with the advice of a group of eminent authorities from hospitals, universities, government research laboratories, and the pharmaceutical industry. It was felt that a need for such a book existed because of the rapid pace at which drugs have been developed and because the public has been confused by claims and counter-claims, politics and partisanship, half-truths and misinformation. The book gives authentic information about the field of pharmaceuticals including their promise and potential as well as limitations and possible harmful side effects. A wide variety of drugs are discussed, including contraceptives, vitamins, psychiatric drugs, narcotics, antibiotics, anticancer agents, diabetic drugs, and many others. In addition, there are chapters on heredity and drugs, testing drugs, and possibilities for the future. The story of the historical development of many of the products is presented throughout with the sketches. The book is recommended for anyone interested in modern remedies.

377. U.S. Food and Drug Administration. Bureau of Drugs. Office of Scientific Coordination. **National Drug Code Directory. June 1972.** Washington, GPO, 1972. 1v.(various paging). index. $4.50pa. (FDA) 72-3027. Stock No. 1712-0150.

This directory is a computer-produced listing designed to link national drug codes to the products which they represent. A packaged drug product is identified by a nine-character, alpha-numeric, segmented code with the first three characters identifying the labeler (the manufacturer usually), the next four the drug product, and the last two the basic trade package size. The drug product and the code which represents it is defined by product name, generic name (where available for single ingredient products), labeler's name, dosage form, route of administration, strength, legal status, package size, and package type. Section A of the directory is arranged alphabetically by product name; Section B is arranged by established (generic) name; Section C is the list of codes in numeric sequence. There is also an appendix of manufacturers' names, addresses, and the shortened name used in the main listing. About 2,400 products are identified, and more are to be added to the system from time to time.

This publication is important because it establishes a standardized identification system for drug products. One can take an unknown capsule, for instance, and by the code marking on it, identify the product. Also, it is possible to use the codes in various computer-based systems.

378. Wilson, Charles O., and Tony E. Jones. **American Drug Index 1973.** Philadelphia and Toronto, J. B. Lippincott Co., 1973. 717p. $10.25. LC 55-6286. ISBN 0-397-50290-7.

This annual publication has been compiled to identify and correlate the many pharmaceutical products which are available. There is considerable need for this index as drugs and drug products have multiplied rapidly and a large number of similar products exist. The listing is arranged alphabetically with numerous cross-references. Generic names (or common names), brand (or trademark), and chemical names are listed as well as *U.S. Pharmacopeia* and *National Formulary* synonyms that are in general use. Listing the variety of names is an outstanding feature of the work as many lists are arranged by one kind of name only. Also, it is possible to find drugs or drug combinations when only one major ingredient is known. The data included with each entry is concise but adequate: manufacturer, composition, available forms, sizes, dosage, and use. The publication is most useful to physicians, pharmacists, dentists, nurses, sales personnel, and students, teachers and librarians in the fields incorporating pharmaceuticals. It is highly recommended.

10. MENTAL HEALTH

379. Association of Hospital and Institution Libraries. Committee on Bibliotherapy and Subcommittee on the Troubled Child. **Bibliotherapy:
Methods and Materials.** Chicago, American Library Association, 1971.
161p. bibliog. index. $5.95. LC 75-165199.

This handbook surveys the developments of bibliotherapy and/or therapeutic
library service. There are two parts: the first presents a foundation for executing
a therapeutic program and suggests methods, and the second lists books useful
for young people facing difficulties in adjustment. The latter takes up more than
half the book. Each title is annotated, and theme, audience, reading level, and
interest level are indicated. The annotated list is divided into separate sections
listing books that have been found to be helpful in the treatment of such problems as hostility, retardation, failure in school, sibling rivalry, parent-child
relationships, and sexual maladjustment. One chapter of part 1 deals with services to the physically and mentally ill, to the retarded, to the offender, to alcoholics, and to drug users.

The publication should prove of interest and value to clinical psychologists, physicians, nurses, chaplains, teachers, and social workers as well as librarians.

380. Ciba Foundation Symposium. **The Mentally Abnormal Offender.** Edited
by A.V.S. de Reuck and Ruth Porter. Boston, Little, Brown and Co.,
1968. 260p. bibliog. index. SBN 7000-1363-6.

This publication records the proceedings of an international conference. The
papers are written at a high level by experts. The presentations are grouped into
three sections as follows: (1) Antisocial behaviour and its treatment and care,
(2) Social problems, (3) Legal problems. The book discloses many different
approaches that are being made in the management of the mentally abnormal
offender in different countries and between different disciplines.

381. Conley, Ronald W. **The Economics of Mental Retardation.** Baltimore,
Johns Hopkins University Press, 1973. 377p. bibliog. index. $15.00.
LC 72-12345. ISBN 0-8018-1410-3.

This book is written for the college level audience that has had little background
in mental retardation or economics. Economists, professionals associated with
mental retardation, politicians and civil servants, and concerned citizens will be
interested in it. The author, who was with the President's Committee on Mental
Retardation when the work was begun, has explored the extent and demographic
characteristics of mental retardation, the causes of it, the characteristics of programs providing services to the retarded, and the employment and earnings of the
group. He also makes a cost-benefit analysis. In the last chapter, ways to improve
services are discussed. The author points out that a new kind of program, community care for the retarded in group homes or in other forms of community
residence, has been growing rapidly. He supports these efforts but warns that

institutional care should not be abandoned, at least before problems of continuity of care, fire regulations, transportation, and the like have been solved in the community. Also, the development of sheltered work in regular employment settings is mentioned as a possible goal not yet in sight. The book contains 63 tables of statistical material.

382. Feldman, Saul, ed. **The Administration of Mental Health Services.** Springfield, Ill., Charles C. Thomas, 1973. bibliog. index. $18.75. LC 72-11611. ISBN 0-398-02804-4.

The editor of this multi-authored work feels that mental health services have changed a great deal of recent years and that administration of these services has grown very difficult. Expenditures now exceed $5 billion annually. There is a need to accelerate understanding of the problems of the administration of such extensive services. The prototype mental health organization of the 1970's is a complex, frequently decentralized service system with various levels of accountability and close ties with other human services. Frequently, mental health services are administered by health professionals with little administrative experience or training, and trained administrators are frequently unfamiliar with the field of mental health. The book is concerned with these and other problems. The titles of the papers presented are as follows: (1) Planning in mental health, (2) Budgeting and behavior, (3) People make programs: personnel management, (4) Financing mental health services, (5) Management information, (6) The sociology of organizations, (7) Interorganizational relations, (8) Community participation, (9) The governmental system, (10) Change and innovation, and (11) Program evaluation. The book is a welcome addition to the literature as little exists in this field.

383. Golann, Stuart E. **Coordinate Index Reference Guide to Community Mental Health.** New York, Behavioral Publications, Inc., 1969. 237p. bibliog. index. (Community Mental Health Series). $9.00. LC 68-59452.

This book is a bibliography of 1,510 references, most of which were published between 1960 and 1967, which is arranged alphabetically by author. Each reference is accompanied by code numbers indicating the subject content. A coordinate index and also a cross reference has been provided to assist the user in a subject approach. The book also contains a list of 47 organizations with addresses called "Other Sources of Information." The bibliography is not really very comprehensive, but an effort was made to achieve representativeness. It mostly lists articles from journals published in the United States. The book should prove most useful for the contiuing education of practitioners and to students who are trying to find their way through the rapidly growing literature in this field.

384. Heck, Edward T., Angel G. Gomez, and George L. Adams. **A Guide to Mental Health Services.** Pittsburgh, University of Pittsburgh Press, 1973. 139p. index. (Contemporary Community Health Series). $6.95. LC 72-92694. ISBN 0-8229-3262-8; 0-8229-5236-Xpa.

This book was written primarily for individuals who will be guiding patients with mental problems in obtaining the assistance they need. It presents basic, practical information about mental health services, practitioners, and treatments. It covers a wide range of mental health topics. It is not a directory of services, but will help the reader search out and evaluate services in a community. Chapter headings are as follows: (1) Mental health and mental illness, (2) Some mental health professions, (3) Diagnosis: defining mental problems, (4) Treatment: solving mental problems, (5) Residential or inpatient treatment facilities, (6) Mental health clinics: outpatient treatment facilities, (7) Mental health treatment programs in the schools, (8) Comprehensive community mental health centers, (9) Mental health services for special populations, (10) Some sources of mental health information, (11) Encouraging citizen participation in mental health activities, and (12) Conclusion.

385. Lamb, H. Richard, Don Heath, and Joseph J. Downing, eds. **Handbook of Community Mental Health Practice.** San Francisco, Jossey-Bass, Inc., 1969. 483p. bibliog. index. LC 72-92886. SBN 87589-040-7.
This book is about the San Mateo, California experience with a program to link together the essential and the supplementary elements of a community mental health program. This was a ten-year program, the first of its kind in the United States. The book should be useful in academic training as well as in operating community programs. All of the contributors to the work were on the staff of the County of San Mateo Mental Health Services Division. They have attempted to write a useful book which can serve as a handbook of practical experience. There is a prologue on "Program antecedents and public health" and an epilogue "From experience to principle." The rest of the text is divided into four parts: (1) Philosophy, administration, and liaison, (2) The direct services, (3) The indirect services, and (4) Program evaluation and training.

386. Martindale, Don, and Edith Martindale. **The Social Dimensions of Mental Illness, Alcoholism, and Drug Dependence.** Westport, Conn., Greenwood Publishing Co., 1971. 330p. bibliog. index. $12.50. (Contributions in Sociology, No. 9). LC 72-133499. ISBN 0-8371-5175-9.
This book is a sociological study which examines the physiological, psychological, and social stresses that contribute to mental illness, alcoholism, and drug dependence. The theory of the authors is that these illnesses represent a failure of socialization in the development process. They cite evidence that the more successful trends in therapy attack the individual's psychology and at the same time transform the social context in which he is operating into an ego-sustaining therapeutic community. Chapter headings are as follows: (1) Contours of the contemporary problem of mental illness, (2) Mental illness and the law, (3) The trauma of commitment to the primary group, (4) Formal and informal organization of the mental hospital, (5) The career of the mental patient, (6) Mental disorders, treatment methods, and the therapeutic community, (7) Return to the community, (8) Alcoholism, (9) Drug dependence, (10) Toward an integrated theory.

387. Moss, Gordon Erwin. **Illness, Immunity, and Social Interaction: The Dynamics of Biosocial Resonation.** New York, John Wiley and Sons, 1973. 281p. bibliog. index. $14.95. LC 72-11782. ISBN 0-471-61925-6.
This study presents a theoretical framework which links social behavior and disease. It is hoped that it will aid medical researchers in using sociological concepts and encourage sociologists to consider biological processes in their work.

Material is provided from a number of experimental and clinical studies to illustrate that illness (or immunity) in an individual may be related to his degree of acceptance in a social or communication network. Chapter headings are as follows: (1) Development of the concept of biosocial resonation, (2) Evaluation of stress models, (3) The central nervous system and perception in biosocial resonation, (4) Autonomic and neuroendocrine processes and changes in susceptibility to disease in biosocial resonation, (5) The biosocial resonation of individuals in social change, and (7) Immunity and relief from information incongruities through social participation.

The author defines "biosocial resonation" as "the continuing reciprocal influences of physiological processes and social behavior in social interaction." The book is written at the level for a student or a professional. It is of particular interest because it brings together work done in various medical, psychological, and social fields.

388. Nichtern, Sol, ed. **Mental Health Services for Adolescents.** Proceedings of the Second Hillside Hospital Conference. New York, Praeger, 1968. 232p. (Praeger Special Studies in U.S. Economic and Social Development). $12.50. LC 68-30682.
This publication includes presentations and part of the discussions presented at the Hillside Hospital Conference held February 25-26, 1967. The Conference highlighted the fact that mental health services for adolescents often have been inadequate. In addition, many traditions followed in services of this kind have had little application to young people. The community, its professional groups, agencies, and programs and the ways that these could be attuned to the needs of the adolescent were examined. The presentations are divided into five groups as follows: (1) Community resources, (2) New horizons in mental health services, (3) The hospital and the adolescent, (4) The milieu of the adolescent, and (5) Results and findings.

389. Schneider, John M., Barnett Addis, and Marsha Addis. **Films in the Behavioral Sciences: An Annotated Catalogue.** 2d ed. Oklahoma City, University of Oklahoma Medical Center, Department of Psychiatry and Behavioral Sciences, Behavioral Sciences Media Laboratory, 1970. 225p.
This catalog covers the field rather broadly, expanding its listings into related areas of the subject. The publication is in two parts: the first lists titles classified according to content, such as learning, psychodynamics, physiological factors in behavior, psychopharmacology, etc. The second part is an alphabetical by title list with annotations and descriptions of the film. All films are 16mm. Distributors are indicated. About 1,300 titles are listed, including a few "underground" films.

390. U.S. National Institute of Mental Health. **Bibliography of Suicide and Suicide Prevention, 1897-1957, 1958-1970.** By Norman L. Farberow. Washington, GPO, 1972. 143p. index. DHEW Publication No. (HSM) 72-9080. $2.00pa. Stock No. 1740-0342.
This bibliography is important because there has been an increased interest in relatively recent years in the problems of suicide and its prevention. As a result,

there has been a marked increase in the number of articles about the subject appearing in the professional literature. This bibliography provides a single reference source for the publications. The bibliography is divided into two periods as indicated in the title above. The first period incorporates and expands the bibliography originally published in the author's book *The Cry for Help* (McGraw-Hill, 1961). The second list has been added to this, making a total of about 4,600 items. A good deal of foreign language material has been included. The list is quite comprehensive, but medical articles, appearing in journals written for physicians, have for the most part been excluded. It is planned that the list will be updated.

391. U.S. National Institute of Mental Health. **Directory of General Hospitals Providing Walk-In Emergency Mental Health Services.** Washington, GPO, 1973. 49p. DHEW Publication No. (HSM) 73-9022. $.90. Stock No. 1724-00304.

This directory lists general hospitals which provide emergency mental health services. Federal hospitals have been excluded as have those that treat only alcoholics and/or drug users. The hospitals listed are arranged by state and secondarily by city. The following information is provided: name, address, phone number, hours and days of operation, geographic and other restrictions, and the name and address of the parent facility.

392. U.S. National Institute of Mental Health. **Directory of Halfway Houses for the Mentally Ill and Alcoholics.** Washington, GPO, 1973. 133p. DHEW Publication No. (HSM) 73-9008. Supt. of Docs. No. HE 20.2402:H13. $2.50.

This directory provides information on the availability of halfway houses throughout the United States. It is intended for use by referring professions, families of potential residents, or the individuals for whom this kind of facility would be appropriate. The facilities provide residential service to the emotionally disturbed, alcoholics, or combinations of these. The directory is arranged by state, and within each state by the primary resident group served. Data given for each facility is as follows: name, address, phone number, established year, geographic area served, auspices, capacity, ages served, sex served, persons served, maximum stay permitted, number of readmissions permitted, and admission requirements.

393. U.S. National Institute of Mental Health. **Mental Health Considerations in Public Health: A Guide for Training and Practice.** Edited by Stephen E. Goldston. Washington, GPO, 1969. 252p. bibliog. (Public Health Service Publication No. 1898). $1.25pa.

This publication is addressed to professional public health personnel who function in the areas of general health administration, medical care and hospital administration, health education, epidemiology, biostatistics, chronic diseases, maternal and child health, public health nursing, family planning and population policies, environmental health, occupational health, and nutrition. Also, mental health specialists such as psychiatrists, psychologists, psychiatric social workers, and psychiatric nurses who seek to contribute and learn from the field of public health can benefit from it. The book contains 12 scholarly papers which were prepared for the National Conference on Mental Health in Public Health Training held at Airlie House in Warrenton, Va., May 27-30, 1968. The relationship between training in public health and mental health was looked at. Titles of the papers are as follows: (1) General health administration, (2) Medical care and hospital administration, (3) Health education, (4) Epidemiology, (5) Biostatistics, (6) Chronic diseases, (7) Maternal and child health, (8) Public health nursing, (9) Family planning and population policies, (10) Environmental health, (11) Occupational health, and (12) Nutrition.

These papers present a framework for training at the professional level in schools of public health, in medical departments of preventive medicine, in other health training centers, and for the continuing education of public health workers.

394. U.S. National Institute of Mental health. Center for Studies of Crime and Delinquency. **Directory of Institutions for Mentally Disordered Offenders.** Washington, GPO, 1972. 24p. DHEW Publication No. (HSM) 72-9055. $.25. Stock No. 1724-0236.

This publication lists mental health and correctional institutions which provide psychiatric care for adult mentally disordered offenders. Included are state, federal, and municipal facilities. Veterans' Administration hospitals and correctional facilities connected with the Armed Forces are excluded. Arrangement is by state. Information provided includes data regarding location, capacity, type of institution, administrative officials, and population classified by sex.

395. U.S. National Institute of Mental Health. National Clearinghouse for Mental Health Information. **Mental Health Directory, 1971.** Washington, GPO, 1971. 480p. (Public Health Service Publication No. 1268 rev.). $3.75. Stock No. 1724-0136.

This directory was part of an effort to help improve the treatment and rehabilitation resources available to the public. It contains information regarding existing mental health resources and is intended for use by both professionals and laymen. It is hoped that it will improve the referral process, suggest services which need to be developed, and promote cooperative efforts within the network of the mental health service agencies. The following lists are presented: (1) Regional mental health offices of DHEW-NIMH, (2) State and territorial mental health authorities, (3) State mental health services and facilities, (4) Mental health associations, and (5) Other sources of mental health information.

396. Victoroff, Victor M., and Hugh A. Ross. **Hospitalizing the Mentally Ill in Ohio.** Cleveland, Press of Case Western Reserve University, 1969. 353p. index. $8.95. LC 68-9430. SBN 8295-0143-6.

This book is intended for physicians, hospital administrators, social workers, clergymen, psychologists, law officers, attorneys, nurses, public health workers, and other interested individuals. The book is of particular value, perhaps, to family physicians as the limited number of psychiatrists available make it necessary that family doctors treat much mental illness. One of the authors is a psychiatrist, the other a professor of law. The volume is divided into two parts. Part 1 is on medical aspects of the subject, and Part 2 is on legal aspects. Although the book specifically deals with the matters in the state of Ohio, other states have similar situations. There is a good deal of appended material in the book which includes a list of psychiatrists in Ohio, psychiatric facilities in Ohio, official forms for admission to psychiatric hospitals in Ohio, probate courts of Ohio, and Ohio organizations concerned with mental health.

11. DRUG ABUSE, ALCOHOLISM, AND TOBACCO USE

397. Aaronson, Bernard, and Humphry Osmond, eds. **Psychedelics: The Uses and Implications of Hallucinogenic Drugs.** Garden City, N.Y., Anchor Books, Doubleday and Co., 1970. 512p. bibliog. index. $2.45. LC 70-103788.

This publication is a collection of articles about psychedelics, or hallucinogenic drugs. Some of the material has been published previously. The approach is psychological rather than physiological or medical. The papers outline the implications of use of these drugs and point up some of the problems. The attitudes expressed are in general sympathetic to the use of these "mind-expanding" substances although a more controlled development of their use is hoped for. The presentation is divided into parts as follows: (1) Introduction, (2) The nature of the experience, (3) Anthropological considerations, (4) Effects of psychedelics on religion and religious experience. (5) Psychedelic effects on mental functioning, (6) Nondrug analogues to the psychedelic state, (7) Therapeutic applications, (8) Sociology of psychedelics in the current scene, and (9) Conclusion.

The viewpoints expressed in the book seem a bit out of date at this writing. There is now a growing feeling that the use of hallucinogenic drugs is very risky as permanent damage to the user is likely and genetic damage is possible.

398. Advena, Jean Cameron, comp. **Drug Abuse Bibliography for 1971.** Troy, N.Y., Whitston Publishing Co., 1972. 419p. index. $15.00. LC 79-116588. ISBN 0-87875-025-8.

This bibliography is the second annual volume which supplements an earlier list compiled by Joseph Menditto called *Drugs of Addiction and Non-Addiction, Their Use and Abuse. A Comprehensive Bibliography, 1960-1969,* by the same publisher. The arrangement of the material is different from that of the earlier volumes; it is divided into two sections, one by title and the other by subject. Complete information about the entries are given in both sections. There is also an author index. Most of the references are to periodical literature, but some books also have been included. The list seems to be rather complete; a large number of bibliographies and periodical indexes were searched in compiling the work. The book will serve the needs of researchers in medical and social sciences and also those of undergraduate students and laymen.

399. Ajami, Alfred M., ed. **Drugs: An Annotated Bibliography and Guide to the Literature.** In collaboration with the Sanctuary, Cambridge, Mass. Boston, G. K. Hall and Co., 1973. 205p. index. $15.00.

This bibliography focuses on drugs of abuse and the so-called "drug culture." References are included on neurological, pharmacological, historical, social, and political implications. The 529 references are divided into several categories: (1) Drugs in physiological psychology, (2) Pharmacology, (3) Drugs in society, and (4) Cultural and philosophical overviews. Two appendices are included in the book; one a summary of scientific information about a limited number of common drugs, and the other a guide to bibliographic and search services available. The work should prove quite useful, particularly on the university level, as large numbers of the references come from the more scholarly scientific journals. There is, however, a sprinkling of the popular.

400. American Hospital Association. **Desk Reference on Drug Abuse.** 2d ed.
      Chicago, American Hospital Association, 1971. 76p. bibliog. $1.65.
This book was prepared mainly for hospitals and their personnel who are involved in providing treatment to drug abusers. It is in four sections. The first is on diagnosis and treatment and has its own separate index. The second section is on the hospital and the law. The third section is an extensive bibliography arranged by type of drug. The last section is a good glossary of "drug culture" language.

401. American Hospital Association. **Who Cares About an Alcoholism Program in the General Hospital?** Chicago, American Hospital Association, 1972. 49p. bibliog. $1.50. ISBN 0-87258-088-1.
The first section of this pamphlet-sized manual asks a number of questions about the care of alcoholics and presents some related facts. The second section presents a number of responses to problems and outlines attendant steps. There are several appendices including a statement of admission to the general hospital of patients with alcohol and other drug problems, a typical history of a chronic alcoholic, physical conditions associated with alcoholism, and others.

402. American School Health Association and Pharmaceutical Manufacturers Association. **Teaching about Drugs: Kindergarten through Twelfth Year.** Kent, Ohio, American School Health Association, 1970. 207p. illus. (part col.). bibliog. index. $4.00pa.
This guide was prepared with the assistance of a large group of scientists and educators with the purpose of assisting teachers in planning programs to educate youth about drug abuse and to upgrade the quality of health instruction. The first part of the book presents suggested curricula for each age group, giving objectives to be achieved, comments, suggested learning activities, and lists of resources and materials. The second part is an excellent group of review papers, each by a noted educator and/or scientist. The last section is a collection of "Teaching Aids" which includes suggestions for discussion groups, a glossary of slang terms related to drug usage, a drug abuse products reference chart, photographs of stimulants, depressants, hallucinogens (in color), and a list of signs and symptoms to help identify drug abusers. Although many feel that there has been an "overkill" on teaching young people about drug abuse, this guide is a good one, and it will assist teachers in planning education about drugs and drug abuse as part of the regular health education curriculum.

403. Andrews, Matthew. **The Parents' Guide to Drugs.** Garden City, N.Y., Doubleday and Co., Inc., 1972. 186p. illus. bibliog. index. $6.95. LC 78-144245.
This guide was prepared by a former drug addict, who is a novelist and journalist, for parents, teachers, and concerned adults. It is surprisingly well done. There are several parts to the work. The first is a short discussion of the drugs of abuse.

The scientific information in this section is a bit weak, but some insight is given into the "drug culture," and information is also included on how the illicit drugs are packaged, prepared, priced, and used. The second part is a discussion of the environment, that is, the home, the school, the street, and the law. The third part discusses therapy and includes short sections on the public hospital, private clinics, psychiatric or individual therapy, and encounter or group therapy. Part four is on the parent and tells what to do; gives a glossary of terms used by addicts; a list of organizations and associations interested in drug education; a state directory of agencies giving emergency aid; suggested readings; recommended films; and not recommended films.

404. Austrain, Geoffrey. **The Truth about Drugs.** Garden City, N.Y., Doubleday and Co., Inc., 1971. 131p. illus. $3.50. LC 70-103729.
This book is written in an unusually interesting fashion and is of note because it is particularly suitable for young people in their teens. It tells the story in an accurate, straightforward fashion describing the use of drugs, their effects, history, reasons for their use, and what is being done about the problem. The author pleads no cases for or against the use of drugs, simply tells the facts, which are pretty depressing. The author is a newspaper reporter.

405. Ball, John C., and Earl D. Chambers, eds. **The Epidemiology of Opiate Addiction in the United States.** With a preface by Griffith Edwards. Springfield, Ill., Charles C. Thomas, 1970. 337p. bibliog. index. $15.50. LC 70-126466.
Following a precedent set in other areas of trouble, the term "epidemiology" is further extended in this book outside the realm of infectious diseases to include addiction. The history of drug addiction in the U.S. is traced to the present time. Questions of etiology and prevention are considered. Research findings are presented, and many statistical tables are included. Research workers, planners of health services, and legislators should be interested in the book. The material is divided into parts, as follows: (1) History and present epidemiology, (2) Patterns of drug use in the United States, (3) Opiate use in selected populations, and (4) Medical aspects of opiate addiction.

406. **Behavioral and Social Effects of Marijuana.** Papers by Ernest L. Abel and others. New York, MSS Information Corp., 1973. 175p. bibliog. index. $15.00. LC 72-13500. ISBN 0-8422-7093-0.
This publication is a collection of papers on the various aspects of the chemistry of marijuana. They are research papers, all published previously (from 1970-72) in leading scholarly periodicals. The articles, although somewhat technical for the average reader, will be of interest because they provide the basis for a chemical understanding of the drug. The papers are grouped by broad subject areas as follows: (1) Effects of marijuana on memory and other aspects of mental performance, (2) "Marijuana psychosis" and various perceptual and behavioral responses to marijuana, (3) Personality and attitude among marijuana users, (4) Sociological and legal aspects of the marijuana problem.

407. Blachly, Paul H., ed. **Drug Abuse: Data and Debate.** Springfield, Ill.,
     Charles C. Thomas, 1970. bibliog. index. $12.50. LC 78-119970.
The papers that make up this publication were presented at the Second Annual
Western Institute of Drug Problems Summer School held at Portland State University, August 11-14 1969. The participants were a very diverse group: educators,
physicians and other health professionals, policemen, students, clergymen, pharmacologists, social workers, youth counselors, drug addicts, and others. Consequently, the book will appeal to a wide audience. A great many aspects of the
problem were discussed. Following is a sampling of some of the topics covered:
the subculture of the criminal narcotic addict, development of treatment programs, the role of laboratory work in the analysis and control of drug dependence,
the psychology of drug abusers, laws, drug use and students, society and drugs,
and speculation on where we should go from here.

408. Blachly, P. H., ed. **Drug Abuse—Now.** Proceedings of the Western Institute
     of Drug Problems Summer School, August 9-13 1971, Portland, Oregon.
     Corvallis, Oregon, Oregon State University, 1972. 230p. $5.00pa.
     SBN 87678-414-7.
The papers printed in this publication were presented at the Fourth Annual Western Institute of Drug Problems Summer School in 1971. A great variety of
aspects of the subject are discussed, including moral dilemmas of physicians
operating treatment programs, problems of the mass media, education, drugs in
the military, the ghetto, and the work place, and drug use among parents. Even
drugs and fashion are discussed. The speakers are recognized authorities for the
most part.

409. Blum, Richard H., and Associates. **Drug Dealers: Taking Action.** San
     Francisco, Jossey-Bass Publishers, 1973. 312p. bibliog. index. $10.75.
     LC 76-187065. ISBN 0-87589-166-7.
This work is a companion volume to several others produced by the same group
as part of its program. The group's aim is to provide information and perspectives
helpful in improving present international drug activities and to be useful where
planning new legislation and programs designed to reduce drug abuse problems
are concerned. This particular volume is concerned with drug traffic. The authors
point out that policies need to be attuned to regional realities. Several chapters
deal with international problems and look at the world-wide situation. There are
four sections of the book: (1) Traffic, (2) Policing, (3) After arrest, and (4) Policy.
There are chapters on the following specific topics: (1) Problems associated with
drug-dealing, (2) Substances in illicit drugs, (3) Marijuana use, distribution, and
control, (4) International opiate traffic, (5) Considerations on law enforcement,
(6) The narcotics law in action: a college town, (7) The narcotics law in action:
a major city, (8) Juvenile detention centers, (9) Prisons, (10) Drug-dealing and
the law, (11) Corrections and treatment, (12) Social response to drug problems,
(13) Future research and policy action, (14) Responsibilities of the pharmaceutical industry, (15) Action in the schools, and (16) Taking action. The book ends
with a plea for nations to share their successes with one another in the hope of
finding better solutions to this international problem.

410. Blum, Richard H., and Associates. **Drugs I: Society and Drugs, Social and Cultural Observations.** San Francisco, Jossey-Bass, Inc., 1969. 400p. bibliog. index. $12.50. LC 73-75936. SBN 87589-033-4.

This volume attempts to provide a perspective on the psychoactive drugs. Information is given on marijuana, LSD, heroin, alcohol, and other related drugs of abuse. The history of drug use is traced and an analysis made of present patterns of use among hippies, more normal citizens, and high school and college students. Also, comparisons of drug use among various cultures are made and the results of prolonged use assessed. Drug associations with crime, religion, educational status, and the like are considered. The author is a psychologist and is director of the Psychopharmacology Project at the Institute for the Study of Human Problems at Stanford University. Much of the material presented in the book is based on investigations conducted at the Institute. A companion volume authored by the same group is called *Drugs II: Students and Drugs, College and High School Observations* (reviewed below).

411. Blum, Richard H., and Associates. **Drugs II: Students and Drugs, College and High School Observations.** San Francisco, Jossey-Bass, Inc., 1969. bibliog. index. $12.50. LC 73-75936. SBN 87589-034-2.

This publication is a companion volume to *Drugs I: Society and Drugs, Social and Cultural Observations* by the same authors. The emphasis in *Drugs II* is on student drug abuse. Chapter headings are as follows: (1) Prologue: students and drugs, (2) Drugs on five campuses, (3) Those who do, those who do not, (4) Student characteristics and major drugs, (5) Student characteristics, minor drugs, and motivation, (6) Correlations and factor analysis, (7) Users of approved drugs, (8) Users of illicit drugs, (9) Bad outcomes on campus, (10) Students' drug diaries, (11) A follow-up study, (12) Student ideologies compared, (13) Life style interviews, (14) Psychological tests, (15) Horatio Alger's children, case studies, (16) Predicting who will turn on, (17) Psychiatric problems, (18) Drugs and Catholic students, (19) Drugs and high school students, (20) Overview for administrators, and (21) Epilogue: students and drugs.

An attempt is made to characterize, perhaps not very successfully, the kind of student who uses or experiments with drugs. It is evident, however, that drug use was very prevalent in schools at the time the book was written—in the West Coast area, at least.

412. Bourne, Peter G., and Ruth Fox, eds. **Alcoholism: Progress in Research and Treatment.** New York and London, Academic, 1973. 439p. bibliog. index. $21.00. LC 72-82638.

The rising concern over the abuse of drugs in the U.S. has brought about recognition of the fact that the major drug problem is alcohol. It is a drug that can be obtained easily and legally, and is socially acceptable. This volume, which was prepared by a number of experts, explores about every aspect of the problem—biochemical effects, cross-cultural studies of drinking patterns, the behavior of alcoholics, the effect on family life, legal aspects, genetic aspects, and treatment. Treatment by private practitioners, nonphysicians, and the success of Alcoholics Anonymous are evaluated. The need for more research and more effective treatment is stressed. Physicians, medical students, social workers, biochemists, and laymen will all be interested in this book. It is excellent, but it does not leave one with the feeling that great progress is about to be made, but rather that there is much to be done.

413. Brecher, Edward M., and the Editors of Consumer Reports. **Licit and Illicit Drugs.** The Consumers Union Report on Narcotics, Stimulants, Depressants, Inhalants, Hallucinogens, and Marijuana—Including Caffeine, Nicotine, and Alcohol. Boston, Toronto, Little, Brown and Co., 1972. 623p. index. bibliog. $12.50. LC 75-186972. ISBN 0-316-15340-0.

This report was undertaken because the editors felt that the illicit drug scene in the U.S. was becoming intolerable. All aspects of drug abuse are taken up, the pharmacology, the effects of drug laws, drug policies, and drug attitudes. Each drug is presented in its historical perspective. It is interesting to note that the "licit" drugs referred to are caffeine, nicotine, and alcohol; and many readers may feel that caffeine and nicotine are not quite in the same class as alcohol. The work is well documented and thorough. It ends with recommendations that the authors hope will point the way to both short-term and long-term improvements in the critical situation. There is no claim that they constitute a panacea. Many readers may feel that implementing the recommendation will not improve matters at all.

414. Bridge, Carl J. **Alcoholism and Driving.** Springfield, Ill., Charles C. Thomas, 1972. 84p. index. $7.00. LC 78-187647. ISBN 0-398-02243-7.

The author's point of view is that the drunk driving arrest can serve as a resource for a study of alcoholism and to clarify alcoholism's relationship to driving. His study shows that most people arrested for drunk driving are alcoholics. He feels that possible improvement of the current drunk driving problem could be brought about through further research along these lines.

The book reviews the general problems of alcoholism very well. There is a discussion of how deterioration, from subtle loss of judgment to extreme deterioration, correlate with driving characteristics. The author feels that alcoholics must be kept off the road until there is a definite remission of the illness. Statistics from other studies are cited, and new insights into alcoholism are described. Chapter headings are as follows: 1) Introduction, 2) Preliminary observations, 3) Conduct of the study, 4) Rating the disease, 5) Review of 200 arrests, 6) Preliminary conclusions from this series, 7) Added illustrative case, 8) Alcoholism and mental illness, 9) Alcoholic drivers not arrested, 10) Alcoholics are drivers, 11) Drug abuse and driving, 12) Interpersonal relationships among alcoholics, 13) Stark realities, 14) The nature of alcoholism, 15) How to deal with the problem?

415. Brill, Leon, and Louis Lieberman, eds. **Major Modalities in the Treatment of Drug Abuse.** New York, Behavioral Publications, 1972. 313p. $12.95. LC 77-174270.

This book has as its objective to present descriptions of the major modalities currently employed in the treatment of drug abusers. It is confined to a discussion of what is being done in the way of treatment and what additional efforts are required to solve the problem of drug abuse and addiction. In the various articles that make up the book, the authors present the treatments they prefer. It is felt, however, that no one treatment is suitable for every case, as addicts have different social and psychological characteristics as well as physical ones.

A number of institutions and agencies are discussed, including the U.S. Public Health Service and Institutional Treatment Program for Narcotic Addicts and the NIMH Clinical Research Center at Lexington, Kentucky, and the Addiction Services Agency of the City of New York. Methadone maintenance is treated, as is the role of religion in the treatment of opiate addiction. The reports on the agencies include the following usually: brief history, staffing, treatment goals, treatment methods, typical case study, findings, pros and cons, and implications for other problems. This book should have implications in the treatment of other social problems, such as alcoholism, vagrancy, prostitution, criminality and delinquency, and mental illness.

416. Brown, Clinton C., and Charles Savage, eds. **The Drug Abuse Controversy.** Baltimore, National Educational Consultants, Inc., 1971. 270p. bibliog. $8.50. LC 77-185832. ISBN 0-87971-002-0.

This book is a collection of formal presentations made at a symposium held October 16, 1970. The speakers were psychiatrists, psychologists, sociologists, ministers, lawyers, and administrators who were familiar with some facet of the topic. They discussed the ways organized society could restrict, prevent, punish, prohibit, modify, alter, dissuade, and eliminate the growing practice of drug abuse. According to the preface, the "controversy" mentioned refers to the differences of opinion between one group who uses drugs which they claim temper and restrict life's experiences and the other group which is vehement in its contention that individuals are suppressed by both law and tradition and seek enlightment, liberation, and extended vision through drugs. The reviewer presumes that this is another way of identifying the "establishment" and the new, young, group of drug abusers. No mention is made of a group who do not use drugs, or who use practically none. Also, it should be mentioned that most scientists hold the view that drugs do not give one "extended vision," hallucinations being a more accurate term.

The book does present a viewpoint that is sometimes presented and therefore is worthy of note, perhaps. Topics covered are as follows: 1) Drugs and the law: a legal controversy, 2) Drugs and the individual: a controversy of ethics, 3) Drugs and the new order: a controversy of change, 4) Drugs and doctors: a treatment controversy, 5) Drugs and conclusions: an unfinished answer.

417. Burg, Nan C. **Forces Against Drug Abuse: Education, Legislation, Rehabilitation: A Selected Bibliography.** Monticello, Ill. Council of Planning Librarians, 1971. 11p. (Council of Planning Librarians. Exchange Bibliography 231). $1.50pa.

The bibliography, the purpose of which is to point out what counterforces are coming to the fore to cope with the problem of drug abuse and how strong these are or may become, lists both articles and books. The compiler has divided these counterforces into three groups: education, legislation, and rehabilitation and has divided the entries accordingly under these topics. The articles listed appear to be well selected from a wide variety of sources.

418. Cahalan, Don, Ira H. Cisin, and Helen M. Crossley. **American Drinking Practices: A National Study of Drinking Behavior and Attitudes.** New Brunswick, N. J., Rutgers Center of Alcohol Studies, Publications Division, 1969. 260p. bibliog. index. (Rutgers Center of Alcohol Studies No. 6). $9.50. LC 70-626701. SBN 911290-37-0.

The authors have attempted to place the problems of alcohol use in realistic context and have made a demographic analysis of alcohol users. They have described man in society using alcoholic beverages and having attitudes about that use. The methods used in making the study are of interest as well as the results of the study. A large amount of statistical data is presented both in the text and in numerous charts and tables. The publication is a valuable and unusual contribution to the study of alcohol and man.

419. Cahn, Sidney. **The Treatment of Alcoholics: An Evaluative Study.** New York, Oxford University Press, 1970. 246p. bibliog. index. $7.50. LC 75-83032.

This book, prepared by a member of the Cooperative Commission on the Study of Alcoholism, is a study of state and local programs and services for alcoholics. The agencies studied are of several types, governmental, voluntary, and private. The strengths and weaknesses of the various approaches to treating alcoholics are discussed, and proposals for improving them are suggested. A major theme of the book is that treatment for alcoholics must be viewed in the context of total community health and welfare activities. The material for the study is based on visits to various communities about the U.S. and Canada, and interviews with persons working with alcoholics. The problems of alcoholics are described and analyzed with particular reference to variations in social class. Although treatment of alcoholics has not been notably successful, the author's recommendations for improvements will be welcomed by those who are working with the problem and by those who are interested in it.

420. Canada. Commission of Inquiry into the Non-Medical Use of Drugs. **Report. Treatment.** Ottawa, Information Canada, 1972. 125p. illus. bibliog. index. $1.75. Catalogue No. H21-5370/3.

This report is a final one on findings, conclusions, and recommendations with respect to treatment of effects of nonmedical drug use. A final report of all findings and recommendations is to be made later. In this report, the various methods of treating the adverse physical and psychological conditions resulting from drug use are discussed. The concepts of the sickness and treatment are discussed first, then follows a brief description of those conditions which call for medical intervention. Then the various goals and kinds of therapeutic intervention are outlined. Other chapters are as follows: treatment of opiate dependence, treatment of high dose amphetamine (speed) dependence, treatment of alcoholism, hallucinogens, short-term medical management, therapeutic communities, organization and coordination of community treatment services, other therapeutic approaches, and cost estimate of a treatment complex.

421. Carone, Pasquale A., and Leonard W. Krinsky. **Drug Abuse in Industry.** Springfield, Ill., Charles C. Thomas, 1973. 172p. index. $11.50. LC 73-228. ISBN 0-398-02801-X.

The material in this book is based on papers and discussion presented at a conference "Drug Abuse in Industry" held at South Oaks, Long Island, New York, in April 1972. The topic is quite timely. Representatives of both management and labor, the academic community, psychiatrists, psychologists, physicians, medical directors of companies, and directors of state agencies were participants. Four basic aspects of drug abuse were presented: 1) The physiological effects, 2) Clinical and treatment aspects, 3) Labor-management views of the problem, and 4) Legal aspects. Included are discussions of therapeutic community models with their pros and cons contrasted to methadone maintenance units; criteria for employment and reemployment; detection and treatment of the drug-using employee; findings of the medical examiner and neuropathologist; how the labor movement sees this major problem; and views and programs of the probation department.

422. Cassel, Russell N. **Drug Abuse Education.** North Quincy, Mass., Christopher Publishing House, 1971. 379p. illus. bibliog. index. $5.95.
LC 77-125922. SBN 8158-0245-5.
This book is a programmed text, designed for self study. It presents useful information to interested individuals on the use of dangerous drugs. It is particularly intended for use with teenagers and young people in the senior high schools of the country, but can also be used by others such as teachers, nurses, and police. The following sections are included: 1) Nature and classes of dangerous drugs, 2) States of effect for dangerous drugs, 3) Nature and types of drug addiction, 4) Reasons for illegal use of dangerous drugs, 5) Treatment programs for drug dependence, 6) Drug abuse education based on rules of evidence, 7) Drug control laws in the United States, 8) The drug users' "Argot" and vocabulary.

423. Clark, Evert, and Nicholas Horrock. **Contrabandista!** New York, Praeger, 1973. 231p. $6.95. LC 72-87296.
This book, which reads somewhat like a novel, is the story of a scheme for smuggling heroin wholesale into the United States by light plane from South America. Eventually the *Contrabandistas* were outmaneuvered and caught by a small but determined group of U.S. narcotic agents and international intelligence operatives. The kingpin of the heroin ring, Auguste Joseph Ricard, was extradited to the U.S. from Paraguay and was tried and convicted in New York federal court. The authors, a *Newsweek* magazine team, have related the story in a fascinating manner.

424. **Controlled Substances Handbook.** Arlington, Va., Controlled Substances Information, Inc., 1972. 1v.(various paging). looseleaf. $20.00.
LC 72-75168.
The purpose of this handbook is to provide information to Bureau of Narcotics and Dangerous Drugs Registrants. The publication contains the text of the Controlled Substances Act, P.L. 91-513 of 1970, an updated version of the regulations, and an explanation of the regulations written in everyday language which can be applied to real situations. Virtually every person who handles drugs must register with the Bureau. This includes manufacturers, distributors, wholesalers, practitioners, such as physicians, dentists, veterinarians, scientists, pharmacies (not pharmacists), and hospitals Sections are included on labeling and packaging

requirements, records and reports, order forms, schedules of controlled substances, and other like matters.

425. Danaceau, Paul. **Methadone Maintenance: The Experience of Four Pro-
     grams.** Washington, Drug Abuse Council, Inc. 1973. 109p. $1.25.
     LC 73-81224.

This publication is the first report of the Council's monograph series. Since the
methadone treatment has become more important during the last decade in
treating heroin addiction, this report is of interest. Four programs are presented
and summarized. These are: 1) The Adolescent Development Program in New
York City, which is a clinic caring exclusively for adolescents from one large
urban high school. Supportive services are emphasized. 2) The Drug Rehabilitation Clinic in New Orleans, a "fee for service" clinic providing methadone without supportive services. 3) The East Boston Drug Rehabilitation Clinic, which has
a primarily white, working class patient population and emphasizes psychological services. 4) La Llave (The Key) Drug Rehabilitation Program in Albuquerque,
developed from the concern of the Chicano community and which operates primarily within that culture. The issue of community control has influenced this
program's development. The author of the report is a journalist and a former
staff director of a U.S. Senate subcommittee. The reports of the programs do
not evaluate them scientifically. They are rather reports of the experience of the
programs.

426. Dawtry, Frank, ed. **Social Problems of Drug Abuse: A Guide for Social
     Workers.** Edited on behalf of the National Association of Probation Offi-
     cers. New York, Appleton-Century-Crofts; London, Butterworths, 1968.
     115p. illus.(col). bibliog. index. $2.65pa.

This book was written to assist practicing social workers. Although it is a British
book, most of what is said applies to situations in the United States as well.
There are two parts presented, the first on the social problem of drugs and the
second on background information on drugs. There is useful information on the
role of the probation officer, clinics, treatment, law, and a social workers' dictionary is included with medical, trade and popular terms in drug lore and literature.
In addition, there is a list of treatment and rehabilitation facilities located in
Great Britain.

427. Densen-Gerber, Judianne. **We Mainline Dreams: The Odyssey House Story.**
     Garden City, New York, Doubleday and Co., Inc., 1973. 421p. illus.
     $9.95. LC 72-89302. ISBN 0-385-00371-4.

This book is a description of one of the most successful programs in the country
for curing drug addicts, the Odyssey House. Written by the founder and director,
the story is told of the rigorous and often unorthodox methods of treatment and
of the early difficulties in getting support for the program. Also, a good deal of
the book is taken up with biographical accounts, a personal story about the author
herself and about the ex-addicts and professionals who run the program. The
author is a distinguished physician and lawyer who showed special concern for
child addicts and addicted mothers when the program was getting underway. The
Odyssey houses have now grown to include 33 establishments in six states which
are flourishing. The treatment seems to work; it is claimed that most of the

addicts treated can return to the community. The book is unusual, fascinating, and presents some insightful ideas about how addicts may be handled. The houses are tough-minded, structured psychiatric therapeutic communities that are most effective with addicts who don't want treatment, but must stay because the courts have sent them there, refuting the idea that an addict must seek treatment himself in order for it to be successful. The Odyssey houses believe in accountability. Residents are held responsible for their actions. It is felt that accountability is part of getting addicts well; the fundamental cause of most addiction is an inability to think in terms of consequences.

428. Drug Abuse Survey Project. **Dealing with Drug Abuse: A Report to the Ford Foundation.** Foreword by McGeorge Bundy. New York, Praeger Publishers, 1972. 396p. $8.95. LC 77-189472.

This book presents the summary of the findings and conclusions of a survey conducted under the auspices of the Ford Foundation in the latter part of 1970 with updating. The group making the study was made up of experts in medicine, psychiatry, law, and economics. The volume contains, in addition to the findings, conclusions, and recommendations, staff papers as follows: 1) The drugs and their effects, 2) Drug education, 3) Treatment and rehabilitation, 4) The economics of heroin, 5) Federal expenditures on drug-abuse control, 6) Altered states of consciousness, and 7) Narcotics addiction and control in Great Britain.

No startling new discoveries were made. The group feels that alleviation of the drug abuse problem will come "through a slow and painful process of social change and accommodation." The major recommendations called for the establishment of an independent Drug Abuse Council, to sponsor basic research, fund treatment and education programs, evaluate treatment approaches, and disseminate information. Such a council was formed under the aegis of the Carnegie Corporation, the Commonwealth Fund, and the Henry J. Kaiser Family Foundation, in addition to the Ford Foundation.

429. Dunn, William L., Jr., ed. **Smoking Behavior: Motives and Incentives.** Washington, V. H. Winston and Sons, 1973. Distributed by the Halsted Press Division of John Wiley and Sons. 309p. bibliog. index. $9.95. LC 72-13271. ISBN 0-470-22746-X.

This publication is made up of papers presented at a conference sponsored by the Council for Tobacco Research—U.S.A., Inc., in January 1972. The conferees, who were a representative group of life, behavioral, and social scientists, were asked to reply to the question "What are the motivational mechanisms sustaining cigarette smoking behavior?" Most experts agree that a pharmacological effect, probably mediated by nicotine, is sought by the smoker under conditions that have an emotional impact. The authors of the papers attempt to outline the underlying mechanisms and processes to explain why 35% of Americans adults smoke. Some of the titles of the contributions are as follows: neuropsychopharmacology of nicotine and tobacco smoking; additional characteristic EEG differences between smokers and nonsmokers; personality and the maintenance of the smoking habit; the relationship of smoking and habits of nervous tension; effects of nicotine on avoidance, conditioned suppression and aggression response measures in animals and man; the effects of smoking on mood change;

smoking attitudes and practices in seven preliterate societies; motivational conflicts engendered by the on-going discussion of cigarette smoking; smoking behavior 1953 and 1970: the midtown Manhattan study; the social sciences and the
smoking problem.

430. Duster, Troy. **The Legislation of Morality: Law, Drugs, and Moral Judgment.** New York, The Free Press, a division of the Macmillan Co., 1970.
274p. bibliog. index. $6.95. LC 72-80469.

This book examines the connection between laws and morals by tracing the history and evolution of narcotic laws. The author's point of view is that narcotics
morality was a direct consequence of legal change and cites many documents to
support his point. The traditional idea is that the opposite situation prevails, that
is, that morality is followed by its codification in law. The author, who is a
sociologist, believes this is true for other current issues and problems.

It is hoped that the volume contributes to both social science theory and to policy decisions on reform of narcotics legislation and the treatment of addicts. The
study should interest sociologists, political scientists, psychologists, lawyers,
legislators, and those interested in the narcotics problem.

431. Eckert, William G., ed. **The Medical, Legal and Law Enforcement Aspects
of Drugs and Drug Abuse: A Bibliography of Classic and Current References.** Wichita, Kansas, Laboratory of St. Francis Hospital, 1972. 97p.
index. $12.00.

The bibliography is preceded by brief text material on narcotic drugs, hallucinogens, and depressants and stimulants. The material was reprinted from recent
issues of newsletters of INFORM (The International Reference Organization in
Forensic Medicine and Sciences.) The compiler is the editor of INFORM. The
bibliography includes 2,500 items, the references taken from many sources such
as the National Library of Medicine publications, and selected abstracts and articles published by INTERPOL and the Legal Index. A subject and author index
has been provided. The list should prove of value to physicians in general practice, psychiatrists, clinical toxicologists, lawyers, law enforcement officers, forensic scientists, and laymen.

432. Eddy, Nathan B. **The National Research Council Involvement in the Opiate
Problem, 1928-1971.** Washington, National Academy of Sciences, 1973.
313p. bibliog. index. $10.50. LC 73-3392.

This book is a report on the work of the Committee on Problems of Drug Dependence (previously known by other similar titles) of the National Research Council. This Committee was for 42 years concerned with the support of laboratory
and clinical research on problems related to drug addiction and dependence, and
in addition, has more recently offered its wisdom and experience to government
agencies responsible for traffic in drugs and concerned with the problems of
addicts. The author, a well-known scientist, spent the major portion of his career
involved in activities relating to narcotics and the affairs of the Committee. The
book is a running account of the work of the Committee and the work done
under its auspices, its deliberations, and conclusions. The Committee has made
important contributions in structure-action relationships of drugs and a better

understanding of drug dependence and addiction. In addition, it has been a major force in promoting cooperation among government and private agencies, including industry, in the interest of public health and to avoid a health hazard. The bibliographies included, which list articles that report on work supported by the Committee, are very extensive, and have their own separate index. In addition, a few letters and documents of interest have been reproduced in an appendix as have facts concerning Committee meetings, membership, research funds, and grant programs.

433. Einstein, Stanley. **The Use and Misuse of Drugs: A Social Dilemma.** Belmont, California, Wadsworth Publishing Co., Inc., 1970. 86p. bibliog. index. $1.25pa. LC 79-107371.

This small book is part of the series called "Basic Concepts in Health Science." There are eight chapters as follows: 1) Introduction, 2) Drugs: problems, considerations, and definitions, 3) Drug users: their characteristics, patterns of drug use, and behavior, 4) Drugs: types, uses, and effects, 5) Misuse of drugs and the community's response, 6) Treatment and legal control of drug use, 7) Economics of drug use and misuse, and 8) Further considerations. The author, who is Executive Director and founder of the Institute for the Study of Drug Addiction in New York City, says his guiding philosophy is 1) that alcoholism and drug addiction are but two of a number of behaviors that are tied together generically (drug addiction, gambling, smoking, overeating, alcoholism), and 2) that the most meaningful way to view any of these problems is by use of an epidemiological frame of reference: host, agent, environment, and their interactions. He concludes that the state of scientific knowledge, the skill of caretaker staffs, community attitudes and values, the types and goals of treatment programs, education and training, public policy, and economics must be understood before any large-scale success is experienced in the treatment of drug addiction. Also, the philosophy of progress through chemistry must be kept in mind. And lastly, we must come to terms with the fact that at present our society reinforces rather than inhibits the misuse of drugs.

434. Fort, Joel. **Alcohol: Our Biggest Drug Problem.** New York, McGraw-Hill Book Co., 1973. 180p. illus. bibliog. index. $6.95. LC 72-12746. ISBN 0-07-021598-7; 0-07-021599-5pa.

The author of this work, who is a physician, explains his point of view regarding the use of alcohol. He has crusaded for having it recognized as a drug and as a major drug problem and to stop alcohol advertising. He treats alcohol in the same context as marijuana, heroin, or cocaine. He also crusades for better treatment for alcoholics. In addition, the flourishing alcohol industry is severely criticized. The book is interesting as the viewpoint presented is a somewhat new one and is one that is currently getting attention.

435. Frykman, John H. **A New Connection: An Approach to Persons Involved in Compulsive Drug Use.** San Francisco, Scrimshaw Press, 1971. 116p. bibliog. $2.25. LC 74-156775. ISBN 0-912020-12-1.

This book is a guide that may be of value to counselors, teachers, social workers, correction officers, and others working with persons who have drug abuse problems. The author sees drug abusers as persons with low self esteem, high approval needs, and deficient problem solving techniques. This book is intended for those who want to have a better understanding of these people. It suggests ways to create a climate of trust, rapport, and communication in which a troubled person will feel free to examine his feelings. Chapter headings are as follows: 1) Observations on drug abuse and its treatment, 2) Counseling: attitudes and actions, 3) Dependent relationships: bereavement, 4) Group work: comments and suggestions, 5) Basic drug information, 6) Coping with drug crises and withdrawal, 7) Drug treatment programs: organization and operation, 8) Glossary of drug-related slang terms. The author has had a good deal of counseling training and experience with drug users.

436. Gamage, J. R., and E. L. Zerkin. **A Comprehensive Guide to the English-Language Literature on Cannabis (Marihuana).** Beloit, Wisconsin, STASH Press, 1969. 265p. index. $5.95.

This comprehensive bibliography deals with all areas of the subject including the medical, psychiatric, psychological, pharmacological, chemical, biochemical, botanical, sociological, anthropological, religious, and legal. The main section is arranged alphabetically by author, and an abstract accompanies each entry giving significant findings, the general position of the author, and the methodology used in reports of research. The subject section gives full citations also, but not the abstracts. The author index included seems to be of limited value as the main list is arranged by author. However, it does assist in locating articles by co-authors. The journals covered, which are listed, are mostly on the scholarly research level.

437. Gerard, Donald L., and Gerhart Saenger. **Out-Patient Treatment of Alcoholism: A Study of Outcome and Its Determinants.** Toronto, University of Toronto Press for the Alcoholism and Drug Addiction Research Foundation of Ontario, 1966. 249p. bibliog.(Brookside Monograph No. 4). $10.00. SBN 8020-3153-6.

This report is based on a study undertaken in 1957 to 1962 to determine the results of treatment services for alcoholics. The main objectives were to secure a picture of contemporary clinic treatment of alcoholism in the United States and to develop suitable standards for the evaluation of treatment offered in alcoholism clinics. The following questions were asked and answered: 1) What kinds of patients come to state-supported alcoholism clinics? 2) What kind of treatment is offered? 3) What changes take place in the patients? and 4) To what extent is change related to the characteristics of patients and/or the treatment provided? Some of the findings will surprise many therapists. For instance, drugs such as barbiturates, vitamins, and tranquillizers in outpatient treatment were not very effective. The drug Antabuse (disulfiram) was found to be rather effective, however. Psychiatric therapy was not as effective as treatment by internists. Perhaps more significant was the finding that the therapy used should match the pathology of the patient. His personality structure, social and cultural milieu, and attitude toward himself and the world should be considered. The study cut across the disciplines of psychiatry, public health, sociology, and psychology and should be of value to professionals in these fields and to laymen who are interested.

438. Gibbins, R. J., with the assistance of B. W. Henheffer and A. Raison. **Chronic Alcoholism and Alcohol Addiction: A Survey of Current Literature.** Toronto, Alcoholism Research Foundation, 1953. 57p. bibliog. (Brookside Monograph No. 1). $6.50. LC 55-31954. ISBN 0-8020-7014-0.

This publication makes a distinction between "chronic alcoholism" and "alcohol addiction." The outstanding criterion in the latter is the inability to break with the habit. Also, addicts are designated as primary or true addicts and secondary addicts. The author does explain, however, that there are a variety of classifications of abnormal drinkers used. The literature of the subject is explored and the findings of researchers reported. Although the book is old, the material seems to be pertinent and of interest still, perhaps because relatively little progress has been made in dealing with the problem of alcoholism. The material is presented in three parts: etiology, psychological investigations of alcohol addiction, and treatment.

439. **Grassroots.** Madison, Wisconsin, published cooperatively by the Student Association for the Study of Hallucinogens, Inc. (STASH) and the National Coordinating Council on Drug Education. 1971– . About six volumes, looseleaf. $85.00 per year.

This publication, although curious and unconventional in format, is invaluable for those wanting information on drug abuse. Materials covering all aspects of the subject are sent out monthly to subscribers to be inserted in the looseleaf binders. The material is reprinted from many sources. In addition, some pamphlet and newsletter publications are included with the subscription than can be inserted also. The materials which are furnished are divided into well-chosen subject areas. Some of these are: history, socio-cultural aspects, psychology, epidemiology, drug education, speakers clearinghouse, ongoing research, prevention, community action, underground digest, treatment and rehabilitation, law and public policy, street drugs, grants and contracts, upcoming meetings, alcohol, narcotics, stimulants, hallucinogens, cannabis, and other drugs. Also, books, films, and other audio-visuals are evaluated.

Two of the *Grassroots* volumes are special publications. One, called *Grassroots Directory of Drug Information and Treatment Organizations*, a state-by-state listing of drug group services, is reviewed separately as is the other which is called *Speed: The Current Index to the Drug Abuse Literature*.

The *Grassroots* materials are very useful, particularly to students preparing papers on various aspects of drug abuse, community groups, speakers, and many others.

440. **Grassroots Directory of Drug Information and Treatment Organizations.** Madison, Wisconsin, Student Association for the Study of Hallucinogens, Inc. (STASH) and the National Coordinating Council on Drug Education. 1971– . looseleaf.

This publication comes with a subscription to the *Grassroots* publication which is reviewed separately. The directory is a looseleaf volume to which new listings and corrections are made from time to time. The arrangement is alphabetical by state. Included are such organizations as counseling and referral services, detoxification programs, drug analysis, programs, education and information services, free clinics, government agencies, hotlines, inpatient services, law enforcement agencies, methadone maintenance, outpatient services, and religious drug use. The information about each agency includes such things as name, address, phone, description of programs and services, publications, clientele, financial data, and names of staff and officers.

441. Halpern, Susan. **Drug Abuse and Your Company.** American Management Association, Inc., 1972. 145p. index. (An AMA Research Book). $11.50. LC 79-184053. ISBN 0-8144-5294-9.

This is an important book because the recent increase in drug abuse has made it every company's problem among employees. The intent of the book is to make known the extent of the problem, the experiences of other companies, and what is being done to alleviate the situation. The material is based on surveys from 231 companies, interviews with about 75 company executives, and available literature.

There are four chapters as follows: 1) Highlights for management, 2) Detection methods, 3) Dealing with the problem, and 4) Recommendations. Also included are three appendices: A) Drug chart, B) Terminology, and C) Legal questions and answers. In addition, there are a number of exhibits presented such as sample laboratory procedure for urine screening for drugs, drug policies and policy statements of various companies, and excerpts from drug treatment programs. It is hoped that other companies can profit from the information presented in implementing their own policies and programs.

442. Healy, Patrick F., and James P. Manak, eds. **Drug Dependence and Abuse Resource Book.** Chicago, National District Attorneys Association, 1971. 581p. bibliog. $10.00pa. LC 78-149765.

The editors read and evaluated many hundreds of articles, then selected and reprinted in this volume the ones they thought represented the best on its topic, regardless of the age of the article. The papers are grouped under four classifications as follows: 1) The problem of drug dependence and abuse and the role of law in a free society, 2) The problem of drug dependence and abuse and the role of education and preventive programs, 3) The problem of drug dependence and abuse: the social perspective, 4) The problem of drug dependence and abuse: the medical perspective. In addition, there are some useful appendices; especially valuable is an annotated bibliography of books, pamphlets, paper presentations and articles and an annotated listing of films, filmstrips, video tapes and film distributors. Also, a glossary of slang terms is included.

The position of the National District Attorneys Association is that the only solution to the drug problem is education, and it hopes that this presentation will assist in that task.

443. Herner and Company, comps. **Directory of On-Going Research in Smoking and Health, 1972.** 4th ed. Washington, GPO, 1972. 301p. DHEW Publication No. (HSM) 72-7523.

This is an international directory of research pertaining to smoking and its relationship to health. It includes activities in the agricultural, biochemical, medical, behavioral, psychological, and related fields. 578 research projects are described. The descriptions are arranged alphabetically by the name of the performing organization, the principal investigators, project title, objective, methods or approach, results to date, future plans, project dates, source of financial support, and references. There are several indexes: subject, principal investigators, sponsors, geographical, and organizations.

444. Hershey, Martin H., ed. **Drug Abuse Law Review—1971**. Albany and New York, Sage Hill Publishers and Clark Boardman Co., Ltd., 1971. 767p. bibliog. index. $29.50. LC 73-163724. SBN 87632-045-0.

This is the first volume of a projected annual series that will attempt to collect the best current periodical literature dealing with the legal aspects of drug abuse. The book covers the following topics: informative drug knowledge, sociological problems—treatment, legislative and legal concerns, statistical information, international and foreign approach.

445. Hochman, Joel Simon. **Marijuana and Social Evolution** . . . . Englewood Cliffs, N. J., Prentice-Hall, Inc., 1972. 184p. bibliog. index. $5.95. LC 72-8952. ISBN 0-13-556217-1. 0-13-556209-0pa.

The author's point of view is that marijuana has replaced alcohol as the drug that is "in" among young people as the great regulator of human emotions. This book attempts to give more information on the effects of the drug within the context of society. The conclusions are based on surveys, interviews, and literature sources.

446. James, W. Paul, Clifford E. Salter, and H. George Thomas. **Alcohol and Drug Dependence**. London, King Edward's Hospital Fund for London, 1972. 98p. illus. bibliog. index. £1.50pa.

This report correlates therapeutic principles with the planning and design of facilities for the treatment of alcoholism and drug dependence. The authors have studied facilities in England, Scotland, and the United States and describe some of them and include floor plans. Considerable attention is given to the staff/patient ratio. Also, recommendations are given about what should be done in the future to cope with the problem. The need for prevention measures, training of staff, and additional research are pointed out.

447. Johnston, Lloyd. **Drugs and American Youth**. A report from the Youth in Transition project. Ann Arbor, Mich., Institute for Social Research, University of Michigan, 1973. 273p. bibliog. index. $7.00. LC 71-190022. ISBN 0-87944-120-8pa; 0-87944-133-X.

This book presents research which is a part of a large nationwide study of adolescent boys begun in 1966 under the primary sponsorship of the U.S. Office of Education. The study, called *Youth in Transition*, followed a panel of young men from 1966 to 1970. The main objective of the study was concerned with the causes and consequences of dropping out of high school; however, several additional areas were studied, one of which is reported in this book. Chapter headings are as follows: 1) An introduction to the study, 2) The use of drugs during and after high school, 3) The attitudes of youth toward drug taking, 4) Background and intelligence related to drug use, 5) Drugs and the high school experience, 6) Paths taken after high school, 7) Drugs, delinquency, and alienation, and 8) Summary and policy implications. The report contains a great deal of valuable statistical data. The most important conclusion is that all in all it was found that the amount of non-addictive illegal drug use has been much less for young people of the U.S. than the media has been suggesting and its effects far less serious than most Americans have assumed.

448. Jones, Kenneth L., Louis W. Shainberg, and Curtis O. Byer. **Drugs and Alcohol.** 2d ed. New York, Harper and Row, 1973. 162p. illus. bibliog. index. $5.00. LC 72-12003. SBN 06-043429-5.

This book, according to the authors, presents the basic information vital to young people when making important decisions concerning their potential use of drugs, including alcohol. This basic information, a good deal of it scientific, is accurate and well-presented. The illustrations and diagrams are unusually helpful. In addition, laws and restrictions governing drug distribution are discussed; medical use of drugs is investigated; and drug groups are placed within a continuum of actions and effects on the central nervous system. Also, the part emotional and psychological problems play in drug and alcohol abuse are taken up. A good glossary is included.

449. Josiah Macy, Jr., Foundation. **Medical Education and Drug Abuse: Report of a Macy Conference.** New York, Josiah Macy, Jr., Foundation, 1973. 17p. $2.50pa.

This small pamphlet is a summary report of a conference held October 16-18 1972 in New York City. The foundation and Rockefeller University invited 30 individuals representing broad interests in medical education to meet in conference to consider the problem of drug abuse and to emphasize prevention and treatment. The names of the participants are included, a group of well-known individuals from the basic science and clinical departments of medical schools, federal and state agencies, professional associations, and the pharmaceutical industry. The report is very short and abbreviated, but it points out the major responsibilities and the role of medical education where drug abuse is concerned.

450. Labin, Suzanne. **Hippies, Drugs, and Promiscuity.** Translated by Stephanie Winston. New Rochelle, N.Y., Arlington House, 1972. index. $7.95. LC 70-189375. ISBN 0-87000-156-6.

The author, who is a native Parisian, traveled thousands of miles to observe the hippie members of the counterculture in the U.S., Canada, France, England, Italy, Germany, Sweden, the Netherlands, India, Nepal, and Afghanistan. She talked with the young people, policemen, parents, and diplomats, and read the hippie press. The book is well-written in the style of case histories and the novel. The reader is given a tour of the hippie world and a view of their drugs, clothes, hygienic habits (or lack of them), and their philosophy of life. There is good deal about drug use and descriptions of them. At the end, the author makes a plea for the young people to change their ways before it is too late. She says the newspapers have not exaggerated the seriousness of the problem. The number of runaways is very large, and never in history has drug abuse been so widespread.

451. Levine, Samuel F. **Narcotics and Drug Abuse: Being a Volume of the Criminal Justice Text Series.** Cincinnati, W. H. Anderson Co., 1973. 438p. illus. (col.) bibliog. index. $12.00. LC 73-80937.

This book was written by an officer of the law to help police officers and others who are involved with drug abuse problems such as legislators, physicians, educators, scientists, and governmental enforcement agencies. The book will assist the reader in understanding the practical mechanics of drug investigation and bring about some understanding of the broader social context in which the problem must be encountered and dealt with. Chapter headings are as follows: 1) Introduction, 2) The drugs of abuse, 3) Development of illicit traffic in narcotic drugs, 4) The evolution of narcotics and dangerous drug laws, 5) Comprehensive drug abuse prevention and control act, 6) International and national police organizations, 7) State and local enforcement organizations, 8) Case initiation and objectives, 9) Effective case development, 10) Field tests and abuser identification, 11) The crime of addiction, 12) Comprehensive treatment and rehabilitation, 13) Abuse prevention and youth, 14) Officers' case experience. In addition, there is an appended glossary of terms and a section on community drug abuse prevention programs.

452. Lieberman, Florence, Phyllis Caroff, and Mary Gottesfeld. **Before Addiction: How to Help Youth.** New York, Behavioral Publications, 1973. 131p. bibliog. index. $7.95. LC 73-7803. SBN 87705-112-7.
This book was written for parents in order to help them and their children in preventing drug addiction. The authors are social workers who have had a good deal of experience with drug abusing adolescents. The book is written in practical terms with an attempt made to include a broad perspective of the social environment, a critique of treatments used, and a discussion of the adolescent and his family. The book is in three parts; the first deals with the problem, the second, therapy, and the third is an exploration of social and philosophical issues and broader concerns.

453. Lingeman, Richard R. **Drugs from A to Z: A Dictionary.** New York, McGraw-Hill, 1969. 277p. bibliog. $6.95. LC 68-30559.
This book, which is a lexicon of terms from the world of drug abuse, was written for laymen by a layman. Many slang terms are included and their origin traced when possible. Eric Partridge's works on slang were used for assistance. Also, the drugs, mostly the mind altering type, are discussed from a pharmacological and sociological point of view. Several physicians were interviewed by the author, and Dr. Herbert Berger of the New York Medical College wrote the introduction to the dictionary. The book has four appendices which are lists of drugs; the longest one is a list controlled by law under the Drug Abuse Control Amendment of 1965.

454. Louria, Donald B. **Overcoming Drugs: A Program for Action.** New York, McGraw-Hill Book Co., 1971. 233p. bibliog. $6.95. LC 74-151499.
The author of this book, a physician and noted authority on the drug problem, gives advice on how to deal with drug abuse. He addresses a number of specific social groups as can be seen from the chapter headings: 1) Where it's at—and why, 2) Approaching young people, 3) Questions and answers, 4) A program for parents, 5) An approach to education, 6) Proposals for communities, 7) Rules and regulations, 8) The laws—proposals for legislators, and 9) Final thoughts.

The author's point of view is that education, both preventive and remedial, is the best approach to ending drug abuse. He suggests a curriculum for schools and special training for teachers. He also presents a 15-point program for communities. The book will be of most value to parents, educators, legislators, and physicians.

455. McIlwain, William. **A Farewell to Alcohol.** New York, Random House, 1972. 143p. $5.45. LC 72-5121. ISBN 0-394-47610-7.

This book is a personal narrative about an alcoholic and his treatment at Butner, a rehabilitation center for alcoholics in North Carolina. The story is well written (the author is an outstanding writer and newspaper editor) as well as honest and touching. The methods of treatment used are of interest, and while the author does not claim successful results for most of the patients, some were apparently cured as he himself was.

456. Maddox, George L., ed. **The Domesticated Drug: Drinking among Collegians.** New Haven, College and University Press, 1970. 479p. bibliog. index. $9.00. LC 78-92543.

This book attempts to present a balanced view of drinking among American college students. The collegian of today is seen as a commentary on the generation that produced him and is a prophecy of the generation that will provide leadership in the near future. The editor sees alcohol as at best a partially domesticated drug, and while much alarm has been expressed about drug abuse among the young, much more trouble continues to be associated with alcohol use. He feels that there is some slight comfort, however, in that the situation is not as bad as it might be given the peculiarities of the American way of drinking. The book is a collection of papers divided into three sections. The first group constitutes a perspective; the second is a group of empirical studies; and the third contains several articles on implications. Each paper is by a different expert; a few have been published previously. The material should prove of particular interest to the college student and to college administrators and research investigators, especially in the social sciences.

457. **Marihuana: Biochemical, Physiological and Pathological Aspects.** Papers by Peter B. Dews and others. New York, MSS Information Corp., 1973. 289p. bibliog. index. $18.50. LC 72-13833. ISBN 0-8422-7094-9.

This book is a collection of papers on various aspects of the chemistry of marijuana. With the exception of one article, they are all research papers, all published previously (from 1970 to 1972) in scholarly periodicals. The paper that is the exception is a summary of the Second Annual Report to Congress from the Secretary of Health, Education and Welfare "Marihuana and Health," 1972. Many of the articles are somewhat technical for the average reader, but the first section, which takes up more general problems of marijuana and health, is not. In any case, the reports will assist the reader in a chemical understanding of the effects of the drug. Other sections of the book are concerned with the following topics: 1) Pathological aspects of marihuana use, 2) Localization of cannabinol derivatives in brain and their effects on central nervous system metabolism, 3) Metabolism of cannabinol derivatives and various physiological effects, 4) Chemical identification and synthesis of cannabinol derivatives, and 5) Cannabis, the marihuana plant.

458. Menditto, Joseph, **Drugs of Addiction and Non-Addiction, Their Use and Abuse: A Comprehensive Bibliography, 1960-1969.** Troy, N.Y., Whitston Pub. Co., Inc., 1970. 315p. index. $10.00. LC 79-116588.

This bibliography of about 6,000 entries is a comprehensive guide to research materials in the field of addiction. It includes citations to books and essays, doctoral dissertations, and periodical literature, the latter being divided into "general" and "scientific" categories. The references are arranged under the following headings: amphetamines and stimulants, barbiturates and tranquilizing drugs, lysergic acid diethylamide, marijuana, narcotic addiction, narcotic rehabilitation, narcotic trade, narcotics, narcotic control, narcotic laws and legislation, narcotics and crime, narcotics bibliography.

The intent is to supplement the original bibliography annually. Two supplements, for 1970 and 1971, compiled by Jean Cameron Advena, have appeared. Also, five-year cumulations are planned.

459. Mercer, G. W. **Non-Alcoholic Drugs and Personality: A Selected Annotated Bibliography.** Toronto, Canada, Addiction Research Foundation, 1972. 77p. index. $2.00. (Addiction Research Foundation Bibliographic Series No. 4).

This selected bibliography of 181 items is a listing of publications which meet the following criteria: 1) They deal with cannabis, psychedelic, amphetamine, tranquilizing, and narcotic drugs; 2) They deal with human beings rather than animals; 3) They deal with hard data in the form of tests, interviews, comparative sampling and the like; and 4) They are not just philosophical treatises on drugs and drug use. For the most part, the publications included have been published in the last 20 years. Most of the references are to journal articles, although some books are included. The annotations are well-written, and the bibliography should prove quite useful.

460. Meyer, Roger E. **Guide to Drug Rehabilitation: A Public Health Approach.** Foreword by Jerome H. Jaffe. Boston, Beacon Press, 1972. 171p. bibliog. index. $5.95. LC 76-179152. ISBN 0-8070-2772-3.

This book, written by a professor of psychiatry who has had long experience with drug rehabilitation and research, attempts to evaluate and review all the known efforts at drug rehabilitation. The author urges that a multiplicity of approaches be used, depending on needs and resources. The book is divided into three sections; the first is on heroin addiction, the second on treating other forms of drug abuse, and the third, a public health approach to treatment. Treatments discussed are methadone maintenance and narcotic-blocking drugs; civil commitment programs; voluntary psychological treatments including traditional approaches, confrontation style groups and therapeutic communities, exhortative groups and aversive treatments. The book is simply written and will be of value to law enforcement officials, clergymen, community leaders, as well as mental health professionals, physicians, and high-level policy makers. The author has hopes that community programs can be effective in dealing with this difficult problem.

461. Musto, David F. **The American Disease: Origins of Narcotic Control.** New Haven, Yale University Press, 1973. 354p. bibliog. index. $10.95. LC 72-75204. ISBN 0-300-01537-2.

This well-documented historical work explores the various early attempts at a solution of the drug abuse problem on the international, federal, and local levels.

The attempts at reform and control, the relationships between legislative processes and various interested groups such as social reformers, politicians, the American Medical Association, pharmacists, manufacturers, addicts, and others are discussed. A good deal of emphasis is put on the way laws actually have worked out in practice. The author is also concerned about what to do with addicts—punish them, attempt to cure them, maintain them as they are, or what? The history of "cures" for drug addiction is presented, and the author concludes that for the most part they have failed. Clinics are discussed, and the relation of drug control to Prohibition receives attention. Most of the book deals with the 1920s and 1930s, but the subject is brought up to the present time with special emphasis on marijuana. The author, who is a historian and physician, has made a thorough study of the subject and has located much material.

462. Nahas, Gabriel G. **Marihuana—Deceptive Weed.** New York, Raven Press, 1973. 334p. bibliog. index. $12.50. LC 72-76743. ISBN 0-911216-39-1.
The author of this book has come to the conclusion, shared by many scientists, that the innocuousness of marijuana is being overstated and its dangers underestimated. This book presents a general account of the plant and the history of its use, and also the scientific and medical evidence about it. The author is a physician and pharmacologist. Chapter headings are as follows: 1) From Bhang to Delta-9-THC: four thousand years of history, 2) Botany—the unstabilized species, 3) Chemistry: the elusive Delta-9-THC and its active metabolites, 4) Toxicology and pharmacology, 5) Clinical pharmacology, 6) Cannabis intoxication and mental illness, 7) Social aspects, and 8) General summary and conclusion. The book is important because it gives a realistic, medically responsible approach with a fresh outlook in a controversial field.

The author concludes that "It is deceptive to consider marijuana intoxication as a youthful fad, similar to many which have occurred in the past . . . . Drug taking is symptomatic of the dissatisfaction and the craving for fulfillment of disillusioned youth seeking new values. Such fulfillment cannot be found in any lasting way through any type of intoxication. To make marijuana, or any other hallucinogenic drug, available will in no way solve the social malaise which has beset the youth of America and its Western allies. One may also wonder how long a political system can endure when drug taking becomes one of the prerequisites of happiness. If the American dream has lost its attraction, it will not be retrieved through the use of stupefying drugs. Their use only delays the young in their quest to understand the world they now live in and their desire to foster a better world for tomorrow."

463. **Narcotics and Drug Abuse A to Z.** Vol. 1-3. Queens Village, New York, Social Service Publications Division of Croner Publications, Inc., 1971. Looseleaf. Kept up to date with quarterly supplements. $18.00 per year per volume. LC 78-173860.
This publication is a looseleaf directory, dictionary, and guide to information sources concerned with drug abuse. There are six sections in each volume as follows: 1) Dictionary. A compilation of terms germane to the field of drugs, narcotics, and drug addiction, 2) Drugs and Narcotics. Most frequently abused drugs are profiled, 3) Who's Who. An attempt has been made to list medical and

program directors of the facilities given in the book, as well as executives of
"umbrella" agencies, and those involved in various drug addiction programs,
4) Bibliography. A compilation of better known works, 5) Miscellaneous. Gives
the more important facts and dates regarding drugs and addiction in telegram
style, as well as a list of organizations, 6) Directory of Facilities and Organizations.

All sections are identical in each of the volumes except Section 6, the Directory
of Facilities and Organizations, which varies according to the section of the
country covered. Volume 1 covers the northeast section of the country, Volume
2 the west, and Volume 3 the rest of the country. The publication should be of
particular value to judges, law enforcement agencies, guidance counselors,
teachers, clergymen, and parents.

464. National Association for the Prevention of Addiction to Narcotics. **Fourth
National Conference on Methadone Treatment. Proceedings.** Co-sponsor:
National Institute of Mental Health. New York, National Association for
the Prevention of Addiction to Narcotics, 1972. 557p. $8.00.
This publication includes most of the formal papers presented at the Conference
which was held in January, 1972. The papers leave little doubt that methadone
is an effective tool in the management of narcotic addiction, although it is not a
wonder drug. There is uncertainty about the extent to which patients can be
withdrawn from Methadone. Significant developments brought out are that a
national organization of Methadone programs has been established, and that
these programs require the concerted effort of staff members with diverse educational, vocational, economic, and ethnic backgrounds. Other conferences are
being planned.

465. National Coordinating Council on Drug Abuse Education and Information,
Inc. **Common Sense Lives Here: A Community Guide to Drug Abuse Education.** Washington, National Coordination Council on Drug Abuse Education and Information, Inc., 1970. 104p. $3.00.
This handbook is intended for community groups and individuals concerned about
the problem of drug abuse. It is not intended for professionals in rehabilitation
work, officers of the law, or medical specialists. It includes some basic facts about
drugs, discusses the makeup of communities, and shows some links between community life and the forces that lead to drug abuse. Action guidelines and strategies are developed which can be applied to almost any community. Also included
is a list of agencies that can be of assistance and a glossary of slang terms used in
the world of drugs. Note: The issuing body of this publication is now called the
National Coordinating Council on Drug Education.

466. National Coordinating Council on Drug Abuse Education and Information,
Inc. **Directory.** Washington, National Coordinating Council on Drug Abuse
Education and Information, Inc., 1970. 90p. $3.00.
This directory lists alphabetically members (which are organizations, not indivi-
duals), including separate listings for federal agency members and state affiliates.
Also included are position statements of some of the organizations. Information
about the Council itself is given, telling how it began, purposes, support, officers,

and trustees. There is no index but the Table of Contents is alphabetical and will serve as such. In the listing of the member organizations, information on purposes, officers' names, and lists of publications are included. Note: The issuing body of this publication is now called the National Coordinating Council on Drug Education.

467. National Coordinating Council on Drug Education. **Drug Abuse Films.** 2d ed. Washington, National Coordinating Council on Drug Education, 1971. 55p. index. $3.00.

This publication lists and evaluates drug abuse audiovisuals. It is intended as a guide only and will not altogether eliminate the need to preview films. Most of the entries in the guide are for films, but there is also a section of other audiovisuals including filmstrips, slides, transparencies, and recordings. With each entry the following is given: year, intended audience, producer, source, rental price, purchase price, details (such as running time, color or black and white, sound or silent, etc.). There follows a synopsis and an evaluation. Some entries are starred as being unusually noteworthy, and some are denoted questionable. A list of the evaluation panelists is included. Many are well-known; some are scientists, some with other areas of expertise. Also included is a list of the Council's member organizations and background material about the council.

468. National Institute for Drug Programs. Center for Human Services. **Bibliography on Drug Abuse: Prevention, Treatment, Research.** Washington, Human Service Press, 1973. 222p. index. $7.95. LC 73-77472.

This volume is the first of a series of publications intended to provide information in the field of drug abuse, prevention, rehabilitation, and research. The work is made up of 366 references to publications, each with an abstract of the cited material. The references are divided into two large groups, drug treatment approaches and society and drugs. Under each there are numerous subheadings. The references are to books and periodical articles.

The compilers feel that the bibliography points up at least two important facts. The first is that there is a trend toward the development of a variety of approaches used in treatment of drug abuse; the second is that there is a notable lack of crucial research and analysis being done in the field, resulting in few publications of value.

469. Nelkin, Dorothy. **Methadone Maintenance: A Technological Fix.** New York, George Braziller, 1973. 164p. bibliog. index. $6.95. LC 72-96071.

The author's point of view is that methadone maintenance is essentially a chemotherapeutic "fix" for heroin addiction. The methadone treatment consists of giving the drug methadone in place of heroin, and dependence is transferred to methadone. It has become the predominant means of dealing with the heroin problem because there have been no other successful developments for dealing with the poorly understood problems of the addict. The effect of methadone is similar to that of heroin; it is itself addicting. The treatment remains controversial. Many feel that addiction is a moral, psychological, and legal problem as well as medical and that a purely medical treatment such as methadone maintenance does not get to the roots of the problem.

A Syracuse, New York, program was selected for study in this book, although the development of the program is considered in its larger national context. Chapter headings are as follows: 1) The addict and society, 2) Methadone maintenance, 3) Problems, politics, and treatment programs: a community study, 4) The organization of a methadone program, 5) The addict as patient, 6) The limits of a technological fix.

The book concludes that methadone programs have value and serve to reduce the heroin needs of street addicts. However, more positive rehabilitation measures should be developed to support drug-free programs including self help efforts.

470. Pace, Denny F., and Jimmie C. Styles. **Handbook of Narcotic Control.** Englewood Cliffs, N. J., Prentice-Hall, Inc., 1972. 95p. illus. bibliog. (Prentice-Hall Essentials of Law Enforcement Series). $3.50pa; $7.50. LC 75-37962. ISBN P-0-13-380469-0; C-0-13-380477-1.

This publication is an overview of problems concerned with drug abuse. Basic information is given which will be of particular help to the law enforcement officer. While some attention is given to the educational efforts of social agencies and referral of drug abusers to hospitals and agencies that attempt to rehabilitate drug users, particular attention is given to making arrests when other efforts have failed to cope with the problem user. The book contains sections on identifying the common drugs, a brief glossary of scientific terms, a discussion of the Comprehensive Drug Abuse Prevention and Control Act of 1970, sections from federal laws governing drugs, and a list of references, films, and other audio visual media.

471. Popham, Robert E., and Carole D. Yawney, compilers. **Culture and Alcohol Use: A Bibliography of Anthropological Studies.** 2d ed. Toronto, Canada, Addiction Research Foundation, 1967. 52p. (Addiction Research Foundation Bibliographic Series No. 1). index. free.

The purpose of this bibliography is to bring together the principal anthropological literature on drinking behavior in different cultures, whether it is customary or pathological. The principal sources of references were the periodicals: *Alkoholpolitik, American Anthropologist, British Journal of Addiction, Human Organization, Quarterly Journal of Studies on Alcohol; The Classified Abstract Archive of the Alcohol Literature*, Rutgers Center of Alcohol Studies; and references from relevant books and articles. The bibliography is arranged by broad topics as follows: 1) Non-literate peoples, 2) Literate peoples, 3) Ancient peoples, and 4) Theoretical studies.

472. Richardson, Winnifred, and Byran E. M. Cooke. **A Bibliography on Drugs: By Subject and Title.** Minneapolis, Burgess Publishing Co., 1972. 60p. index.

This brief bibliography lists references on drug abuse, by title, under about 15 broad subject categories. Book, periodical, and pamphlet references are included. There is a special section of bibliographies, a list of pertinent periodicals, and a list of sources where free and inexpensive materials may be obtained. Most of the references are to articles about drug use among young people and educating them regarding the hazards.

473. Rickles, William H., Benjamin Chatoff, and Charlotte Whitaker. **Marijuana: A Selective Bibliography, 1924-1970.** Los Angeles, UCLA Brain Information Service, 1970. 34p. $3.00.

This annotated bibliography is selective rather than comprehensive, but an attempt has been made to cover several facets of the problem in a representative way. Scientific literature has been selected for the most part.

The bibliography lists alphabetically by author 192 references, mostly to periodical articles, with brief annotations. Also included is a detailed Table of Contents which can serve as an index as it refers to the articles by number and is broken down by type of article. The following categories have been identified: cannabis and its origin, pharmacological effects, clinical studies and case reports, therapeutic assessment, sociological and legal issues, and reviews and overviews.

474. Roebuck, Julian B., and Raymond G. Kessler. **The Etiology of Alcoholism: Constitutional, Psychological and Sociological Approaches.** Springfield, Ill., Charles C. Thomas, 1972. 260p. bibliog. index. $11.95. LC 71-87672. ISBN 0-398-02392-1.

This book presents various points of view on the causes of alcoholism. Recent theories which have appeared in the literature during the years 1940 to 1971 are examined. Three major categorical approaches are explored, the constitutional, the psychological, and the sociological. The suggestion is made that an interdisciplinary approach to the problem is the best one, and a plea is made for further studies along these lines.

475. Scher, Jordan M., ed. **Drug Abuse in Industry: Growing Corporate Dilemma.** Springfield, Ill., Charles C. Thomas, 1973. 312p. index. $11.95. LC 73-227. ISBN 0-398-2809-5.

This work explores the extent and seriousness of the drug abuse problem in industry. Such matters as serious thefts, accidents, poor work performance, chronic absenteeism, and lowered company morale and loyalty are examined. The reader is told what signs and symptoms to look for when drug abuse is suspected. Ways of helping the drug user are suggested. The book is divided into several main parts with several chapters in each. The chapters are written by various authors. The parts are: 1) General considerations, 2) Drugs in industry, 3) The impact of the drug abuser, 4) Law and drug abuse, 5) Rehabilitation and industry, 6) Alcoholics in industry, and 7) Special problems. Also included is an appendix of definitions and a primer on drugs.

476. Schmidt, Wolfgang, Reginald G. Smart, and Marcia K. Moss. **Social Class and the Treatment of Alcoholism: An Investigation of Social Class as a Determinant of Diagnosis, Prognosis and Therapy.** Published for the Addiction Research Foundation. Toronto, University of Toronto Press, 1968. 111p. bibliog. index. (Brookside Monograph of the Addiction Research Foundation No. 7). $6.00. ISBN 0-8020-3207-9.

This book is a report on a study which observed a sample of patients of a public clinic in order to determine the influences of class position on the therapy used in each case. Drinking patterns and the clinical picture of alcoholism differed among the social classes and, as might be expected, the treatments assigned differed. The book is important because there has been a rapid increase in the number of public institutions that treat alcoholism, and the possibility that class status affects the diagnosis and care of the patient should be explored in order to discover new and better methods of treatment.

477. Smith, David E., David J. Bentel, and Jerome L. Schwartz, eds. **The Free Clinic: A Community Approach to Health Care and Drug Abuse.** Beloit, Wisconsin, STASH Press, 1971. 206p. bibliog. $5.00. LC 70-183532.
This publication of three parts contains the proceedings of the First National Free Clinic Council Symposium held January 31 to February 1, 1970, Free Clinic Position Papers, and the National Free Clinic Survey. The "Free Clinics " with which the publication is concerned deal mainly with drug abuse problems, and more is meant by the term "free" than that there is no charge per patient visit. It also means that there is little or no red tape about forms and papers and that there is also freedom from conventional bureaucracy, moral judgments, etc. The publication is of interest because the clinics seem to be surviving in spite of many problems, such as financing, staffing, personnel, and unorthodox approaches. The publication includes a list of 61 such clinics which initiated service during 1967 to 1969 and were still in operation on January 1, 1971. Many of the institutions are short-lived, but new ones are being initiated.

478. Smith, David E., and John Luce. **Love Needs Care: A History of San Francisco's Haight-Ashbury Free Medical Clinic and Its Pioneer Role in Treating Drug Abuse Problems.** Boston, Little, Brown and Co., 1971. 405p. illus. bibliog. $8.95. LC 77-121434.
This book tells the story of the Haight-Ashbury Free Medical Clinic which was the first free community medical center to treat drug abusers. Also, a great deal of material is presented about the Haight district of San Francisco and its decline from a neighborhood of flower children to a crime-ridden ghetto. The book is illustrated with many photographs of the district and its people, many of them shocking and depressing. The multitude of drugs that have to be dealt with, the incredible variety of diseases are described. The only hope offered is that clinics like the one described will reach the alienated groups that have such a desperate need.

The book ends by saying that the free clinics may be clumsy models for the delivery of health services in the future, but that they have demonstrated some important things. They have gained a wide popularity by respecting the needs and the imperfect humanity of their patients; they have minimized red tape in dealing with people; they have pioneered in the use of paramedical volunteers; and in addition, they have proven their ability to reach alienated economic, racial and philosophical minorities. The senior author is a physician and the Medical Director and co-organizer of the clinic. The co-author is a journalist and is Public Affairs Director of the clinic.

479. Smith, David E., ed. **The New Social Drug: Cultural, Medical, and Legal Perspectives on Marijuana.** Englewood Cliffs, N. J., Prentice-Hall, Inc., 1970. 186p. bibliog. $5.95. LC 77-104863.

The editor of this collection of papers (which are reprinted from other sources) feels that the prohibition of alcohol and the illegality of the use of marijuana are similar situations. He says that alcohol is the social drug of this generation and pot the social drug of the next generation. He thinks this situation has contributed to widening the generation gap in America.

The papers are divided into five subject sections as follows: 1) Pharmacology and classification, 2) The issue of marijuana abuse, 3) Marijuana as a social issue, 4) The issue of marijuana regulation, and 5) Marijuana as a political issue.

The book attempts to place this difficult problem in proper perspective, although there seems to be no good solution to it nor is one outlined. It is felt that the "irrational" point of view of the present generation will not be modified; but the prediction is made that the next generation will place marijuana in its "proper perspective." It is not made clear just what that "proper perspective" is.

480. Sonoma County Drug Abuse Council. **Drug Abuse: Information and Resource.** Santa Rosa, California, Sonoma County Drug Abuse Council, 1971. 142p. bibliog. $4.50pa.

This publication contains a good deal of miscellaneous information about drugs of abuse which is useful for reference. The following sections are presented: 1) Classification of drugs, 2) Glossary of slang terms, 3) Cocaine, 4) Hallucinogenic drugs, 5) Marijuana, 6) Narcotics, 7) Sedatives, 8) Stimulants, 9) Volatile liquids, 10) History of federal drug laws, 11) California drug laws, 12) Usage and arrest figures, 13) Effects of arrest and conviction (adults and juveniles), 14) Motivation, 15) Treatment of drug dependence, 16) Referrals, and 17) Bibliography (books, periodicals, and pamphlets).

481. Speck, Ross V., and others. **The New Families: Youth, Communes, and the Politics of Drugs.** New York, Basic Books, Inc., 1972. 190p. index. $6.95. LC 78-174825. SBN 465-05018-2.

The author of this book, a psychiatrist, with a team of psychiatrists, psychologists, and anthropologists, visited youth communes in an effort to understand them and what their members were achieving. The book describes the communal life with the daily activities, the sexual patterns, the role of women, household arrangements, and especially the use of drugs, which seemed to be the main bond between the members of the groups. The author is quite tolerant of the drug abuse by the young people and believes that the new life styles and new values are preparing for the future of our world in a basic new humanistic way. He thinks that acceptance of their ideas may be necessary for our survival, even.

The study of the youth groups was done during 1966 to 1969. At the present time it does not appear that the youths and their new life styles, communes, and the like have had as much influence as the author felt they would. However, the scene as presented and the point of view expressed probably were "relevant" at the time of the study.

The reviewer cannot resist a comment on the role of the women as the book (probably accurately) reports it. The girls were unbelievably passive, nonassertive, and dependent. The women's liberation movement could find no comfort here!

482. Stamford Public Schools, Stamford, Conn. **Stamford Curriculum Guide for Drug Abuse Education.** Chicago, J. G. Ferguson Publishing Co., 1971. 96p. bibliog. $4.25. LC 70-134585.

This guide is intended to assist in programs in drug abuse education in schools from grades four through senior high school. Objectives and recommendations for the implementation of a program are presented. Then there is a curriculum guide for each grade (or grades) worked out in practical detailed fashion. There are also several useful appendices, such as current laws, lists of films, a bibliography, addresses for resource material, and a glossary of drug abuse terms.

483. Student Association for the Study of Hallucinogens. **Directory of Drug Information Groups.** Directory staff, Rita Grossman and others. Beloit, Wisconsin, STASH Press, 1970. 183p. index. $4.50. LC 75-136212.

This directory serves as a resource guide to organizations concerned with drugs and drug information, including data on drug education and counseling and treatment programs. The information included with the entries was supplied by each organization and prepared from questionnaires. The organizations are arranged alphabetically by name under the states. Some entries include a good deal of information, some very little. Besides address, most give the name of a person to contact. The longer entries include such information as purpose of the organization, publications, programs, services, research, financial data, and officers. It is planned that the list will be updated frequently.

484. Terry, Charles E., and Mildred Pellens. **The Opium Problem.** With a new Foreword by John C. Ball and a new Preface by Charles Winick. Bureau of Social Hygiene, Inc., 1928; repr. Montclair, N. J., Patterson Smith, 1970. 1042p. index. bibliog. $25.00. LC 76-108232. SBN 8785-115-0.

This classical work, which has generally been regarded as the single most comprehensive work in the field, is also a source book with many passages from famous writers of the past included. An appraisal of these reports is provided. The work is limited to discussion on what are known today as "hard narcotics"—heroin, morphine, paragoric, codeine, and other narcotic analgesics. There are five areas of the drug abuse problem explored: 1) The history of use in the U.S., including the extent of chronic use, 2) The life course of addiction from onset to death, with emphasis on different types of addicts, 3) The medical aspects of addiction, including tolerance, dependence, and withdrawal, 4) American and European treatment programs, and 5) Legal control of opium abuse under local, state, federal, and international auspices. This landmark book is serving as a foundation for further current research on the problem.

485. **The Treatment of Drug Abuse: Programs, Problems, Prospects.** Raymond A. Glasscote, and others. Washington, Joint Information Service of the American Psychiatric Association and the National Association for Mental Health, 1972. 250p. $7.00. LC 70-187294.

The authors of this work attempt to show realistically what a community can do about a drug abuse problem and how effective a program may be. The book reports on nine programs that exist presently to help drug addicts. The conclusion is that none of the presently available approaches can be expected to be successful with more than a small percentage of drug abusers, and that all approaches combined will have a quite limited effect. The authors take no position for or against any particular approach; they simply discuss the features of each. A great deal of detailed information is given objectively about the well-known programs presented. Chapter headings are as follows: 1) Introduction, 2) Drug abusers—then and now, 3) Theories about the cause of drug abuse, 4) The history of treatment, 5) Present approaches, 6) The status of programs in mid-1971, 7) What might be done, and 8) What one gets for the effort. The nine drug treatment programs discussed are: 1) Beth Israel Medical Center, New York City, 2) Daytop Village, New York, 3) California Civil Addict Program, 4) Illinois Drug Abuse Program, 5) Teen Challenge of Northern California and Nevada, San Francisco, 6) Drug Dependency Treatment Program, St. Louis, 7) The Connecticut State Program, 8) Connecticut Mental Health Center, New Haven, 9) Mendocino State Hospital, Talmage, California. The book is highly recommended for individuals involved in community programs to assist with the drug abuse program.

486. Trice, Harrison M., and Paul M. Roman. **Spirits and Demons at Work: Alcohol and Other Drugs on the Job.** Ithaca, New York, New York State School of Industrial and Labor Relations, Cornell University, 1972. bibliog. index. $5.00. LC 72-619517. ISBN 0-87546-034-8.

Since the literature on drug abuse is growing at such a rapid rate, the authors have presented this book as a guide through some of this material hoping it will be of value for both work-organization personnel and behavioral scientists. Also, they have offered a program of action for work organizations for the management of alcohol and drug abuse. Alcohol is the primary focus of this book, as it is seen to be America's major drug problem. The material presented is based on research studies from scholarly journals and monographs. Chapter topics are as follows: 1) Drinking, deviant drinking, and work, 2) Drugs, youth, and the work world, 3) Opiates, nonopiates, and their users, 4) Job-based risks for deviant drinking and drug use, 5) Job behaviors of deviant drinkers and drug abusers: specific impacts in the work place, 6) Reactions of supervisors to deviant drinkers and drug users, 7) The strategy of constructive confrontation, 8) Union-management cooperation and conflict, 9) Therapeutic alternatives for deviant drinkers and drug users.

487. U.S. National Clearinghouse for Drug Abuse Information. **National Directory of Drug Abuse Treatment Programs.** By Deena D. Watson, Washington, GPO, 1972. 381p. $2.75.

The directory is an expansion of an earlier listing *Directory of Narcotic Treatment Agencies in the United States 1968-1969.* A descriptive outline of 1,300 treatment programs is given, arranged by state. The object of the compendium is to present a referral source for people in need of services as a result of the abuses of opiates, amphetamines, barbiturates, hallucinogens, solvents, and other substances, (excluding alcohol). The listing is restricted to treatment and rehabilitation facilities; services related to drug abuse education and prevention were not included. Information given about each program includes: name, address, phone number, name of officer in charge, type of program, services, admission requirements, clientele, and number and type of staff.

488. U.S. National Clearinghouse for Mental Health Information. **Bibliography on Drug Dependence and Abuse, 1928-1966.** Washington, National Institute of Mental Health, 1967. 258p.

This bibliography of more than 3,000 entries was compiled primarily for specialists and research workers in the field. It includes citations to books, monographs, journal articles, legal documents, and reports of congressional hearings and investigations relating to drug dependence and abuse. The materials are organized under categories as follows: general material, incidence and prevalence, sociological factors, treatment and rehabilitation, attitudes and education, pharmacology and chemistry, psychological factors, and production, control and legal factors. The bibliography is not entirely complete for the period covered, but is quite comprehensive.

489. U.S. National Clearinghouse for Smoking and Health. **Bibliography on Smoking and Health. 1972.** Washington, GPO, 1973. 314p. index. DHEW Publication No. (HSM) 73-8719. (Public Health Service Bibliography Series No. 45).

This bibliography includes items added to the Technical Information Center of the National Clearinghouse for Smoking and Health from January to December, 1972. Earlier volumes were published, beginning in 1968. There are author, organizational, and subject indexes. Most of the citations are to scholarly journal articles and each includes a rather detailed abstract.

490. U.S. Public Health Service. **The Health Consequences of Smoking.** January 1973. Washington, GPO, 1973. 261p. index. DHEW Publication No. (HSM) 73-8704. $1.85. Stock No. 1723-00064.

This report is the seventh in a series issued by the Public Health Service over the years which reviews and assesses the scientific evidence linking cigarette smoking to disease and premature death. This report reiterates, strengthens, and extends the findings of earlier reports that smoking is a health hazard. Contents are as follows: 1) Cardiovascular diseases, 2) Nonneoplastic bronchopulmonary diseases, 3) Cancer, 4) Pregnancy, 5) Peptic ulcer disease, 6) Pipe and cigar smoking, and 7) Exercise performance.

491. Waller, Coy W., and Jacqueline J. Denny. **Annotated Bibliography of Marijuana (Cannabis sativa L.) 1964-1970.** University, Miss., Research Institute of Pharmaceutical Sciences, School of Pharmacy, University of Mississippi, 1971. 301p. index. $7.00.

Most of the 1,112 publications listed in this bibliography are from scientific periodicals. Material for the lay press has been omitted in most instances. Many foreign language materials have been included. The articles are arranged alphabetically by author. The plan is to supplement the basic list from time to time, and a 1971 supplement has been issued. By making use of an earlier work "The Question of Cannabis, Cannabis Bibliography," N. B. Eddy, United Nations Commission on Narcotic Drugs, E/CN7/479, 1965, one can trace the literature up to 1972.

492. Weisman, Thomas. **Drug Abuse and Drug Counseling: A Case Approach.** Cleveland, Press of Case Western Reserve University, 1972. 193p. bibliog. index. $5.95. LC 75-170154. ISBN 0-8295-0223-8.

The intent of this book is to help counselors deal with people who have problems involving drug abuse. It attempts to provide a foundation of pharmacological knowledge that will help the counselor build confidence and skill in his work. Each chapter of the book deals with a different drug or group of drugs. Chapter headings are as follows: 1) The narcotic analgesics, 2) Alcohol, 3) Hypnotics and tranquilizers, 4) Amphetamines and cocaine, 5) Hallucinogens, 6) Marijuana, and 7) Caffeine and nicotine. There is a short expository section, a true-false question section, and a set of case problems for each chapter. The material presented is easy to understand and practical, and the approaches suggested are probably as effective as any.

493. Welt, Isaac D., ed. **Drug Information for the Health Professions.** Proceedings of the First Conference on Drug Information for the Health Professions. Supported by PHS Research Grant from the National Library of Medicine to the New York Academy of Sciences. Held at Princeton, New Jersey, June 4 to 7, 1967. New York, Gordon and Breach, 1969. 465p. bibliog. index. $7.50. LC 70-84478.

This publication records the proceedings of an interdisciplinary conference which included representatives of most of the health professions and some information science experts. The subjects considered deal with what it is that members of the health professions and health services want to know about drugs, what the professions consider that they should know about drugs, and thirdly some of the difficulties that are involved in getting the information. The "state of the art" is presented. Section headings are as follows: 1) Introduction. The present situation and communication and information science, 2) What practicing physicians want to know about drugs and why, 3) What practicing physicians should know about drugs and why, 4) Difficulties of members of the health professions in obtaining drug information they want and should have, 5) General discussion and summary.

This publication is of particular value to health science librarians and drug information specialists as well as to health science professions in general.

494. Whipple, Dorothy V. **Is the Grass Greener? Answers to Questions About Drugs.** Washington, New York, Robert B. Luce, Inc., 1971. 224p. bibliog. index, $5.95. LC 73-129135.

The author of this publication is a physician who has practiced pediatrics for many years. This book discusses all drugs in common use (including alcohol) in a question and answer style in understandable language suitable for young readers. As is customary in dealing with young people, the book does not argue against drug use in obvious fashion but presents factual information. The implication is that the reader will decide himself on whether or not to use drugs from the material presented. Actually, the facts are probably argument enough against drug use.

Chapter headings are as follows: 1) What drugs are and what they do, 2) Marihuana and hashish, 3) LSD and other psychedelics, 4) Opium, morphine and heroin, 5) Amphetamines, 6) Down drugs—the barbiturates, 7) Cocaine, 8) Glue, nutmeg and others, 9) Alcohol, 10) The people who use drugs today, 11) Prevention, treatment and rehabilitation, 12) Drug laws and how they came to be passed, 13) What the drug laws have accomplished, and 14) Other ways of tackling the drug problem.

495. Wiener, R. S. P. **Drugs and Schoolchildren.** New York, Humanities Press, 1970. 238p. bibliog. index. $7.50. SBN 391-0038-1.

This book is of interest because drug use by school children is considered a serious problem and is growing. The study upon which the book is based was done on British children in the London area between the ages of 14 and 19. The study was a sociological investigation to provide an assessment of the situation and to devise a policy for dealing with it. Questionnaires were given to over 1,000 children. Answers from drug users and nonusers were compared. It was found that the behavior, attitudes, and knowledge of the users and nonusers differed consistently. The author includes a discussion of what should be done about the drug problem. He also considers the effectiveness of several different educational media, including films. The research methods used are outlined in some detail. The book is in three parts: 1) The problem and the background to the hypotheses, 2) Methodology, and 3) Results, discussion and recommendations.

496. Williams, John B., ed. **Narcotics and Hallucinogenics: A Handbook.** rev. ed. Beverly Hills, Calif., Glencoe Press, 1967. 277p. bibliog. $5.95.

This is a compendium of information obtained from those having had actual experience in various phases of drug abuse problems, particularly law enforcement officers. Many topics are included, but emphasis is on the addict; the drugs; controls; the local, state, federal, and international efforts to control drugs; the illegal sale and use of drugs; and drug addiction. The publication is divided into three main parts: 1) General problems, 2) Causes of addiction, descriptions of addicts, and criminal behavior, and 3) Treatment of addicts. The handbook will be of particular value to physicians, educators, psychologists, sociologists, investigators, and police officers.

497. Winek, Charles. **1971 Drug Abuse Reference.** Bridgeville, Pa., Bek Technical Publications, Inc., 1971. 100p. $2.00. LC 73-155732.

This small book is intended for parents, teachers, and students. It attempts to define words used by drug abusers, scientists, and others concerned with drug use. There are five sections: 1) General terms, 2) Drug abuse terms, 3) User slang, 4) A list of drugs and chemicals commonly abused, and 5) An educational source guide which includes short lists of books, pamphlets, and films on drug abuse. The latter is perhaps the least useful section as it is short and little information is given about the material. The dictionary sections are quite useful. The compiler is a toxicologist and professor of pharmacology.

498. Zinberg, Norman E., and John A. Robertson. **Drugs and the Public.** New York, Simon and Schuster, 1972. 288p. bibliog. index. $8.95. LC-71-189748. SBN 671-21165-X; 671-21196-Xpa.

This book makes a plea for what is called a "more rational drug policy"; specifically, it advocates the careful and restrained availability of abused drugs in the hope that this will alleviate the drug abuse problems of the world for the common good. Chapter headings are as follows: 1) What is the drug issue? An overview, 2) Public attitudes toward illegal drug use, (3) Drug use and drug users, 4) The problem of research, 5) The British experience, 6) The drug laws, 7) The costs of the drug laws, 8) Alternatives for drug control. Many will not agree with the authors' reasoning. The reviewer does not find it convincing, although it is a more permissive point of view recently advocated by some.

12. THE ENVIRONMENT

499. Aldrich, James L., and Edward J. Kormondy. **Environmental Education: Academia's Response.** Washington, Commission on Undergraduate Education in the Biological Sciences, 1972. 77p. bibliog. (Commission on Undergraduate Education in the Biological Sciences. Publication No. 35.). Available free of charge from the American Institute of Biological Sciences. LC 77-188609.

This publication points out some of the ideas and patterns which have taken shape in institutions in the area of environmental education. Descriptions of programs at three different kinds of institutions are presented: 1) Those at large, multipurpose universities, 2) Undergraduate, liberal arts colleges, and 3) Experimental colleges. It is hoped that the report will prove to be a step toward identifying and answering questions about the role of environmental studies in higher education.

500. Beatty, Rita Gray. **The DDT Myth: Triumph of the Amateurs.** Foreword by Francis A. Gunther. New York, John Day Co. in association with San Francisco Book Co., 1973. 201p. bibliog. index. $6.95. LC 72-12084. ISBN 0-381-98243-4; 0-381-90007-Xpa.

This book points out that the news media are generally inclined to emphasize the attention-getting "bad" rather than the prosaic "good" even in fields so technical and complex as modern pest control with chemical pesticides. A plea is made for sanity, prudence, and proper perspective on the part of everyone in this matter. The author believes that the anti-DDT campaign has been based on faulty research, emotionalism, overreaction to the book *Silent Spring*, and the overzealous activities of amateur ecologists. She believes that control of insect-borne diseases, the feeding of populations of underdeveloped nations, and the public health and agricultural wealth of our own country are at stake. It is the reviewer's opinion that reputable scientists agree with her. Ms. Beatty is not a scientist, but a journalist, although her advisers are, and the author of the Foreword is a well-known entomologist and chemist. This book should be read by all, particularly public and government officials who have been misled by propaganda. The evidence in favor of DDT has been made accessible to laymen by this well-documented publication.

501. Bennett, Gary F., and James W. Hostman. **A Bibliography of Books on the Environment: Air, Water and Solid Wastes.** Toledo, Research Foundation of the University of Toledo for the American Institute of Chemical Engineers, Water Committee, 1969. 52p. $20.00

The references of this bibliography are divided into three large subject areas: water, air, and solid wastes. These areas are further subdivided by specific subject. Included are technical and nontechnical books and related books. There is also a section of conference proceedings and journals.

502. Bonn, George S., ed. **Information Resources in the Environmental Sciences.**
     Papers presented at the 18th Allerton Park Institute, November 12-15,
     1972. Champaign-Urbana, Ill., University of Illinois Graduate School of
     Library Science, 1973. 238p. bibliog. LC 73-75784. ISBN 0-87845-037-8.
There has been such a proliferation of materials and diverse points of view of
various agencies, organizations, and spokesmen in the field of environmental
sciences that it was felt necessary to direct attention to this matter by holding an
Institute. This publication records the papers presented at an Allerton Park Institute which are concerned with information sources, their production, development and use. Titles of the papers are as follows: librarians as environmental
activists; government agencies; information resources in environmental sciences:
an academic viewpoint; environmental information from other organizations;
scientific and educational society activity in the environment sciences; getting
down to earth: the call of Stockholm upon the information services; a guide to
environmental information services of the private sector; national information
centers, facilities and services for the environmental sciences; regional environmental libraries; state and local environmental information centers, facilities,
and services; federal resources and environmental programs; the school media
specialist as activist; selecting and evaluating environmental information resources
in public libraries; coping with environmental information resources; Durkeim
and Weber in wonderland; or, building environmental collections for the real
world.

Librarians and libraries in this field will find the book of considerable value.
There is much good text material, and in addition, there are excellent bibliographies, lists of agencies and the like included.

503. Boughey, Arthur S. **Contemporary Readings in Ecology.** Belmont, Calif.,
     Dickenson Publishing Co., Inc., 1969. 390p. bibliog. $8.00. LC 68-56011.
This book is a collection of 22 papers, reprinted from a variety of sources. The
contributions are divided into four groups: 1) Taxonomy, 2) Evolutionary
ecology, 3) Population ecology, and 4) Community ecology. Each paper was
selected because it depicted a trend, the ideas therein presenting a new concept
or a challenge to an old one. The papers are quite technical as most come from
scholarly journals. However, some insights can be gained from them by the
reader less familiar with scientific presentations.

504. Chute, Robert M., ed. **Environmental Insight: Readings and Comment on
     Human and Nonhuman Nature.** New York, Harper and Row, 1971. 241p.
     bibliog. index. $4.00. 70-141170. SBN 06-041285-2.
This book is written for undergraduates who are not majoring in biology. It will
also be of interest to others who are interested and who want to gain some biological insight. It is hoped that the reader will get a new perspective, gain new
ideas and concepts and make new observations about himself and his surround-
ings. The book is a collection of research reports and review papers selected
largely because they are interesting and provocative. They are divided into six
parts as follows: 1) Man in/and/or nature, 2) Systems and cycles, 3) The monkey-
wrench in the watchworks, 4) Other cultural pressures on the environment, 5) The
fateful exponent, population, 6) The remorseless working of things.

505. Cook, Robert S., and George T. O'Hearn, eds. **Processes for a Quality Environment**. Green Bay, Wisconsin, University of Wisconsin, 1971. 166p. $2.50. LC 72-169181.

This publication presents the papers of a conference held in 1970 and attended by invited participants who discussed the materials and strategy for environmental education that they had been developing and implementing. The aim of the conference was to help develop an integrated model plan by which a school system could implement environmental concepts and materials effectively into its instructional program. The viewpoint expressed was that this education should be interdisciplinary and should pervade the spirit of all teaching at all levels. Titles of the papers are as follows: Introduction: environmental education and survival university, 1) Environmental education: value reorientation, 2) Conceptual schemata in environmental education, 3) Formation of environmental values: a social awareness, 4) Environmental education and psychological behavior, 5) An environment for leisure: the challenge multiplied, 6) Environmental education: approaches for curriculum development (K-12), 7) The role of ERIC in environmental education, 8) Operation models: (a K-12 program in Maine; Massachusetts Audubon Society Program; Environmental education in the arts; and a U.S. Forest Service Program), 9) The challenge of environmental education.

The papers should prove valuable to educators who are interested in environmental education.

506. Cooley, Richard A., and Geoffrey Wandesforde-Smith. **Congress and the Environment**. Seattle, University of Washington Press, 1970. 277p. illus. bibliog. index. $8.95. LC 76-103295. SBN 295-95056-0.

This publication poses the question of whether or not the American political system, Congress in particular, can cope with the economic, esthetic, and other problems raised by the deterioration of the environment. The book presents a number of case studies, and each chapter surveys a relatively recent piece of legislation to determine how Congress handled the environmental problem in question. The chapters are as follows: 1) Prologue: environment and the quality of political life, 2) Indiana Dunes National Lakeshore: the battle for the Dunes, 3) Presidential proposal and congressional disposal: the High Beautification Act, 4) The Wilderness Act: a product of congressional compromise, 5) Controversy in the North Cascades, 6) Economics, aesthetics, and the saving of the redwoods, 7) Meeting the costs of a quality environment: the Land and Water Conservation Act, 8) Water projects and recreation benefits, 9) Water quality: a question of standards, 10) Junked autos: an embodiment of the litter philosophy, 11) Wild and scenic rivers: private rights and public goods, 12) Aircraft noise abatement: a case of congressional deafness, 13) International control of the ocean floor, 14) National policy for the environment: politics and the concept of stewardship, 15) Conclusions: congress and the environment of the future, 16) Epilogue: environment and the shaping of civilization. Also, broad issues are raised, such as the cost of a quality environment and conflicts between local and national interests, and the need to balance private property rights with public good. The authors feel that the outlook is depressing.

507. Cralley, Lester V., ed. **Industrial Environmental Health: The Worker and the Community.** New York, Academic, 1972. 544p. bibliog. index. $24.00. LC 70-187243.

The public concern over environmental conditions in industry brought about a need for this book. It brings together material on topics relating to safety and health in industrial plants. Each of the 15 sections was written by a person well-known in the field. Attention is centered on evaluating the health hazards covered by the Occupational Safety and Health Act of 1970. The section headings are as follows: 1) Epidemiologic studies of occupational diseases, 2) Toxicology, 3) Noise, 4) Nonionizing radiation, 5) Ionizing radiation, 6) Engineering approach to analysis and control of heat exposures, 7) Evaluation of chemical hazards in the environment, 8) Hazard evaluation and control, 9) Personal protective devices, 10) New and recurring health hazards in industrial processes, 11) Contributions of ergonomics in the practice of industrial hygiene, 12) Air pollution, 13) An empirical approach to the selection of chimney height or estimation of the performance of a chimney, 14) Water pollution, and 15) Agriculture now.

The sections vary in their approach and in their coverage and value. Some are technical, some are philosophical, and some superficial. The book is, however, of value to certain groups such as industrial hygienists, engineers, chemists, toxicologists, and physicians as it will bring them up to date on what is new in at least some of the areas.

508. Durrenberger, Robert W., comp. **Dictionary of the Environmental Sciences.** Palo Alto, Calif., National Press Books, 1973. 282p. illus. $7.95. 78-142370. ISBN 0-87484-150-X.

This dictionary was prepared to assist people in understanding the environmental terms used which come from various disciplines. Students, professionals, and laymen will find it valuable. A broad range of terms are included from such fields as economics, engineering, geology, geography, anthropology, architecture, botany, zoology, agriculture, and a number of others. It is particularly strong in geoscience terms.

509. **Ecology, Conservation, and Environmental Control: Career Opportunities.** Chicago, J. G. Ferguson Publishing Co., a subsidiary of Doubleday and Co., Inc., 1971. 211p. illus. index. $6.95. LC 77-134012.

This publication was designed for students who are interested in doing something to help save the environment and want careers in this area, and for counselors, teachers, and parents who also are interested. The book surveys the two-year post high school programs related to ecology which are offered by many junior, community, and technical schools. There is a chapter on each of the following programs: civil technician, environmental health technician, fish culture technician, food processing technician, forestry technician, marine life technician, nuclear technician, ornamental horticulture technician, park and recreational land management technician, physical oceanographic technician, physical radiologic technician, soil reclamation and conservation technician, urban planning technician, water and wastewater technician, wildlife and conservation technician. The book is illustrated with attractive photographs of workers at their jobs. Some material is included that originally appeared in other books.

510. Edwards, Clive A. **CRC Persistent Pesticides in the Environment.** Cleveland, CRC Press, A Division of the Chemical Rubber Co., 1970. 78p. bibliog. $10.50.

This book originally appeared as part of an article in the journal *CRC Critical Reviews in Environmental Control*. The persistent pesticides in question, particularly the organochlorine insecticides, have been of tremendous benefit to mankind by controlling disease and increasing yields of crops. A serious problem has arisen because as populations increase the need for food increases, and it follows that the use of pesticides will increase. This has resulted in a residue of the persistent pesticides in air, rainwater, dust, rivers, the sea, in the bodies of aquatic and land animals, birds, and in human beings. The largest residues appear in the tissues of animals near the top of the food chain, which, of course, includes man. The author stresses that these residues have not really been assessed as to importance. They do not seem to threaten any species with extinction or even diminish its numbers. Also, there is little evidence of any illnesses resulting. However, the spread of these chemicals is a cause of anxiety until more is learned about their possible long-term effects. This publication reviews the current state of knowledge in this area and gives comparative data on the amounts of residues currently in the environment. The hope is that the review will stimulate interest and demonstrate the need for further research and possible legislation. An extensive bibliography of 322 references is included.

511. Environmental Science and Technology. **Pollution Control Directory, 1973-1974.** Special Issue, vol. 7, no. 12, November 1973. Easton, Pa., American Chemical Society, 1973. 136p. $1.50.

This special issue is published each year in November. It is in eight main parts: 1) Dealers and supply houses in the U.S., an alphabetical by state listing of dealers and suppliers, 2) Professional consulting services: a listing of companies offering consulting services only, 3) Instruments and equipment: manufacturers listed alphabetically under product headings, 4) Chemicals: manufacturers listed alphabetically under product headings, 5) Services: alphabetical listing of companies which offer services and consultants that also manufacture, distribute products, and offer other services, 6) Books and authors: a listing of books on the environment which were reviewed in the journal, 7) Trade names: alphabetical list for products intended for the environmental field, 8) Company directory: alphabetical listing of manufacturers and suppliers of the products and services listed in this directory.

512. Fortune Editors. **The Environment: A National Mission for the Seventies.** New York, Harper and Row, 1970; repr. Chicago, Time, Inc., 1969. 220p. illus. $1.25. LC 73-119639.

The contents of this book originally appeared in *Fortune* magazine, the October 1969 and February 1970 issues. There are statements at the beginning from both President Nixon and Senator Muskie to suggest to the reader that the problem of the environment is not a partisan issue. The book contains 13 chapters, each on a different area of pollution. There are reports on the limited progress that has been made in reform and the major steps that still remain to be taken. The writers do not search for scapegoats, but suggest that environmental clean-up will be a large task for everyone and harder to achieve than many of its advocates suggest. Some of the chapter topics are as follows: the limited war on water pollution, industry starts the big clean-up, cars and cities on a collision course, it's time to turn down all that noise, and conservationists at the barricades.

513. Frear, Donald E. H., comp. and ed. **Pesticide Handbook-Entoma.** 24th ed. Published in consultation with the Entomology Society of America and the National Pest Control Association. State College, Pa., College Science Publishers, 1972. 279p. $6.00. $4.50pa. LC 52-44516.

This annual publication contains a wide variety of miscellaneous information of value to anyone interested in pest control. A great deal about safety is included. The largest section of the book is an alphabetical list of commercial products by trade name. Active ingredients are given and the name of the manufacturer. In another section, products are arranged according to use, and still another section is a manufacturers' list. In addition, information about regulations, equipment, antidotes, applications, compatibilities, hazards, and safety is included. A list of Poison Control Centers set up with the assistance of the U.S. Public Health Service has been inserted on colored pages.

514. Freeman, A. Myrick, III, Robert H. Haveman, and Allen V. Kneese. **The Economics of Environmental Policy.** New York, Wiley, 1973. 184p. index. $6.95. LC 72-7249. ISBN 0-471-27787-8; 0-471-27786-4pa.

The objective of this book is to depict the problem of environmental quality as an economic problem. In order to resolve this problem the authors feel that knowledge and analyses developed by economists, natural scientists, political scientists, and lawyers should be used. Materials balance is emphasized. Viewed as an economic problem, the problem of environmental degradation is seen as a result of the failure of the market system to efficiently allocate environmental resources among their alternative uses. An economic system such as ours depends on voluntary exchanges of goods and services in markets to determine the relative value of things and how much of them to produce. Our system does not work for "common property" such as environmental resources. The book emphasizes the need to bring environmental resources into the economic system.

No prior background in either economics or the natural sciences is needed to understand the book. It is appropriate as a text for economic principles applied to public policy issues or for a survey course in environmental problems. Chapter headings are as follows: 1) Environmental quality: an economic problem, 2) The environment and the economy, 3) Some facts about environmental pollution, 4) The market system and pollution, 5) The economic principles of pollution control, 6) Public policy for water pollution control, 7) Public policy for air pollution control, 8) Environmental management: some issues, and 9) Environmental management: an overview.

515. Gorden, Morton, and Marsha Gorden. **Environmental Management: Science and Politics.** Boston, Allyn and Bacon, 1972. 548p. illus. bibliog. index. $9.95. LC 70-188224.

This book is concerned with developments that have arisen out of the efforts put forth to solve the problems of the environment. The authors and/or compilers feel that we must now mix political considerations with the technical aspects of environmental management. They also feel that overspecialization is partially responsible for our plight, and that it must be overcome.

This book is largely made up of a collection of articles by well-known individuals. These articles are heavily technical but point out problems politically oriented people must face up to. Each chapter is made of several articles. General chapter headings are as follows: 1) Uncertainty: new demands on the sciences, 2) Complexities of interactions: foreseeing consequences, 3) Generation of wastes: unclosed materials cycles, 4) Values: the best ecosystem, 5) Research for environmental management: needed knowledge, 6) Environmental management: needed skills, 7) Implementation: from science to application, and 8) Conclusions: can we manage the environment?

516. Hagevik, George. **Planning for Environmental Quality.** Monticello, Ill., Council of Planning Librarians, 1969. 12p. (Council of Planning Librarians. Exchange Bibliography 97). $1.50.
This bibliography is designed to assist interested individuals with the problems, issues, institutional contexts, and content of the subject area of planning for environmental quality. Book and periodical references are both included. This listing is divided with subject headings as follows: scope and content of environmental planning; political and institutional setting; the environmental planning process; general systems theory; ecology and public policy; the new conservation and environmental quality; water quality management; air quality management; solid wastes management; and noise control.

517. Harte, John, and Robert H. Socolow. **Patient Earth.** New York, Holt, Rinehart and Winston, Inc., 1971. 364p. illus. bibliog. index. $4.95pa. LC 77-148032. ISBN 0-03-086571-9; 0-03-085103-3pa.
This book tells about the work of those who are diagnosing and attempting to heal the environmental illnesses of the earth. It also imparts a good deal of information of use to those who are interested in joining in like activity. The first two chapters are historical. One is on the Dust Bowl of the 1930s and the other about the Classic Maya civilization. Then 10 contemporary case studies are presented on the following topics: cities, low-sulfur fuels, abortion, helium conservation, DDT, nuclear power on Cayuga Lake, herbicide use in Vietnam, Project Sanguine (a radio wave project), the Mineral King natural forest area, and the Everglades. In addition, there is a section on equilibrium with nature, and also one on constraints on growth. The presentation is somewhat technical in certain sections, but in general it is not above the reading level for most individuals. The book is interesting and somewhat timely although somewhat controversial since recent developments such as the energy crisis have brought about a general change of view on some of the problem areas discussed.

518. Helfrich, Harold W., Jr., ed. **The Environmental Crisis: Man's Struggle to Live with Himself.** New Haven and London, Yale University Press, 1970. 187p. $1.95. LC 79-105456. ISBN 0-300-01312-4cl. 0-300-01312-2pa.
This publication is based on a lecture series organized by the Yale School of Forestry with funds from the Ford Foundation. The objective was to analyze technological aspects of the environmental crisis and to probe moral, economic,

and social facets as well. The contributors are distinguished authorities in science, law, regional planning, economics, and government. The problems are seen as water and air pollution, mismanaged natural resources and open spaces, increasing and unplanned populations, urban congestion, and mismanagement of our national energies. It is hoped that the papers presented will stimulate a search for practical solutions. Titles of the papers are as follows: 1) Playing Russian roulette with biogeochemical cycles, 2) The plight, 3) Water modification in the service of mankind: promise or peril? 4) Famine 1975: fact or fallacy? 5) The harvest of the seas: how fruitful and for whom? 6) The green revolution: agriculture in the face of population explosion, 7) The search for environmental quality: the role of the courts, 8) The federal research dollar: priorities and goals, 9) Man against nature; an outmoded concept, 10) The dilemma of the coastal wetlands: conflict of local, national, and world priorities, 11) Fun and games with the gross national product: the role of misleading indicators in social policy, 12) The federal government as an inadvertent advocate of environmental degradation.

519. Henderson, Kay, ed. **Pollution: Sources of Information.** Proceedings of a one day conference held at the Library Association, London, October 27, 1972. London, Library Association Reference, Special and Information Section, 1972. 102p. bibliog. index. ℒ2.50. SBN 85365-435-2.

This publication records the papers presented at a conference sponsored by two British organizations, the Library Association Reference, Special and Information Section and the ASLIB Transport and Planning Group. There were six speakers, two representing "consumer" and four "suppliers." Four of the speakers were experts in the field of information. All of them presented large numbers of references to literature of importance. An additional reading list has also been supplied. The titles of the presentations are as follows: 1) Pollution; the information problem, 2) Information needs of the research worker, 3) Air pollution, 4) Noise pollution, 5) Marine pollution, 6) General documentation on pollution and sources of freshwater pollution, solid wastes, pesticides and radioactivity. In addition to the subject index supplied, also included is an index to organizations, authorities, and institutions. While the publication is British, many American sources have been included.

520. Hodges, Laurent. **Environmental Pollution: A Survey Emphasizing Physical and Chemical Principles.** New York, Holt, Rinehart and Winston, Inc., 1973. 370p. illus. bibliog. index. $7.95. LC 72-79645. ISBN 0-03-086328-X.

This book was written as a textbook or as a supplementary work for courses dealing with environmental concerns. It is also of value to educated laymen as a scientific introduction to pollution and its control. The physical sciences are emphasized rather than the biological. Historical and current statistics have been included in order to show the progress that has been made in overcoming some types of pollution and yet to demonstrate the magnitude of existing problems. Chapter headings are as follows: 1) The growth of population, production, and consumption, 2) Air pollution: introduction, 3) Air pollution: meteorology and climatology, 4) Air pollution: industrial emissions and classical smog, 5) Air pollution: motor vehicle emissions and photochemical smog, 6) Noise, 7) Water pollution: introduction, 8) Water pollution: municipal, 9) Water pollution:

industrial and commercial, 10) Agricultural pollution, 11) Pesticides, 12) Solid wastes, 13) Thermal pollution, 14) Radiation, 15) Electric power generation, 16) Foods, drugs, and cosmetics, 17) Pollution in foreign countries, 18) Economic and legal questions, 19) Legislation. In addition, there is an appendix which includes lists of books and periodicals dealing with the environment and a list of addresses of sources of information on the subject.

521. Hook, Ernest B., Dwight T. Janerich, and Ian H. Porter, eds. **Monitoring, Birth Defects and Environment: The Problem of Surveillance.** New York, Academic, 1971. 308p. bibliog. index. $8.50. LC 70-179925.

This book is based on a Symposium held in Albany, New York on October 19-20, 1970, sponsored by the Birth Defects Institute of the New York State Department of Health. The Institute brought together a distinguished group of scientists who presented papers centered in the critical area of the environment and its influence on heredity and birth defects. The goal of surveillance as considered in this publication is to monitor the incidence of malformations and mutations in the population to detect the introduction or the increase of unsuspected mutagens and teratogens in the environment. The rationale, problems, and costs of various approaches to the question are discussed. Several possible surveillance systems are described, and methods for improving, refining, and elaborating the monitoring are presented. The markers discussed include fetal wastage, major and minor malformations, and somatic mutations. The book should interest pediatricians, teratologists, geneticists, epidemiologists, biochemists, and public health officials.

522. International Atomic Energy Agency in collaboration with the World Health Organization. **Nuclear Power and the Environment.** Vienna, International Atomic Energy Agency, 1973. 85p. $2.00. STI/PUB/321 (rev.)

This is an information booklet in regard to nuclear power and its importance, preservation of public health and safety, and the environment. Chapter headings are as follows: 1) The role of atomic energy in meeting future power needs, 2) Radiation protection standards, 3) Safe handling of radioactive materials, 4) Other impacts, 5) Public health considerations. The material presented is very timely as we have reached the place where public acceptance of nuclear power may be as important as the technology itself.

523. Jones, Kenneth L., Louis W. Shainberg, and Curtis O. Byer. **Environmental Health.** San Francisco, Canfield Press, 1971. 118p. illus. bibliog. index. $2.50pa. LC 71-146370. SBN 06-384366-8.

This book is written with the positive viewpoint that although environmental disaster is a real threat, man will act to save his environment before it is damaged beyond hope. The first section of the book deals with man and his environment, and includes material on health hazards, substandard housing, and the urban environment. The second section takes up population dynamics and includes discussions of world population problems and resources and controlling population. The third section is on conservation, and presents discussions of resources such as food, recreational resources, pollution, and effective conservation action. Useful statistical tables are included throughout.

524. Kilbourne, Edwin D., and Wilson G. Smillie, eds. **Human Ecology and Public Health.** 4th ed. New York, Macmillan Co.; London, Collier-Macmillan, Ltd., 1969. 462p. illus. bibliog. index. $12.50. LC 69-18251.

Earlier editions of this book were called *Preventive Medicine and Public Health.* The new edition is a bit broader in scope as the title indicates. The subject encompasses demography, human and microbial genetics, epidemiology, clinical medicine, systems analysis, and health services administration. 15 distinguished scientists and experts contributed to the volume which is suitable for medical and other advanced health professions' students and graduate students of public health. It is also of value for public health administrators, physicians, public health nurses, and other interested individuals. The material is presented on a somewhat advanced level, however. The book has three main divisions: human ecology and human disease; public health—problems and practice; and the administration of health services.

525. Klausner, Samuel Z. **On Man and His Environment.** San Francisco, Jossey-Bass, Inc. 1971. 224p. bibliog. index. $7.50. LC 77-146736. ISBN 0-87589-086-5.

This book takes a sociological approach to the problem of the environment. It begins with the characteristics of human society and takes a sociological look at the environment. The book points out that we cannot apply knowledge about cleaning up the environment that we do not yet have. We are cautioned against rushing into clean-up programs that we are ill equipped to implement. The author proposes the establishment of university-based institutes to develop the knowledge about man in relation to the environment and calls for more research before we attempt applications. He suggests further research in the areas of psychology, sociology, economics, anthropology, and geography. The institutes could be set up utilizing existing social and behavioral science faculties. Later interdisciplinary integration would come about. The proposals seem reasonable, although perhaps the part of the physical and biological sciences has been neglected in the author's outline. Chapter titles are as follows: 1) Retreat from man-environment studies, 2) Populations and their resources, 3) How physical facts become social facts, 4) Elements for an environmental theory, 5) Rediscovery of the environment, 6) Social implications of filth and noise, 7) Recreation as social action, and 8) Social policy for the environment.

526. Knobbe, Mary L. **Air Pollution: A Non-Technical Bibliography. Annotated.** Monticello, Ill., Council of Planning Librarians, 1969. 9p. (Council of Planning Librarians. Exchange Bibliography 83). $1.50.

This selective annotated bibliography lists general nontechnical publications which will fill the needs of local officials of the community, but not scientists. Most of the references are to periodical articles. The bibliography is grouped into several parts as follows: air pollution studies, by city, county, or state; control devices and methods; legislation, administration and economics; source and source emission studies; models and use of computers; standards and criteria; and a list of periodicals cited.

527. Kogan, Benjamin A. **Health: Man in a Changing Environment.** New York, Harcourt, Brace and World, Inc., 1970. 642p. illus. bibliog. index. $9.50. LC 78-113709. ISBN 0-15-535580-5.

The central and recurring theme of this book is that we must seek and find ways to achieve harmony between man's inner and outer ecosystems. Chapters 1 and 2 explore the meanings of health and relate them to ecology; Chapters 3 and 4 describe some of the inbalances between man's internal and external environments; Chapter 5 traces the historical course of disease and its impact on history; Chapter 6 is historical also with a view to the future; Chapter 7 and 8 are concerned with body functions and structure and chronic impairment to them; Chapter 9 deals with nourishment; Chapters 10 and 11 explore man's personality development and anxieties as they relate to the environment; Chapter 12 is on drugs of abuse; Chapter 13 is on overpopulation problems and reproduction; Chapters 14 and 15 explore the significance of courtship, sex, and marriage; Chapter 16 is on birth and the problems involved; and the final chapter explores the role of the individual in the pursuit of health for all. The book was prepared with the help of a large group of scientists, but it draws heavily on the social sciences and the humanities as can be seen. The text is suitable for college students or intelligent laymen.

528. Krenkel, Peter A., and Frank L. Parker, eds. **Biological Aspects of Thermal Pollution.** Proceedings of the National Symposium on Thermal Pollution, Sponsored by the Federal Water Pollution Control Administration and Vanderbilt University, Portland, Oregon, June 3-5, 1968. Nashville, Vanderbilt University Press, 1969. 407p. bibliog. index. $7.95. LC 75-92265. SBN 8265-1144-9.

This book contains the symposium papers which are concerned with thermal pollution in the nation's lakes, rivers, estuaries, and coastal waters. Thermal pollution refers to the degradation of water by heat which is usually caused by the discharge of hot condenser-cooling water into streams, lakes, etc. Temperature rise affects most chemical, physical, and biological processes in water. Most of the thermal pollution taking place is caused by manufacturing industries and electric power generating plants. Since the need for more power is so great, this is a very timely topic. Not a great deal is known yet about thermal pollution. The symposium brought together well-known engineers, scientists, and government officials. The papers are of particular interest to fisheries biologists, sanitary engineers, water resources managers, and other concerned individuals. The discussions presented here will help establish a baseline for future research on the subject.

529. Lund, Herbert F., ed. **Industrial Pollution Control Handbook.** New York, McGraw-Hill, 1971. 1v.(various paging). illus. index. glossary. $29.50. LC 70-101164.

Since public concern over and legislation affecting environmental pollution is growing so rapidly, this book makes a major contribution. The handbook is designed to show how to reduce waste discharges using the latest technology. An impressive group of contributors assisted with the presentation, most of them from industry. The first section of the book takes up the evolution of industrial pollution control. In the second section, every major industry where pollution is a problem has been described in a separate chapter. These industries include foundries, plating, pulp and paper, foods, chemicals, textiles, pharmaceuticals, aerospace, and a separate review of European plant practices is presented. The last section is on pollution control equipment and operation.

The book is of particularly value for those who are seeking background information, the details of legislation, quality standards, control systems, and community relations.

530. National Foundation for Environmental Control, Inc. **NFEC Directory of Environmental Sources.** 2d ed. Introduction by Myer M. Kessler; Charles E. Thibeau, editor; Peter W. Taliaferro, associate editor. Boston, Distributed by Cahners Books, Division of Cahners Publishing Co., Inc., 1972. 457p. index. $25.00. LC 78-158971.

This directory lists many sources of information on the environment, such as government agencies, citizens' organizations, publications, etc. Names, addresses, and other important data on each source are given. There are 15 chapters as follows: 1) U.S. government—executive agencies, 2) U.S. government—legislative committees, 3) U.S. government—independent agencies, 4) Citizens' organizations, 5) Professional occupational organizations, 6) Trade associations, 7) Educational institutions and organizations, 8) Abstracts, directories, and indices, 9) Published bibliographies, 10) Additional information sources, 11) Conference and symposium proceedings, 12) Documents and reports, 13) Serials and periodicals, 14) Books, and 15) Films and filmstrips. Many groups can make good use of this directory. It will interest private citizens, legislators, conservation and action groups, government agencies, industry, and the technological community. The chapter on educational institutions will be of interest to those contemplating a career in the environmental sciences, and to institutions planning environmental programs. Libraries will be interested in the literature sources listed.

531. Purdue University. Radiological Control Committee. **Radiological Control and Health Physics Handbook.** Lafayette, Ind. Purdue University, Radiological Control Committee, 1971. 61p.

While this handbook was prepared for use of the staff and students of Purdue University, others engaged in work with ionizing radiation will find it useful. In general, the publication does not restate specific Atomic Energy Commission and state regulations regarding the use of radioactive materials and radiation producing devices, but pertains only to the use of such at Purdue University, giving regulations and procedures set up for personnel working with or using radioactive materials there. However, the handbook has been submitted to the Atomic Energy Commission and the Indiana State Board of Health for approval.

Such topics are included: administration of the radiological control program, regulations governing use of radioactive materials (including procedures for procurement, use, transfer, disposal of wastes, and personnel monitoring), regulations governing use of X-rays, guidelines for particle accelerators, and health physics regulations.

532. Revelle, Roger, and Hans H. Landsberg, eds. **America's Changing Environment.** Boston, Houghton Mifflin Co., 1970. 314p. illus. bibliog. index. $6.95. LC 69-15028.

In this book, 20 different economists, political scientists, city planners, and conservationists discuss urgent problems of the environment. Some of the essays appear for the first time in the publication, but others appeared originally in slightly different form in the Fall 1967 issue of *Daedalus*, the journal of the American Academy of Arts and Sciences. The essays are divided into six subject areas: 1) Ecology as an ethical science, 2) Water, air, and land, 3) Economics and politics, 4) The humane city, 5) Playgrounds for people, and 6) Roles of eduction.

There are discussions on how serious the problems are, what society thinks of them, how they can be dealt with, the changes in our national values and priorities that are necessary if degradation is to be stopped, and what society is willing to pay for. The most important contribution of the book is its attempt to show how damage can be averted. The fact that this will be expensive in terms of dollars is pointed out.

533. Rossano, A. T., Jr., ed. **Air Pollution Control: Guidebook for Management.** Stamford, Conn., Environmental Science Service Division, E. P. A., Inc., 1969. 214p. illus. bibliog. $15.00. LC 72-101407.

This text was written to present basic principles of air pollution control in such a manner that both technical and nontechnical persons can gain from it. Each chapter was written by an expert. Diverse aspects of the field are treated, including chemistry, engineering, meteorology, biology, law, and administration. The first half of the book is devoted to a description and evaluation of the problem, and the last half takes up specific approaches to the elimination or control of air pollution. The chapter headings in the last half are as follows: measurement and control of community malodors, engineering control of air pollution, air pollution control in the chemical industry, source testing procedures, administrative and regulatory aspects of air pollution control, and legal aspects of air pollution.

534. Schoenfeld, Clay, ed. **Outlines of Environmental Education.** Madison, Wisconsin, Dembar Educational Research Services, 1971. 246p. bibliog. $8.95. LC 78-149599.

This volume contains articles collected from the 1969-70 and 1970-71 issues of the *Journal of Environmental Education*. The aim of the book is to help professionalize the new field of environmental education. The editor hopes that it will help inject deep-digging research, practical field approaches, and imagination to the field. Educators involved in new environmental science curricula will find the book of particular interest. The papers are arranged by subject as follows: 1) The environmental decade, 2) Defining environmental education, 3) The schools encompass environmental education, 4) Environmental studies come to the campus, 5) New learning laboratories in field and factory, 6) Adult education for ecological action.

535. Sherrod, H. Floyd, ed. **Environmental Law Review—1970.** Albany, N. Y., Sage Hill Publishers, Inc.; New York, Clark Boardman Co., Ltd., 1970. 704p. bibliog. index. $29.50. LC 70-127585. SBN 87632-043-6.

This publication collects in one place some of the most notable writings of the year in the environmental law field. This is the first of what was expected to be an annual compilation. This first volume contains material published in early

1970, 1969, and some articles of special significance which appeared in 1968. There are several parts to the volume as follows: 1) The theoretical framework, 2) Particular pollution problems, 3) Legislative and administrative action, and 4) Judicial action. Part 3 is subdivided into four parts: an overview, air pollution, water pollution, and land use. The book should prove useful to ecology students, lawyers, scientists, and to the lay public.

536. Strobbe, Maurice A., ed. **Understanding Environmental Pollution.** St. Louis, Mosby, 1971. 357p. bibliog. $5.95. SBN 8016-4823-8.
This publication is a collection of articles which should prove useful for use in environmental courses in colleges and as a guide and handbook to the understanding of the different parameters of environmental pollution control. It provides the necessary background that will suggest the action that might be taken by the community or the individual. The book is divided into two sections; the first is on environmental problems. The authors of the papers are prominent people. Those of the first section present a variety of opinions which provide a cross section of the field. The articles in the second part provide evidence of accomplishments in the field. There are five appendices included. These are: 1) Supportive references, 2) Selected films on environmental issues, 3) Glossary, 4) National conservation organizations, 5) Laboratory tests and demonstrations.

The 49 articles cover a great variety of subjects. To name a few: pollution in the Great Lakes, ocean pollution, thermal pollution, DDT and other pesticides and herbicides, population pollution, air pollution of many kinds, and waste water renovation.

537. Thomas, William A., ed. **Indicators of Environmental Quality.** Proceedings of a Symposium held during the AAAS meeting in Philadelphia, Pa., December 26-31, 1971. New York, Plenum Press, 1972. 275p. bibliog. index. (Environmental Science Research, vol. 1). $18.50. LC 72-86142. ISBN 0-306-36301-1.
This rather technical publication presents primarily physical, chemical and biological aspects of the subject. However, social consequences of actions are recognized throughout the volume, and one author directly discusses the social aspects of environment. It is the intention of the editor to help provide objective measures of environmental quality that can be made comprehensible to all segments of society. Indicators and indices which measure variables and provide overall composite values for environmental shifts are examined. The current state of the art is surveyed.

538. Turk, Amos, Jonathan Turk, and Janet T. Wittes. **Ecology, Pollution, Environment.** Philadelphia, Saunders, 1972. 217p. illus. bibliog. index. $3.95pa. LC 74-176218. ISBN 0-7216-8925-6.
Two aspects of environmental science are stressed in this book. The first is subject matter in the realm of the physical sciences, and the second concerns the decisions people make about environmental problems, the social problems and issues. The aim of such an approach is to lead to final judgments that do not bring unwanted results. This procedure is sometimes called "rationalizing the trade-offs." Chapter headings are as follows: 1) Introduction to ecology,

2) Agricultural environments, 3) Pesticides, 4) Radioactive wastes, 5) Air Pollution, 6) Water pollution, 7) Solid wastes, 8) The growth of human populations, 9) Thermal pollution, 10) Noise.

539. U.S. Council on Environmental Quality. **The Federal Environmental Monitoring Directory.** Washington, GPO, 1973. 105p. $.80. Stock No. 4111-0016.
The term "monitoring" is defined in this instance as systematic and continuing observations of environmental parameters that are collected nationally. Many different kinds of environmental monitoring sites are now operating all over the United States. Monitoring information is needed to assess status and trends in the condition of the environment. The directory is a list of sources (agencies) that provide such monitoring information. It should be stressed that nearly every agency listed sponsors a publication (or publications) which are described with the entry.

The agencies are divided into six groups by kind of information they are involved with. These are as follows: 1) Underlying factors such as population, economic development, and urbanization, 2) Resources such as water, timber, energy, minerals, land, etc., 3) Ecological factors such as climate, natural disasters, and wildlife, 4) Pollution such as air, water, radionuclides, pesticides, noise, and toxic substances, 5) Man-made environment such as housing, transportation, aesthetic values, occupational environment, recreation, and cultural resources, 6) General sources; sources that cut across categorical boundaries.

540. U.S. National Science Foundation. **Student-Originated Studies Projects, 1971. Abstract Reports.** Presented at the Meetings of the American Association for the Advancement of Science, Philadelphia, Pennsylvania, December 28-29, 1971. Edited by Berton F. Hill. Washington, National Science Foundation, 1972. 334p. (NSF 72-22).
This publication contains summaries of projects carried out by 1,100 college students at a number of colleges and universities. The program was initiated by the National Science Foundation in 1969 as a vehicle through which students could express their concern constructively about the nation's well-being and also with the hope that some of the participants would be drawn to a career in the environmental field. Although the projects were carried out on limited budgets mostly by undergraduates, they are quite impressive. The abstracts are arranged by broad topics as follows: 1) Resource utilization studies, 2) Water quality studies, 3) Urban and rural studies, and 4) General environmental studies.

541. Wagner, Richard H. **Environment and Man.** New York, W. W. Norton, 1971. 491p. illus. bibliog. index. $7.50. LC 74-141581. SBN 393-09986-5.
This book attempts to pull together all the aspects of the man-environment field. It is not an exhaustive treatment as the subject coverage is broad. It is a general introduction to environmental problems for the non-scientist, student, and general reader, and can be used as a textbook. Problems such as air and water pollution, biocides, chemical and biological warfare, radiation hazards, overpopulation, and the growing food crisis are discussed. The volume is in six parts as follows: 1) Man in the landscape, 2) Natural traumas become pollutants, 3) Man makes new traumas, 4) The biotic world and man, 5) Man's urban

environment, and 6) The people problem. The material presented is well-written, interesting, and covers the field adequately and sensibly. The author ia a professor of botany.

542. Wang, J. Y. **Introduction to Environmental Studies: (Human Ecological Problems). Syllabus.** San Jose, Calif., Milieu Information Service, 1970. 320p. index. bibliog.

This publication is written as a textbook for the beginner in environmental studies or for the general public. It covers most of the major problems of the field. The first seven chapters present factors and facts of the human environment, including the physical, biological, and social aspects. Chapters eight through ten introduce the processes which lead to environmental crises. The last two chapters stress methods of abatement and solutions to the problems, and long term considerations are discussed in the last chapter. Also included is a glossary and annotated bibliography. Chapter headings are as follows: 1) Man and his environment, 2) The air, 3) The water, 4) The land, 5) Living conditions, 6) Urban society, 7) Rural environments, 8) Balances of nature, 9) Imbalances of nature, 10) Human environmental crises, 11) Prediction and control, and 12) Future prospects. The author is a professor of meteorology.

543. Watts, D. G. **Environmental Studies.** London, Routledge and Kegan Paul; New York, Humanities Press, 1969. 118p. bibliog. $3.00. SBN 7100-65167 cl.; 7100-65175pa.

This publication is of particular interest because environmental studies have recently been introduced in many schools and colleges. However, there has been little written on the theory and research of the subject. This book attempts to fill that gap by surveying the ground for a structural theory.

The book is organized as follows. Chapter 1 examines and philosophically analyzes the terminology and concepts employed in discussing environmental studies and introduces the themes to be discussed in later chapters. Chapter 2 describes the historical roots of the environmental idea from Locke to Piaget. Chapter 3 goes on to discuss the relationship between the environment and the learning of infants, children, and young adults. Chapter 4 presents an interpretation of the objectives, concepts, and organization of environmental studies courses. Chapter 5 presents possibilities and problems and considers some aspects of methodology.

544. Winton, Harry N. M., comp. and ed. **Man and the Environment: A Bibliography of Selected Publications of the United National System, 1946-1971.** New York and London, Unipub, Inc./R. R. Bowker Co., 1972. 305p. index. $7.00. LC 72-739. ISBN 0-8352-0536-3.

The aim of this bibliography of more than 1,200 entries is to call attention to valuable kinds of information and publications emanating from the United Nations system. They are not as widely known and distributed as they should be. Most of the publications listed are for sale, and include monographs, dictionaries, bibliographies, directories, yearbooks and other periodicals, and filmstrips. In addition, a number of newsletters and public information pamphlets available free have been included. The entries are arranged by broad subject and four indexes, author, series and serials, title, and subject are provided.

545. World Health Organization. **Health Hazards of the Human Environment.**
Prepared by 100 specialists in 15 countries. Geneva, World Health Organization, 1972. 387p. bibliog. index. $11.00.

This book was compiled for the benefit of health authorities and others concerned with environmental problems. Since the subject covers so vast a range, the treatment is synoptic. More details can be learned by consulting the references given. Part 1 deals with environmental hazards from the standpoint of the media, e.g., air, water, food, insects and rodents, and other community influences, e.g., home, workplace, and culture. Part 2 deals with each specific contaminant and hazard. Part 3 is on surveillance and monitoring. Part 4 approaches environmental health hazards from the standpoint of public health operations and the principles and practice of intervention and control procedures.

13. PATENT MEDICINE, QUACKERY, AND QUESTIONABLE BELIEFS

546. Carson, Gerald. **One for a Man; Two for a Horse: A Pictorial History, Grave and Comic, of Patent Medicines.** New York, Doubleday and Co., Inc., 1961. 128p. illus. bibliog. index. $6.50. LC 61-5590.

This book reproduces pictures and advertising of the "cures" and health devices of long ago and also includes text material about the medicines, their promoters, and the methods used to sell them. The publication is amusing, very handsome, and tells a good deal about our American heritage in such areas as medical history, advertising, publishing and mass distribution, public health, social legislation, taste and recreation, and the level of culture of the time as well. Some of the companies mentioned still exist and are reputable today. The pictures were taken from the holdings of libraries, historical societies, and private collections, including the author's own. This work is exceptionally well done.

547. Consumer Reports Editors. **The Medicine Show: Some Plain Truths about Popular Remedies for Common Ailments.** Rev. ed. Mount Vernon, N.Y., Consumers Union, 1970. 272p. illus. index. $2.00pa. LC 73-112645.

This book is addressed to individuals who have come to question both the propriety and the quality of over-the-counter drug advertising, particularly the television commercial. The authors feel that the public needs better medical education than it gets from advertising and offer the book as a guide. The material is reliable and well-presented. The reviewer does feel, however, that the average intelligent layman already knows most of what is presented and that he does not, as a rule, take advertising very seriously anyway.

548. Fuller, John G. **200,000,000 Guinea Pigs: New Dangers in Everyday Foods, Drugs, and Cosmetics.** New York, G. P. Putnam's Sons, 1972. 320p. index. $7.95. LC 72-79521. SBN 399-11000-3.

This work is a kind of sequel to an earlier book published about forty years ago called "100,000,000 Guinea Pigs" by Arthur Kallett and F. J. Schlink. The guinea pigs referred to are the consumers of the United States (the number has doubled since the earlier book was written). The authors of both books express their concern about the food additives, drugs, and other dangers that manufacturers expose the public to. The author of the present volume does not seem to have medical training as the author of the earlier work had. The book is written in a sensational style, and there is no scientific documentation included for anything presented. The U.S. Food and Drug Administration and various manufacturing corporations are sharply criticized, and tough laws are called for. In an attempt to evaluate this book, this reviewer would say that some of the criticism presented is valid; many individuals do have severe reactions to common drugs, cosmetics, and food products. However, usually these materials do no harm to most people, and they do serve some useful purpose, perhaps doing more good than harm. Also, there is good scientific evidence that many products already taken off the market because of the potential hazards they pose are very benefi- cial in many instances. The reviewer feels that the consumer should be educated about these matters, and then be allowed to decide himself whether or not he wants to use them. Tougher laws frequently cause great inconvenience and do not help.

549. Hechtlinger, Adelaide. **The Great Patent Medicine Era: or Without Benefit of Doctor.** New York, Grosset and Dunlap, Inc., 1971. 248p. illus. $14.95. LC 70-122554.

This book is lavishly illustrated with pictures and text from 19th century domes- tic medicine books, and a large number of advertisements are reproduced for things like Indian Snake Root Oil, Dismal Swamp Chill and Fever Tonic, and other patent medicines. There is even a selection of pages from a Sears Roebuck Catalog of drugs produced in 1906. The material for the volume was drawn from the author's own collection, and she has supplied short introductions to each sec- tion. While the book has little scholarly appeal, it is a handsome publication, interesting and amusing, and offers a look at the American past when no pure food and drug laws existed, and the patient largely treated himself.

550. Stabile, Toni. **Cosmetics: Trick or Treat?** Introduction by Congressman James J. Delaney. New York, Hawthorne Books, 1966. 223p. bibliog. index. $4.95. LC 66-24522.

This book, written by a journalist, points out the need for legislation to protect the public against harmful cosmetics. It is written in a somewhat sensational and perhaps exaggerated style. However, it is well for the public to be aware that cosmetics may not be entirely safe, particularly for people who have a tendency toward allergies. Also, as the book points out, advertising claims are not reliable, and the price of cosmetic products is unduly high.

551. Turner, James S. **The Chemical Feast: The Ralph Nader Study Group Report on Food Protection and the Food and Drug Administration.** New York, Grossman, 1970. 273p. bibliog. index. $6.95. LC 73-112515.

This much publicized book is the report of a study of chemical food additives and the Food and Drug Administration's involvement in protecting the public against harmful ones. The study was done in 1968 by a group of young law stu- dents and/or lawyers. Few, if any, scientifically trained individuals were involved. The group reported on such matters as cyclamates (artificial sweeteners), the enforcement of federal regulations concerning foods, hidden ingredients in foods, food-borne disease, the food industry, the history of food and drug legislation, and the difficulties the FDA has encountered in its operation. The material for the book was collected partially from library searching, but evidently depended very heavily on interviews. The study team's concern was that not enough is being done to protect the public against harmful additives.

Many of Nader's views are controversial, as there is considerable feeling that the evidence he presents is more emotionally based than scientific, and that useful products have been withdrawn from the market for no sound reason, as for instance, the cyclamates.

552. U.S. Food and Drug Administration. **A Study of Health Practices and Opinions. Final Report.** Philadelphia, National Analysts, Inc., 1972. Reproduced by National Technical Information Service, U.S. Department of Commerce. 340p. (PB-210 978). $6.00.

The purpose of the study was to investigate fallacious or questionable health beliefs and practices, and susceptibility to them. The following areas were investigated: use of vitamin pills and other nutritional supplements, without a physician's guidance; use of "health food"; weight reduction practices; use of laxatives or other aids to bowel movements; self-diagnosis of ailments; self-medication for serious ailments; practices in the diagnosis and treatment of arthritis/rheumatism; practices in the diagnosis and treatment of cancer; health practitioners used; hearing aids and medication; "aids" to quitting smoking; and general health-related attitudes and opinions.

The data was collected by a large national survey and individual and group depth interviews with people known or suspected to hold questionable beliefs. The numerous conclusions of the study are outlined in detail. In general, it can be said that a wide-spread lack of understanding of the potential dangers of ineffective treatments was suggested.

553. Wade, Carlson. **Health Tonics, Elixirs, and Potions for the Look and Feel of Youth.** West Nyack, N.Y., Parker Pub. Co., 1971. 236p. index. $6.95. LC 71-151659. ISBN 0-12-384545-1.

This book has much the same slant as the patent medicine and quackery books of old, but the "tonics, elixirs and potions" referred to are "health foods" or "natural foods" rather than drugs. There seem to be no harmful remedies mentioned, but it is doubtful that many of the potions will live up to the claims made for them; e.g., stimulating hair growth and curing arthritis.

554. Young, James Harvey. **The Toadstool Millionaires: A Social History of Patent Medicines in America before Federal Regulation.** Princeton, N.J., Princeton University Press, 1961. 282p. illus. bibliog. index. $6.00. LC 61-7428.

This book is a history of proprietary medicines in the United States from the early 18th century to the enactment of national legislation in the early 20th century. The various stages in the development of patent medicine promotion are outlined. In some chapters, case histories are related to illustrate the situation that prevailed at the time. The author also makes some attempt to explain why the public was (and to some extent still is) so gullible as to buy these nostrums. He feels, however, that a full answer lies hidden in the mystery of human motivation.

The title of the book refers to a quotation by Oliver Wendell Holmes which says, "Somebody buys all the quack medicines that build palaces for the mushroom, say rather, the toadstool millionaires."

14. SPECIFIC DISEASES

555. Archuleta, Michael, and Alyce J. Archuleta. **Sickle Cell Anemia: A Selected Bibliography for the Layman.** San Diego, Calif., Current Bibliography Series, 1972. 21p. (Current Bibliographies Series No. 1). $1.50. P. O. Box 2709, San Diego, Calif. 92101.

Since sickle cell anemia has received a good deal of attention recently in the popular press, this bibliography should prove useful in many libraries, particularly those that serve a large number of blacks, as this inherited disease affects only Negroes ordinarily. Although the bibliography is intended primarily for laymen and public libraries, biomedical libraries may also find it valuable. Most of the material listed was published within the last five years. References are to general periodical, medical journal, and newspaper articles and to pamphlets, documents, and films.

556. Goode, Stephen H., comp. **Venereal Disease Bibliography, 1966-1970.** Troy, New York, Whitston Pub. Co., 1972. 613p. index. $22.50. LC 71-189843.

This publication is a very comprehensive bibliography of the world literature of venereal disease covering the five-year period, 1966-1970. It is to be supplemented annually. The following bibliographies and indexes were searched in compiling the references: *Bibliographic Index, Books in Print, Canadian Periodical Index, Cumulative Book Index, Cumulative Index to Nursing Literature, Current Index to Journals in Education, Current Literature of Venereal Disease, Education Index, Index to Legal Periodicals, Index Medicus, Index to Periodical Articles Related to Law, International Nursing Index, Public Affairs Information Service, Readers' Guide to Periodical Literature, Social Science and Humanities Index.* Since such a wide and disparate group of indexes was covered, the bibliography can serve the needs of several kinds of users. It should be of interest to medical scientists on several levels, undergraduate and graduate students, nurses, psychologists, sociologists, political scientists, etc.

While the work appears to be well done, the arrangement is a bit odd. Each bibliographic entry is given twice, once in a straight alphabetical by title listing, and once in a subject listing. While the book is usable enough this way, it seems unnecessary to repeat each entry since numbering them would have made it possible to list each complete reference only once if a subject index were included referring to the numbered items. The book does have an author index with references to pages where an author's work is listed.

The book is recommended and is of considerable importance because venereal disease is now a major socio-medical problem.

557. U.S. National Institutes of Health. **Digest of Scientific Recommendations for the National Cancer Program Plan.** Bethesda, 1973. 1v.(various paging). DHEW Publication (NIH) 74-570.

In 1971, the President and Congress of the United States indicated the need for an overall plan for an intensified attack on cancer. The National Cancer Institute and the National Advisory Cancer Council called upon the scientific community to participate in the development of the National Cancer Program Plan. Many planning sessions were held to develop this program. A strategic plan and an operational plan were developed. This publication outlines the objectives of the overall plan in digested form. There are seven objectives, as follows: 1) Develop the means to reduce the effectiveness of external agents for producing cancer; 2) Develop the means to modify individuals in order to minimize the risk of cancer development; 3) Develop the means to prevent transformation of normal cells to cells capable of forming cancers; 4) Develop the means to prevent progression of precancerous cells to cancers, the development of cancer from precancerous conditions, and spread of cancers from primary sites; 5) Develop the means to achieve an accurate assessment of a) the risk of developing cancer in individuals and in population groups and b) the presence, extent and probable course of existing cancers; 6) Develop the means to cure cancer patients and to control the progress of cancers; 7) Develop the means to improve the rehabilitation of cancer patients.

558. U.S. National Institutes of Health. **The Strategic Plan: National Cancer Program.** Bethesda, January 1973. 1v.(various paging). DHEW Publication (NIH) 74-569.

In 1971, the President of the United States and Congress indicated a need for an overall plan for an intensified attack on the cancer problem. The National Cancer Institute and the National Advisory Cancer Council asked assistance from the scientific community to develop the National Cancer Program Plan. A strategic plan and an operational plan were developed. This publication presents the strategic plan. At this writing the operational plan publication is still in preparation. There are five parts to this publication as follows: 1) Introduction; 2) National Cancer Program strategy: 3) Implementation strategy; 4) Five-year projection of cancer research; and 5) National Cancer Program resource projections. There are many supporting statistical charts and tables included.

15. OTHER TOPICS

559. **Biofeedback and Self-Control: An Adline Reader on the Regulation of Bodily Processes and Consciousness.** Chicago, Aldine-Atherton, 1971. 806p. bibliog. index. $17.50. LC 71-167858. ISBN 202-25048-2.

This publication is a sourcebook of materials in the new field of biopsychology, biofeedback. The most important articles were selected from scientific periodicals by six well-known psychologists and collected into this volume. What the studies suggest is that with modern technological devices, man may be able to exercise voluntary control over many body and brain functions that were once considered as being beyond such control. This includes such functions as heartbeat, blood pressure, and stomach acidity. The articles are arranged by broad subject as follows: heart rate; blood pressure and vasomotor responses; electrodermal activity; salivation, urine formation, and gastric motility; electroencephalographic activity; electromyographic activity; methodology: what is conditioning?; classical conditioning; yoga, zen, and autogenic training; voluntary control and hypnosis; and voluntary control, consciousness, and physiology. The reader contains only articles published before 1970. The publication is to be supplemented with an annual volume covering current material.

560. **Civilization and Science: In Conflict or Collaboration?** A Ciba Foundation Symposium. Amsterdam, Associated Scientific publishers (Elsevier, Excerpta Medica, North Holland), 1972. 227p. bibliog. LC 77-188826. ISBN Excerpta Medica, 90-219-4001-9; American Elsevier, 0-444-10351-1.

This book records the proceedings of a symposium meeting where scientists, politicians, economists, and historians from a number of countries reviewed the origins of today's conflicts between civilization and science and the supposed lack of value orientation in science. It is pointed out that most countries have reduced science budgets or have made no increases of recent years. Also, there has been a world-wide anti-science movement. Scientists have been challenged because they have not become more socially responsible. (At the present writing, it seems that this anti-science trend may be reversed in the face of the energy crisis.) The aim of the book is to encourage the placement of science exactly where it belongs in the scale of human values, not too low or not too high.

Titles of the papers are as follows: 1) The problem defined; 2) Some reflections on the theme of science and civilization; 3) The historical background to the anti-science movement; 4) Anti-science: observations on the recent 'crisis' of science; 5) The responsibility of scientists to the community: a discussion; 6) Science: a consequence of science policy or an expression of culture? 7) Science, technology and the political response; 8) Science and trans-science; 9) Science and the military; 10) Science in Spanish and Spanish-American civilization; 11) Some economic aspects of science; 12) Scientific research and long-term growth; 13) The need for a science of civilization; and 14) Summing-up.

561. Cobb, A. Beatrix. **Medical and Psychological Aspects of Disability.** Springfield, Ill., Charles C. Thomas, 1973. 365p. bibliog. index. (American Lecture Series Publication No. 868). $13.75. LC 72-86997. ISBN 0-398-02653-X.

This book was written primarily to assist the rehabilitation counselor in becoming familiar with the medical and psychosocial concepts surrounding common disabilities. Also, it is hoped that the reader will develop a better understanding of the total rehabilitation process. A number of diseases are discussed, each by a different contributor or contributors, and the educational, psychological, and rehabilitation factors of each is brought out. Chapter titles are as follows: 1) An approach to interdisciplinary communication in rehabilitation; 2) Medical aspects of heart disease; 3) Psychological aspects of heart disease—implications for rehabilitation workers; 4) Psychological consideration in hemiplegia; 5) Stroke patients: their spouses, families and the community; 6) The multiple dysfunctions called cerebral palsy; 7) Amputations and amputees; 8) Respiratory diseases; 9) Respiratory disorders and the rehabilitation process; 10) Diseases of the kidney; 11) The gastrointestinal system; 12) Medical and psychological factors pertinent to the rehabilitation of the epileptic; 13) Rehabilitation medical aspects of hearing disorders; 14) Education and social factors in the rehabilitation of hearing disabilities; 15) The path of light; 16) Psychological adjustment to blindness.

562. Gubrium, Jaber F. **The Myth of the Golden Years: A Socio-environmental Theory of Aging.** With a foreword by David O. Moberg. Springfield, Ill., Charles C. Thomas, 1973. 225p. bibliog. index. $9.75. LC 72-88494. ISBN 0-398-02703-X; 0-398-02757-9pa.

The author of this work is searching for a theory that can help bring about good personal and social adjustments for older people. He is looking for a way to promote social conditions that will facilitate their coping with life and foster morale, happiness, life satisfaction, comfort, etc. He has developed a new socio-environmental approach to aging to overcome the weaknesses of other theories such as the activity and disengagement theories. His theory introduces a blend of the other theories and possibly overcomes some of their weaknesses. The chapter titles are as follows: 1) Current theories of aging; 2) A socio-environmental approach to aging; 3) Social contexts and activity norms; 4) Individual contexts and activity resources; 5) The social psychology of contexts; 6) Group-consciousness and age-concentration; and 7) The myth of the golden years.

The book will be of interest to social workers, physicians, counselors, clergymen, nurses, attorneys, and those working in geriatrics such as gerontologists, sociologists, psychologists, and their students.

563. Guild, Warren R., Robert F. Fuisz, and Samuel Bojar. **The Science of Health.** Englewood Cliffs, N.J., Prentice-Hall, Inc., 1969. 532p. illus. bibliog. index. $10.00. LC 68-10420.

This book is a health science text suitable for a college course. Written by physicians, it is a blend of physiology and pathology. It is unusually well illustrated with photographs and line drawings which supplement the text. The following subjects are considered: a modern concept of health; the cellular basis of life, heredity and genetics; the heart and blood vessels; the respiratory system; the digestion and absorption of food; the reproductive systems; marriage and parenthood; the nervous system, sight, and sound; the endocrine glands; the blood; bone, muscle, physical fitness, and fatigue; the skin; the kidneys and body fluids; nutrition and drugs; tobacco; alcohol; narcotics, stimulants, and hallucinatory drugs; origins and development of personality; the psychosexual development of the personality; puberty, adolescence and young adulthood; mental mechanisms; disturbances of mental health; the communicable diseases; community health; national and international health; and environmental health. A list of films is also included.

The book will be useful as a reference source for many individuals such as undergraduate students, public health workers, and many laymen as it is reasonably simple but authentic.

564. Karlins, Marvin, and Lewis M. Andrews. **Biofeedback: Turning on the Power of Your Mind.** Philadelphia, J. B. Lippincott, 1972. 223p. bibliog. index. $5.95. LC 79-39759. ISBN 0-397-00855-4.

Biofeedback is a new technique which presumably allows individuals to control the state of bodily processes, health, and well-being through the power of the mind. No drugs are used. It has long been assumed that the involuntary nervous system, which regulates such bodily functions as heartbeat, digestion, and the generation of different sorts of brain waves, was beyond an individual's power to control. Biofeedback research suggests that if such functions are made apparent to the individual, by translating them into light or sound signals, or by some other means, he can be trained to control them. Biofeedback training has been used to alleviate insomnia, anxiety, pain, muscular tics, and in treating headaches, and stroke victims. Biofeedback machines are now available to the public, and the authors provide some advice on buying and using them. The authors have provided good bibliographic references to scientific studies although the book is written in a somewhat popular style. The conclusion made is that biofeedback training will allow the individual to control and guide his own destiny to an extent not possible before.

565. King, Lester S. **The Road to Medical Enlightenment, 1650-1695.** London, Macdonald; New York, American Elsevier, 1970. 209p. bibliog. index. LC 79-111293. British SBN 356-03126-8; American SBN 444-19685-4.

The author, who is an editor of a medical periodical and professorial lecturer in the history of medicine, emphasizes the works of five men: Riverius, Van Helmont, Boyle, Sylvius, and Sydenham, all brilliant scientists of the late 17th century. In addition, he discusses briefly a few others, such as Digby, Nedham, Twysden, Glanvill, Stubbe, some Italian reactionaries, and Hooke. The last section deals at some length with Friedrich Hoffman, whose work, *Fundamenta Medicina* (1695) is perhaps the best synthesis of what was the new medicine. The book is scholarly, and the material is presented in such a manner to give insights into these men's ideas and works.

566. Larson, Leonard A., and Herbert Michelman. **International Guide to Fitness and Health: A World Survey of Experiments in Science and Medicine Applied to Daily Living.** Sponsored by the International Committee on the Standardization of Physical Fitness Assessments, with the assistance of the People-to-People Sports Committee, Inc. New York, Crown Publishers, Inc., 1972. 210p. illus. bibliog. index. $6.95. LC 72-89847. ISBN ISBN 0-517-501465.

This book, written by an authority in the field of physical education, is an outgrowth of the work of the International Committee on Standardization of Physical Fitness Assessments which was formed in 1964, prior to the Olympic Games in Tokyo, for the purpose of correlating the scientific information on the subject of exercise and to pursue further experimentation. This book attempts to present the scientific findings in terms understandable to the layman, but professionals also will find it valuable. Its primary purposes are to stimulate people to engage in daily physical activities and to promote sports activities. Much practical information has been included. One can find out how much of any given physical activity it takes to balance off calories so that weight control programs can be effective. Methods are explained and information given to create a personal program, both for children and adults. The book is the first of its kind and is quite authentic. Chapter headings are as follows: 1) What exercise can do; 2) Fitting exercise to your requirements; 3) Other factors associated with exercise, 4) How can personal requirements for exercise be determined? 5) Individual exercise requirements be met? 7) Regulating your program; and 8) Measuring progress. Also incuded are appendices: 1) Basic programs (daily requirements with illustrations); 2) Medical examination prerequisite to physical activity; and 3) Members of the International Committee on Standardization.

567. Metzger, Norman, and Dennis D. Pointer. **Labor-Management Relations in the Health Services Industry: Theory and Practice.** Washington, Science and Health Publications, Inc., 1972. 360p. $17.50. LC 72-95547.

Labor relations in the health services industry have recently gained widespread attention. There has been a marked increase in collective bargaining activity even among health professionals. This text presents a thorough theoretical and pragmatic treatment of the subject. The authors trace the development of the movement, discuss the means of and reasons for union organizational drives, discuss negotiations, labor laws, strikes, and state their views on the need for a national hospital labor relations policy. The volume contains a large amount of statistical data given in tabular form throughout. This material has considerable reference value. There is no general index, but a good Table of Contents of Tabular Data (called "Index of Tables") is included.

The book gives both sides of the issues and makes definite recommendations. It also allows the reader to examine the issues and make his own conclusions.

568. Payne, Buryl. **Getting There without Drugs: Techniques and Theories for the Expansion of Consciousness.** New York, Viking Press, 1973. 204p. bibliog. (An Esalen Book). $7.95. LC 72-75747. SBN 670-33763-3.

In the past several years, psychedelic drugs have been used as a way of achieving a more conscious state. While they have evidently provided many people with mystical-like experiences (some maintain they are in reality hallucinations), the drugs have had serious and disturbing side effects. The author of this book maintains that by following his instructions, a series of meditational exercises, a reader can repossess nonverbal realms of experience that guide him in his search for transcendent awareness. Chapter headings are as follows: 1) Where are we? 2) Sensory awareness—expanding ordinary consciousness; 3) Living here and now; 4) Transcending here and now; 5) Meditation; 6) The way of the machines—biofeedback training; 7) Essence and personality; 8) What is time? Is it now? 9) Psychological time; 10) Transcending space-time; 11) A fifth dimension; 12) The we field; 13) Life and death and life and death and life . . .; 14) Where are we?

569. Shepard, Thomas H. **Catalog of Teratogenic Agents.** Baltimore, Johns Hopkins University Press, 1973. 211p. index. $10.00. LC 72-12350. ISBN 0-8018-1408-1.

This is an important book because defects that exist at birth create societal problems of great magnitude. Knowledge of the causes and prevention of these defects is very limited, but some are evidently due to teratogenic agents. A further problem is that the teratogenic literature is dispersed throughout the biomedical publications and is difficult to locate. The main purpose of this publication is to link the information on experimental teratogens with congenital defects in human beings. The agents listed in the book include chemicals, drugs, physical factors, and viruses. The literature has been surveyed and this listing or catalog compiled making use of a computer. Each listing includes a main entry with synonyms. This is followed by an account of some of the work published including the species used for the study, dose, gestational age at time of administration, and type of congenital defect produced.

The catalog will be most useful for physicians, geneticists, pharmaceutical chemists, and environmentalists.

AUTHOR AND TITLE INDEX

SUBJECT INDEX